W9-AEP-216

The Real World
of Liberalism

David Spitz

The Real World of Liberalism

**The University
of Chicago Press**
Chicago and London

David Spitz (1916–79) was professor of political science at Hunter College and at the Graduate Center of the City University of New York. Among his publications are *Patterns of Democratic Thought*; *Democracy and the Challenge of Power*; and *The Liberal Idea of Freedom*.

The University of Chicago Press, Chicago 60637
The University of Chicago Press, Ltd., London

Printed in the United States of America
89 88 87 86 85 84 83 82   54321

Library of Congress Cataloging in Publication Data
Spitz, David, 1916-
    The real world of liberalism.
    Includes index.
    1. Liberalism. 2. Conservatism. I. Title.
JC571.S7723   320.5'1   81-16262
ISBN 0-226-76973-9   AACR2

To my daughters
Deborah and Janet
who have remained faithful to the liberal
principles in which they were nurtured.
Con amore

Contents

Foreword

David Spitz died suddenly on March 23, 1979. His work on this book was almost, but not quite, completed. A first draft of the final chapter, including about three-quarters of the text on Hayek, was typed. Notes for the remainder lay on his desk, along with his plans for the concluding section on the current crop of new conservatives. Because normally we worked together closely, I was able to reconstruct the manuscript with some accuracy and to finish the chapter as I believe he would have written it. Nevertheless, it is only fair to say that, for David Spitz, first drafts served to clarify his own thoughts and were always more expansive than later versions. Habitually, he pruned in a second draft and then polished in a third. The pruning I have attempted, because his intentions were already on paper, but not the polishing (from which I refrained as a matter of piety as well as inability). Stylistic differences from the rest of the book may thus be apparent in the final chapter.

The Introduction to this volume is the product of a similar editing process. I reworked David Spitz's extensive notes into a text with as much fidelity to his formulations and priorities as possible. His desire to defend liberalism from those he believed had misrepresented its message, and to make clear the authentic Millian position with respect to common contemporary attacks on liberalism, was so strong that, I felt, it justified an effort to communicate what he had in mind.

The Credo printed at the end of the book is a set of ten commandments for liberals. I have included them, in their obviously unfinished state, for the priorities they reveal and the concerns they express. They substitute, at least in part, for the planned but never written Afterword, entitled "The Real World of Liberalism."

While we will all miss David Spitz's unique conceptual lucidity and great eloquence, I hope, as he did, that these essays will launch the counterattack against liberalism's enemies that is so long overdue.

ELAINE SPITZ

Hunter College, 1980

Preface

No true liberal is afraid of the name because many people who know not what it means run it down or claim for it more virtues than it can bear. Liberalism entails neither wretchedness nor a continuing felicity, only a certain approach to and assessment of the human predicament: a theory of man's nature, his society, and his knowledge. What that theory is, and what therefore is required of liberty and equality to assure a measure of justice, is the theme to which this book is addressed.

Most of the essays reprinted here appeared initially in *Dissent*. I am grateful to Irving Howe, friend and editor extraordinary, for his patience and persistence in extracting them from me. I am especially indebted to my wife, Elaine Spitz, for her love, encouragement, and intellectual combat.

DAVID SPITZ

Introduction

The Question of Liberalism

Ever since Lucifer was banished from the kingdom of heaven, it has been fashionable to focus on demons for the explanation of evil. Liberalism is today such a demon. Both sides of the political spectrum, the new conservatives and the new left, identify the current sorry state of human affairs with liberalism's deficiencies. This is easily understandable, for liberalism is a revolutionary doctrine that calls upon men and women to accept three things—none of which is comfortable: *uncertainty* (no assurance of absolute truth); *tolerance* (even for what is loathsome); and *compromise* (as preferable to nonpeaceful resolutions of conflict). To escape these onerous burdens, it is necessary to expose the inadequacies of liberalism. The case constructed is familiar but nonetheless formidable.

Some indictments turn on a misunderstanding: they identify existing derangements in society—poverty, racism, alienation, crime—with liberalism. They treat these problems, which have existed in all sorts of social systems, even those ruled by conservatives and communists, as if they were intrinsic to liberal principles. Liberalism, of course, is neither their creator nor responsible for their continuance, although it is a way of dealing with them, a method for arriving at solutions (not a preconceived compendium of the solutions themselves). As the essays in this book argue, the liberal approach provides the single best hope of mitigating social ills that we can have. But because it neither despairs of progress nor dispenses packaged remedies, liberalism is a target for everyone with present discontents.

Another persistent misunderstanding confuses liberalism's high regard for individuality with a commitment to individualism or a deprecation of community. Because liberals champion man's capacity to make autonomous decisions adequate to the task of self-protection and the assumption of moral responsibility, some have concluded that liberals view people as separate entities, each creature independent of his historical situation and group affiliations. This is simply not so. While liberals may reject an extreme historicism (and see continuity in human nature at least sufficient to make Homer intelligible to modern audiences), this does not lead to a rejection of man's essential sociality. On the contrary, from John Stuart Mill's famous chapter heading that cites individuality as only *one* of the elements of well-being to John Dewey's book-length concern for the quality of public life, liberals have recognized social interdependency. Indeed, they have been in the forefront of the drives for cooperative social endeavors. Portraits of possessive individualists distort to the point of caricature. The frequency with which John Stuart Mill's obvious interest in participation is cited as an exception to liberal atomism should alert a careful historian to the inaccurate descriptions of liberalism, for Mill is the quintessential liberal, and his descendants have been equally sensitive to the inextricably intertwined interests of man and mankind.

A third shibboleth these essays may help to overcome turns on the alleged moral relativism of liberal principles. Too many writers have not appreciated the difference between skepticism and a prudential allowance for error. It is true that liberals are not absolutists, but it is false to conclude that they are nihilists. Liberals, in fact, have many principles, but these are largely about methods, about fairness, or about inquiry. They inform a variety of rule-making activities, and while good procedures do not lead inevitably to good results, what liberals argue is that "right" results are best achieved by the processes liberals uphold. Their unwavering support of liberty simply cannot be equated with an inability to combat evil or to assert an effective public morality.

Apart from these misconceptions, assaults are often directed against the liberal conception of community, which, according to its critics, places a purely instrumental value on public life and pays inadequate attention to the moral character of citizens. Prominent themes include liberalism's exaltation of pluralism, minimization of tradition, and stress on procedural rather than substantive justice. To understand liberal principles in these areas, it is necessary to examine the shift by liberals from a negative to a positive view of the state, their attempts to reconcile planning and democracy, and their persistent effort to dichotomize public and private life. The essays in this volume touch upon these topics repeatedly.

Does liberal pluralism, for example, weight politics in favor of those already powerful? Surely, in some sense, pluralism diminishes the role of unorganized interests, just as it slights public policies not in the immediate interest of any important group. But pluralism is not another name for liberalism. Again, John Stuart Mill provides the appropriate liberal paradigm, and his concern for the general interest, his distinction between democracy (majority rule) and representative government (consideration of the interests of all), is instructive. Diversity wins plaudits because of the connection between social pluralism and liberty, not because it successfully protects vested interests, as some detractors have claimed. Similarly, Mill's effort to separate self-regarding and other-regarding activities is an effort to provide for individuality, not to restrict government to a night watchman's role. Liberal support of equality, including compensatory mechanisms to readjust conditions so that equal opportunity remains meaningful for all, testifies to this libertarian function of pluralism. So, too, does liberal support of corporate regulation.

Nor does concern for liberty and individuality mean that liberalism lacks ennobling ideals or visions. Nothing in liberal thought precludes them, although liberalism does refuse to impose them on others. Liberals ask only that each ideal be subject to perpetual examination. Admittedly, this reduces the aura of sacredness, but it does not eliminate respect for either tradition or utopian dreams.

Two subjects dear to liberalism's enemies are private property and rationalism. Liberals, the charge goes, favor the private ownership of the means of production and the inheritance of wealth, and this vitiates political equality and conflicts with justice. However, as any reader of Mill's *Chapters on Socialism* knows, liberalism is not wedded to any particular economic order and is able to countenance a wide assortment of property regulations. What is interwoven in the following essays is the concern among liberals for private property's function as a bulwark against government, as a source of power perhaps necessary to counteract an overwhelming or otherwise unchallengeable amount of authority amassed by bureaucrats. The task, as liberals see it, is to balance the requirements of liberty and equality while also maintaining an awareness of the connection between freedom and a maldistribution of power or resources. It is necessary to reflect upon the alternatives and make a reasoned choice among the competing values.

Such rational assessment leads to what has become one of the major topics in modern philosophy. What is rationality? How can anyone embedded in a particular culture, amid the forces of a particular historical moment, ask a neutral question, much less find a value-free answer? Is there only one right answer? Is it discoverable? How? Liberals, according to their accusers, by pretending that people are free-floating decision-makers, take a position that systematically distorts reality and people's places within a political system. Thus, the liberal's plea for rational discussion and choice is merely an ideology that masks the structural elements actually responsible for how a social order operates.

On the left, voices refer to liberalism's "excessive rationality." In the left's antiintellectual phase, especially in the sixties, rationality was held to be "excessive" when it calculated instead of "felt," when it inhibited people instead of liberating their impulses. In its Marxist version, "excessive" means too great a reliance on education for the removal of environmental impediments to clear thinking. Behavior, on this showing, is more determined than liberals acknowledge. Many on the right agree. People, according to Michael Oakeshott, are products of a tradition that so structures their lives that they can make only those incremental changes necessary to keep the human enterprise afloat. Large-scale innovations create new problems but not new solutions. Liberals, therefore, are guilty of attempting to abridge experience with schemes of social engineering that can never work.

B. F. Skinner, from a quite different perspective, also castigates liberal rationality, charging that it depends on a belief that people have minds that make choices; in his view, of course, people do not have minds and merely behave in response to environmental forces. Science, as he understands it, pushes beyond rationalism grounded in human freedom and points to conditioning as the appropriate way to improve the world.

None of the discussions in this book will definitively settle these contemporary controversies about human nature and the role of reason in being, but they do address the central issues in the debate and suggest what a liberal philosophy entails. Consistent with its rejection of human infallibility on any subject, liberalism eschews any extreme form of rationalism that predicates a single correct, knowable solution to any problem. Whether it be allowance for the subtle rule of the passions or for the structural determinants of human behavior, a liberal readily acknowledges restrictions on the ability of a person to reason. What liberals have insisted upon is that only reason can discern irrationality. People must use reason to grasp its limits. And they must practice tolerance to minimize their inevitable errors. In this sense, reason and tolerance are central qualities of a liberal politics.

Current assaults on liberalism from all quarters, then, are based largely on issues confronted in the following essays. These essays continue and amplify the mainstream of liberal thought that flows from John Stuart Mill to Lindsay, Barker, Laski, and Russell in England and to John Dewey, Morris Cohen, and Robert MacIver in this country. Critics of liberalism must come to terms with this tradition, not with some burlesque of it. A generation of political scientists has seemingly been content to fight with Schumpeter's definition of democracy, not Mill's, or to contend with behaviorists who call themselves liberals. The authentic liberal tradition has been sidetracked. It is time to refocus the discussion. Cogent criticisms of liberalism must meet the arguments sustained in this book.

1

Liberal Perspectives:
On Human Nature,
Freedom, Democracy,
and Revolution

On Human Nature, I

If man is a rational animal, it is surely odd that he so often debates questions whose answers must be presupposed before the debate can take place. (I use the term "man" here in its primary dictionary meaning, to denote the human species.) This oddity is particularly pronounced in discussions of human nature.

Consider two of the more perennial questions: Is man an autonomous or a conditioned being? If, or to the degree that, he is an autonomous being, is his reason the servant or the master of his passions?

Now clearly, to discuss these questions at all, one must assume and not look for the answer, that is, one must begin by accepting as true, and therefore rejecting as false, one half of each dichotomy. For if, to take the first question, man is a conditioned animal, molded by forces outside his control and in most cases—as with Freud's (or Marx's, or Marcuse's, or Skinner's) insistence on the importance of unconscious and irrational influences that dominate human behavior—beyond his knowledge, he can only think and act as he has been conditioned to think and act. Then it doesn't really matter what you and I, for example, may say here: for I *have* to say what I am about to say, and you not only *had* to come here, not only *have* to listen to me (or not listen to me, as the case may be), but *must* react as you will. Nothing I may say can possibly change you, and nothing you may say can possibly change me; or, if we are to affect each other, this too is already given by the nature of what has previously been done to us. In effect, we are about to act out a charade, with all the words and actions predetermined for us by forces or actors somewhere out there.

If, however, we are to engage in a meaningful discussion, we can only do so by assuming that we are autonomous or relatively autonomous men, not

All of the essays in this chapter appeared originally in *Dissent*, volume 18 (1970), with the exception of "On Freedom II," which appeared in volume 25 (1978), pages 205–6. All are reprinted by permission of *Dissent*.

conditioned beings, or at best only partially conditioned and hence partially autonomous beings.

Similarly, I must assume that you and I are not only rational but that in some measure at least our reason can indeed govern our passions. This is not to deny that men are, as Hobbes and Hume argued, creatures driven by (perhaps insatiable) desires, and that reason then enters to show us how we may best or most effectively satisfy those desires. Nor is it to deny that some men are often controlled by their passions, and perhaps all men are sometimes controlled by their passions. It is only to insist that in order to understand even this much, in order to know that we are creatures of desire and that reason is an instrument for the satisfaction of those desires, we must do so rationally. We must rationally understand the irrational. Even if we employ seemingly irrational means to move seemingly irrational men to what we take to be rational conduct, we must do so rationally; that is, we rationally employ irrational methods to control irrational men. But then, the rational use of irrationality makes those irrational methods eminently rational.

More than this: what distinguishes man from the other animals is that he not only acts, he gives, or is asked to give, reasons for his actions. He is the one creature on earth who asks the question, Why? Why have you done, or why do you now want to do, A? Why have you not done, or why do you not now want to do, B? And since there is always a plenitude of answers, since there are always reasons, we seek to discriminate among them: we seek to distinguish sensible from incoherent or illogical reasons; reasons that take into account the consequences—as far as we can conceive them—of our actions; reasons that are grounded in empirical reality and not fanciful situations; reasons that carry weight on moral and prudential grounds and do not rest merely on arbitrary preferences. In effect, we seek to make sense out of what would otherwise be a senseless world. We seek reasons that are empirically sound and philosophically sane.

I would dwell for a moment on this last point. For what I contend is that we need not simply causal and functional hypotheses—theories, if you will—to explain human behavior; we also require standards in terms of which, or grounds on the basis of which, we may properly evaluate, justify or condemn, that human behavior. We need to make judgments of right and wrong—about the war in Vietnam, about affirmative action, about cases of civil disobedience, and the like. Hence we are concerned not simply with facts but with ways of looking at facts, with categories that give meaning to those facts. We seek to relate those facts to purposes, to ends on which men are sorely disagreed but with respect to which they cannot avoid taking a stand. This, or at least this, is what it means to be human.

Now, if what I have said is at all persuasive, we must proceed on the assumption that the dichotomies I originally set forth are literally absurd. No matter how socialized, conditioned, manipulated man might be, he still has a measure of choice: he has a mind with which to conceive or to entertain *some* alternatives, and freedom of will to make a judgment among them. Even more, he can conjure up or consider moral principles by which to regulate and guide his behavior, that is, by which to restrain some impulses or desires and to indulge others. He is not only a rational, he is a moral creature. He is also, perhaps distressingly but also challengingly, a responsible creature—both for what he does and, so far as it lies within his powers to control events, for what he allows to be done.

In these terms, it is surely a mistake to ask whether man is solely good (or cooperative, or altruistic) or solely bad (or competitive, or driven only by self-interest) or solely indifferent (or amoral, or apathetic). He is not solely any of these things because he is all of them, though clearly individuals possess and manifest these and other qualities in different combinations and degrees, and not always consistently but variously in response to diverse circumstances. The hangman who plays gently with children, the concentration camp commandant who listens sensitively to a Beethoven quartet—but the point is too obvious to warrant further elaboration here.

Nor is it less absurd to treat seriously the alleged issue of individuality versus sociality, as if these were discrete and antagonistic terms. Clearly, a man is what he is by virtue of the fact that he was born into, and raised in, a community. He is not a man by himself, he is never totally different from everyone else; otherwise we should not be able to communicate with him, understand him, relate to him. Nor is he totally like everyone else; otherwise we should have no problems with him, no collisions, no estrangements, no cause to like or dislike him; we should all think alike, act alike, be alike. Individuality refers to uniqueness in some things; humanity entails likeness in other things. In fact, he is an individual only because he is a social animal. The terms "individuality" and "sociality," far from standing in inherent and consistent opposition to each other—though individuals may and at times do stand in opposition to particular social demands—are and must be mutually sustaining, because complementary, terms.

Even when we turn to more sensible, though controversial, notions of human nature, we are plagued by similar oddities.

What can it mean, for example, to ask whether men are equal or unequal, the same or different? Surely they are not all equal (or unequal) in all things, or at least a man who is superior to another person in one thing (say medical knowledge) may be inferior to that person in other things (say political judgment). When, therefore, we speak of equality we can only refer to certain kinds of equality, or equality in what we take to be the important things. But important for what? and to whom? Surely not simply to the individuals involved, but also to the society whose very notion of the structure of relationships requisite to the building and maintenance of community is at stake. Important, therefore, not only for an individual's but also for society's sense of justice.

Consider in these terms the problem posed by the plank of Carneades: Two persons, neither of whom can swim, are adrift in an open sea, with but a single plank at hand. When they seize the plank, they quickly discover that it will not bear their combined weight. The plank will support one of them, but not both. Which of the two has a legitimate claim to its use, and on what grounds?

If both persons are equal to the point of identity—in age, sex, intelligence, talent, strength, virtue, and the like—there is clearly no ready answer. (Apart, perhaps, from the tossing of a coin or by resorting to the children's game of odd and even fingers, which is purely a matter of chance. Is a lottery, then, the true principle of justice for a society of equals?) For then no differences enter to justify preferential treatment for either. But what if there are differences, say, of age or sex?

In the age of chivalry, if one of the two persons were a woman, the adult male would doubtless—as a gentleman—gallantly abandon himself to the deep. But apart from the fact that not all men are likely to be gentlemen in such circumstances, the advent of the women's liberation movement renders such a gesture inadmissable. In our day, each person—male or female—is now required to grant the other merely an equal right.

If one person is old and the other young, it might be argued that the former has lived his life while the latter should not be denied an equal opportunity to achieve longevity. But what if the older person cherishes the prospect of a few remaining years, and is in addition an Einstein or a Toscanini, while the child is a cretin or an incorrigible scourge? Shall we deny a superior claim to genius? Shall we deprive society of a greater social good?

Shall we then, with Carneades, argue that in such a situation the order of justice ends and the principle of self-preservation begins? If this is in fact the resolution, does it not shift the governing principle from equality to inequality? For then superior cunning or strength rather than (say) virtue prevails; and these are surely as irrelevant to equality as they are to any conceivable principle of political right.

Or shall we, in this dire case, look with the Jesuit teacher Suarez to the Christian principle of charity? Clearly this is most acceptable, provided the person at the other end of the plank is a Christian, and that he will observe the requirements of his religion. But what if both are Christians, or neither is a Christian? Or what if one is a Christian but finds himself or herself psychologically unable to act according to the tenets of this admirable teaching? Will we not once again find force or guile to be the dominating principle?

Assuredly, if a notion of human nature must accord with the realities of practical life as well as with the stipulations of justice, the principle of equality cannot by itself resolve such a conflict between competing egalitarian claims. We need to look outside equality for a standard that will help us decide questions of equality. We need, no less importantly, to understand precisely what we mean when we talk about equality.

If by equality we mean equality of opportunity, we are committed, paradoxically, to inequalities of result; for equality of opportunity, from this standpoint, is no more than a fair instrument for determining allocations of place and power on the basis of natural rather than artificial differences. If by equality we mean equality of condition, then we make difficult if not impossible the emergence of individuality, of differences that enable one person to manifest special gifts and talents not possessed by another. Does equality entail respect for every person's life and liberty? If so, shall we empty our jails, remove the traffic lights, and never, no matter what the circumstances, send men to die on the battlefield?

Let us look a little closer at this idea of liberty, which is surely central to any liberal or socialist idea of what it means to be human. At a minimum, liberty seems to mean the freedom to do what one wants. There is, however, a problem. Men, or some men, often want what is not good for them; in satisfying their desires they fail to satisfy their needs. As Rousseau, Hegel, Marcuse, and others have argued, therefore, they should not be free to do what they want; they should be free only to do what they ought to want, and they ought to want it because it accords with their needs, and consequently with what is right and good. Many, however, are too stupid or ignorant to know what they ought to want, and others are too selfish or wicked to do what they ought to, even though they know full well that they ought to do it. Hence it is necessary for wiser and better men to compel them to act rightly. But in thus being forced to do what they ought to do, what in fact they would themselves do were it not for their ignorance or wickedness, they are actually being forced to do only what they *really* want to do, that is, they are satisfying not their false desires but their true needs. Hence they are *really* free.

If to be human, in other words, is to be free, we can (in this construction) only be human if we correctly understand what freedom means and then act in accord with that understanding. So it is that liberty, which seemed to mean the freedom to act as one wants, turns out to mean the freedom to act as Someone Else wants you to act, that is, coercion in a right cause.

But this is surely an odd use of language and a mistaken idea of liberty. Liberty, if it means anything at all, entails the freedom to choose. In order to choose, there must be alternatives from which to choose, and hence the very real possibility that in choosing one may choose wrongly. But this is not merely a *necessary* risk; it is precisely what differentiates an adult from a child, autonomy and responsibility from dependence. Without the right to choose, whether this be the right or wrong choice, without the right to be wrong, a person is not fully human; he is certainly not free. Accordingly, whatever else we may say about human nature, it is surely the case that without this liberal view of freedom—what may be called *negative* as distinct from *positive* liberty—there can be no humanity.

Take finally the issue of malleability. Is human nature permanent or changing? And if changing, how malleable is man? The answer, I think, is not only that we don't know but that in some respects we don't want to know. The answer, also, is that human nature is probably both, or, perhaps more accurately, it is our conceptions of human nature that are probably both. Let me explain.

Unless there is some permanence to human nature, unless men today are in certain crucial respects very much as they were 500 or 2,000 or more years ago, we could not understand Socrates and Moses and Jesus, Homer and Dante and Shakespeare. That we can read these forebears, understand and learn from them, that we can in fact accept their teachings, or some of their teachings, as relevant and applicable to our lives today, demonstrates that they were like us, they faced many of the same problems we face, and they resolved them in ways we are prepared to consider as appropriate today.

Yet human nature, or at least our conception of human nature, has changed too. Some once thought, and some still think, that half the human race is inferior to the other half; yet today it is abundantly clear that men and women are morally and intellectually alike. And while it is true that human follies have led, in all too many cases, only to further follies, we believe—or some of us believe—that there has also been an appreciable increase in wisdom, or at least that the state of affairs in certain parts of the world today (say with respect to individual freedom) is appreciably better than it had once been. To have moved from slavery through feudalism to capitalism, for example, as even Marx emphasized, was a progressive act. To have moved from dynastic to democratic rule constitutes another great advance. And it would be hard to maintain that these shifts in economic and political arrangements, along with the rise of the great cities and the diffusion of cultures, did not have major effects on human nature, or at least on the natures of those men and women who were once subjects and are now citizens. If and as societies move closer to certain ideal conditions—the further removal of unwholesome restraints, the spread of knowledge, the assurance of peace and material security—the way will be opened for the emergence of new potentials that cannot be fully anticipated.

But I said earlier that in some respects we do not wish to know the answer to the question, how malleable is man? even though the answer to this question might well determine the limits that man's nature would place on our ideal political and social arrangements. Despite (perhaps because of) the Nazi experience, we do not wish to know the ultimate depths of cruelty and degradation to which man's nature can descend. We do not wish to cultivate the kind of conditioning that a Skinner offers us, because we recognize that if man could be made into what Skinner would make of him, he would no longer be recognizably human; he would be a robot. We hold to certain conceptions of humanity and dignity that preclude infinite experimentation.

And this, I think is where we properly end. Man is a protean animal, all the things both noble and base that historians and philosophers have said of him. He is both enlarged and limited by circumstance and by his society's values and practices. But he is molded, above all, by the promises gleaned from the visions that man has held of Man, from moral conceptions of what it means to be a just and decent and complete human being. It was doubtless the realities of man's baseness that led Jeremiah to utter his terrible warning: "Cursed is every man that has faith in man." But it was the realities of man's nobility that led Pietro Spina, the protagonist in Silone's novel *Bread and Wine*, to affirm his promise: "Man doesn't really exist unless he's fighting against his own limits."

We do not know, and we do not want to know, the full nature of human nature; for then not only the mystery but life itself would be at an end. It is only the striving, the testing, the unfolding of that nature that makes possible the dignity and creativity of the creature we call Man.

On Human Nature, II

Most commonly, to inquire into the relationship between human nature and human society is to ask, What opportunities or limitations does society place on the development of man's nature? But this is surely a senseless question, for it presupposes that we know what human nature is, antecedent to and apart from its presence in human society, otherwise we cannot say that social institutions frustrate or promote that nature. Nor can we know what human nature is except as it emerges from and is expressed in and through human society. Hence the individual can never be at war with society, only with its tyrannies.

However, to speak of society's tyrannies is to presuppose a nature that is frustrated or denied, which implies that we do indeed have a conception of man as distinct from and endangered by society. There is an essence prior to and independent of existence. But what is this essence, and how do we know that "it" exists?

Now the essence of a man is that which is peculiar or distinctive to him. But what is peculiar or distinctive to man is in part what is peculiar or distinctive to all men; it is what sets him apart from other beings or things; it is what entitles him to be called human. This quality, whatever it might be, must exist in all men; hence the differences among men—of wisdom or talent or virtue or strength or beauty—are from this standpoint less consequential than what is common to them all. In this respect the essence of a man is the idea of a *human* nature, which is the idea of the common, of equality.

But men who speak of essences generally mean something other than this. They mean that which is peculiar or distinctive to *this* man, that which sets this man apart from other men, that which renders him different, unique, specifically himself. For men are not equally wise or good or talented; they are not identical. Nor do they wish to be. In fact, they esteem the things that set them apart from each other. Hence they press not for equality but for liberty, for the right to pursue their differences, for the right to be unequal. From which it follows that liberty and equality are always in tension.

A society that does not recognize and seek to satisfy both passions—the passion for equality, or the sense of the common, and the passion for liberty, or the sense of the different—is a society that can but aggravate this tension. In this sense we may say that a society that seeks to achieve unity through diversity is more congenial to the demands of human nature than a society that strives for unity through uniformity. But can a society achieve unity through diversity?

This too is a senseless question, for there are degrees of unity and many kinds of diversity, some perhaps that are destructive of any kind of unity—I am thinking here of what is commonly defined as criminal conduct, e.g., theft and rape and murder. If there is to be more than a specific answer to a specific question—what sorts of diversity are compatible with this or that kind of unity?—it can only be a formula that in some measure reconciles both the demands of individuality and the requirements of community. Here perhaps the ancient wisdom of the Greeks applies: we need both the One and the Many.

We need, on the one hand, to satisfy the longings of men to be at one with their own kind, whether this be a family or tribe or city or nation. We need, on the other hand, to provide the conditions that make it possible for the individual to go his own way, to depart from the established traditions, to live differently from the rest of his folk. Each society writes the formula differently. None writes it in such a way as to resolve the tension for all time, or indeed to resolve it completely for its own time. The tension is always there.

This is because the individual is himself a tortured and schizophrenic animal. He is in pursuit of his self, but he does not know what that self is and is consequently unlikely to recognize it should it appear. He does not know who he is, where he has been, or where he is going. But he knows that he is, that he has been, and that he is going somewhere. Where? In pursuit of his needs. But his needs are insatiable, he often mistakes his needs for his desires, and in any case his actual attainments are always less than what is required by his needs or his desires. There is little correspondence between a man's dreams and his capacities, between his estimate of himself and that held of him by others, and consequently between his expectations and his rewards. So he never achieves tranquillity.

The tension also remains constant because social arrangements and practices are themselves but tentative and imperfect approximations of what they are meant to be. What a society is, is never what it was fully intended to be, or even what people may take it to be. Moreover, social arrangements are constantly in process of change. The conflicts that bedevil the self are as nothing compared to those that bedevil a society. The pressures and pulls, the jostlings among men and groups, the systematic demands and accidental occurrences, the internal maneuverings and external impositions, all contribute to the ever-continuing modification of social structures and processes and modes of behavior. There is no equilibrium, if by equilibrium we mean a system in balance. For there is neither fixed system nor permanent balance; there is only movement and disequilibrium; there is always conflict and tension.

But conflict has its advantages too. Here we must part from the Greeks, who perceived in harmony an ideal attainable by reason. Government by the passions, they believed, made for an unruly life. Reason's government of the passions, in contrast, made for that right ordering of capacities and needs that would establish a balanced and harmonious existence.

Apart from the authoritarian potential in government by men of right reason—for surely not all reasoning is right—two difficulties at least attend this conception of human nature and human society. One is the stagnation attendant on quietude. If men and societies are less than perfect, as they always are; if indeed men and societies are somewhat deranged, as in some measure they probably are; then conflict, which is always with us anyway, as it takes the form of competing ideas and strivings for power, is also needed to remedy existing wrongs and to point the way to progressive change. The other is that reason is more often the servant than the master of the passions. It is passion that generally determines what men want; reason then enters to show men how to achieve their desires. Reason may of course help men to order their conflicting desires, even perhaps to arrange them in some sort of hierarchy of values. But reason neither completely silences nor absolutely commands desires. Nor can reason overcome the terrible truth to which Kant, among others, alerted us—that out of the crooked timber of humanity no straight thing was ever made.

So crooked men fall into various points along the jagged path that runs from Left to Right, from the adventurous to the prudent, or timid, from those who press for something they call progress to those who seek to conserve the existing order of things, from those who prize diversity to those who value harmony, or even sameness. These differences exist not merely between men but also within individual man, and just as they tear man and men apart, they ensure that human societies will always be turbulent, never secure. And so we can never go to sleep.

On Freedom, I

In discussions of freedom certain elementary distinctions continue to be blunted or ignored.
● A free nation is not necessarily a nation of free men. A free nation is one that is not subject to alien rule. A free man is one who is not subject to another's restraints. Ghana became a free nation when it threw off the fetters of Great Britain. The people of Ghana did not thereby become free men and women; for they were still subject, among other things, to the laws of their new (and in some respects oppressive) government. Even in the silence of the law men and women are not completely free, for almost always social powers—of the corporation, the labor union, the church, the family, the schools, of other individuals and groups—impose a multitude of restraints.
● *Feeling* free is not *being* free. Men may feel free even when they are restrained: the poet may proclaim the freedom of his spirit even as he sits within prison walls; the slave may sing of his carefree existence even as he tills the fields of his master; the patriotic citizen may feel free even as he abstains from disobedience to laws. Subjectively, men may not feel the burdens of external restraints; but the restraints—and I must emphasize that I speak here of external, not of internal (manipulated) restraints—are nonetheless there.
● There is a difference between doing what you want and doing what someone else believes you should want. To do what you want may be to do what is good; it may also entail doing what is wrong or harmful. Since (it is often said) good men, if they are also rational, do not wish to do wrongful or harmful things, it would seem to follow, in Orwellian fashion, that preventing them from doing what they do not *really* want to do and compelling them to do what they *really* want to do, that is, what some one wiser than they "knows" they really want to do, which is to do only what is good, is not coercion but liberation. But this of course is not so: coercion even in a good cause is still coercion; freedom even if it leads to a painful result is still freedom.
● Freedom is not equality. "Liberty," said a celebrated writer, "is unattainable until the passion for equality has been satisfied." But the passion for equality may never be satisfied, for equality is a multifaceted and paradoxical concept. If by equality is meant equality of opportunity, then restraints against discriminatory practices that render such equality impossible—e.g., disadvan-

tages imposed for reasons of race, religion, sex, education, age, and the like—must be introduced at the several points of origin; even parents might have to be denied the liberty to treat their own children differently (better?) than other parents treat theirs. Paradoxically, morever, equality of opportunity means that men who begin equally may end unequally—a nonegalitarian (and undesired?) result.

If by equality, however, we mean equality of condition, so that men who begin unequally end equally, then restraints must be introduced to impose a uniform level (say) of attainment: a Heifetz or an Einstein will no longer enjoy a greater esteem, a greater position, a greater reward; there would not, in fact, be a Heifetz or an Einstein.

Apart, further, from the inconvenient fact that such equalities—of opportunity and of condition—may be mutually exclusive, or psychologically impossible to sustain, or socially undesirable, they involve not the fulfillment of liberty but its limitation. Clearly, freedom is one value, equality another, and they are not always compatible.

● Freedom is not power, nor power freedom; but power is a condition that makes possible the enjoyment of certain freedoms. Without the power of money, a man may be free to travel but unable to do so; with money he may be able to travel but in the face of a prohibitive law not free to do so. Without the power of knowledge, a man may be free to choose among consumer goods or styles of life but unable to choose wisely; with knowledge he may be able to judge wisely but in the face of limited goods or a state-imposed style of life he may not be free to choose. Thus power lends effectiveness to choice but does not itself constitute the freedom to choose. The absence of power may render formal freedoms unreal.

● A paradox: freedom, which entails tolerance, is itself often intolerable. Men and societies may espouse the principle of freedom but they distrust and even fear it, for freedom enables men to engage in distasteful or loathsome acts, such as picking one's teeth in public, or wearing inappropriate dress, or giving vent to improper thoughts, or committing theft or murder or rape, or befriending or marrying the "wrong" person. To prevent or suppress these and other "intolerable" things, societies impose a variety of moral and legal sanctions. No society, consequently, is ever fully free. Every society fears and excludes some "wrong" freedoms. Every society esteems and seeks to assure the enjoyment of the "right" freedoms.

● Hence freedom in the real world is never a totality. It is never a matter of all or nothing, but always an operating system (even if a confused one) of specific liberties and concomitant restraints. Some freedoms are approved and maintained; others are disapproved and suppressed. And for each freedom that is assured, a restraint is required to prevent interference with its exercise by others. My freedom to enter a church of my choosing entails a restraint on those who would prevent me from worshipping there. My freedom to utter displeasing ideas entails a restraint on those who would otherwise silence me. The issue is never, freedom or slavery. It is always a question of which freedoms for whom, under what circumstances, in what measure, and for what time. Freedoms are always specific, and specific freedoms, if they are to be made real, always require concomitant restraints.

• Systems of freedom are to be defended or condemned on qualitative, not quantitative grounds. A judgment concerning freedom in the U.S. or the U.S.S.R., for example, is not a matter of how many freedoms exist in the one as compared to the other but a matter of which freedoms are enjoyed in the one or denied in the other. If freedoms of speech, of the press, of political opposition are deemed crucial, then lesser freedoms, no matter how numerous, are insufficient to tip the balance.

For these and other reasons, freedom is perhaps the most paradoxical and protean of political terms and the most persistently difficult of all political problems.

On Freedom, II

Only salacious individuals are likely to deny that pornography is a serious problem. It offends many people, and in a particularly objectionable way, because some pornographic displays are often unavoidable. But people are offended by many things, and unless it can be shown that a distasteful item or practice adversely affects their interests and not merely their sentiments, or stands in a necessary (causal) relationship to criminal conduct or seriously impairs rather than marginally troubles a community's quality of life—none of which (with respect to pornography) has yet been conclusively demonstrated— we should hesitate to meet that practice by censorship and other legal sanctions rather than by moral and social disapprobation.

It is of course a familiar stratagem, perhaps derived from our Puritan heritage, to seek to exorcise an evil by legislating against it. But evil is not easily or always eradicated by political fiat, and the use of legal instrumentalities may introduce still greater evils. It may be useful to recall some of these potential (I think highly probable) dangers.

First, who will be the censors—an elegant word for petty bureaucrats—who will distinguish "obscene" from acceptable literature (books, magazines, films, plays, etc.), observing the careful distinction drawn by sober thinkers like Murray Hausknecht between "erotica" and "pornography" and employing standards that yield clarity of meaning and ease of administration rather than extensive and bewildering judicial wrangling?

If censorship is really to work—and here I urge a rereading of Milton's *Areopagitica*—the censors must begin by cataloguing and proscribing all scandalous works already in print, prohibit the importation of all foreign writings until they have been examined and approved, expurgate those works that are partly useful and excellent and partly pernicious, and require all new materials to be submitted prior to publication. Such arduous tasks require censors of unusual quality and diligence, and very many of them to boot. Where will we find them?

By the very nature of the task they are likely to be, as Milton argued, second- or third-rate minds, "illiterate and illiberal individuals" who will refuse their sanction to any work containing views or expressions at all above the level of "the vulgar superstition." Men and women of worth would obviously refuse such an assignment as tedious and unpleasant, and as an immense forfeiture of time and of their own studies. Such censors as we would be likely to get would be a constant affront to serious (for I worry not about scurrilous) writers, and could only do more harm than good.

Second, does legislation in matters of morality produce significant compliance? Can we safely ignore the American experience with laws designed to curb or eliminate prostitution, gambling, the sale and consumption of intoxicating beverages, the use of marijuana and other drugs, and the like? Such legislation has not only been ineffectual. It has created classes of criminals where none existed before; it has contributed to (if not encouraged and perhaps required) the growth of organized crime, including smuggling, the black market, and police corruption; it has promoted a general contempt for, and widespread disobedience of, law; and it has in unacceptable ways invaded the realm of privacy.

Third, is not legislation that seeks to suppress or discourage pornography through heavy taxation intrinsically discriminatory? Will this do more than deny it only to the poor? Is it not enough to torture the limits of liberty? Must we also attack the principle of equality?

A final point. Those who—like the Irving Kristols and Herbert Marcuses of this world—would invoke the law to repress what they do not like mistake the very nature of the goodness they affirm. They would impose their "right" morality on others, but—even if their morality is "right," which is surely contestable—they forget that law as a means of coercion does not ensure but inhibits the truly moral act, which is the free and responsible choice of right action. One is not good when he acts on a choice delegated to others. Indeed, one is then less than human. For what does it mean to be a person, a good person, if not that one himself chooses between good and evil, virtue and vice, truth and falsehood? Those who would deny him that choice, who insist instead that he forsake his reason and his right to free decision-making and place his conscience into their custody, demand that he cease to be a mature and responsible individual. Where, then, do evil and presumption reside?

On Democracy

When asked how in the real world I distinguish a democratic from a non-democratic state, I answer with a single question: who is the leader of the opposition? For without a political oppositon, and the commotion it produces, no state that calls itself democratic deserves the name. I mean by this commotion, of course, not the turbulence engineered by violence, whether spontaneous or directed, but the gentler yet easily visible agitation brought about by the normal activities of constitutionally sanctioned and articulate opposition parties.

Historically, men have generally identified democracy with the notion that the people shall rule—either directly or through representatives, chosen *and removable* by them. The ways in which people organize and exercise this twofold choice of selection and dismissal vary considerably from one democratic state to another; but what is common to them all, and what entitles such states to be called democratic, is the effective realization in some form of this power of choice. This is what is meant by making governments responsible.

Self-styled aristocrats often make the claim that they, and their governments, are no less and perhaps more responsible than are the governments of democratic states; but the claim is a specious one because they mean by responsibility an accounting not to the people but to what they believe to be a "higher" wisdom, which invariably turns out to be a quality of judgment mysteriously incorporated only in themselves. What democrats mean by responsibility is a periodic accounting by those temporarily occupying the seats of power to those who put them there and over whom that power is exercised. Such an accounting, involving as it does both an attack upon and a defense of the government's uses of the powers delegated to it, reduces even the most powerful of men to the role of deputy, to tenants rather than owners of power. In doing so it institutionalizes what may well be the most extreme and revolutionary of political conceptions: the simple if paradoxical idea that *in a democracy the people have a right to fire their boss*.

This proposition—I am tempted to call it perhaps the most important political discovery of the human mind—is not one to which men customarily subscribe. Most men do not think of it as a principle appropriate, say, to the economic and religious realms of human association; and the fact that adults regularly bewail the recurrent manifestations of juvenile delinquency suggests that it is not likely to be accorded governing status in our family life and schools. Yet in democratic states it is the central feature of the polity.

Now, to dismiss a government without suffering the serious consequences of anarchy, we need a group of men ready to step into office at the moment of dismissal. To know whether a government merits dismissal, we need to know what ineffectual or evil things it has done, or what worthy thing it has failed to do. Such knowledge can only be forthcoming if the channels of political criticism are unrestrained; and such an alternative group of men can only exist if there is a party *system*, if there is a lawfully recognized—a legitimate—opposition. Without such a party system and without the free play of conflicting opinions, elections are a vacuous affair and a people cannot effectively and peacefully fire their boss. The rulers cannot be held responsible to the ruled.

This is why, despite all the many other things that political theorists have stipulated as essential to a democratic state, it is sufficient to identify it by the presence of the leader of a viable opposition speaking out against governmental policy without having to suffer the risk of punishment or reprisal.

Now it is fashionable in certain circles to deprecate this understanding of democracy as more formal than real. In reality, or so it is said, oppositions in the so-called democratic states are not to be taken seriously, for they do not differ significantly, in principles or behavior, from the governing party they allegedly oppose; together with the governing party they are but constituent parts of the Establishment. Those states that are termed democratic, moreover, are everywhere disfigured by social and political arrangements that effectively block popular rule and by a manipulated public opinion that enables their governments to bespeak a rhetoric that is belied by their practices; they profess a commitment to liberty, equality, and justice, but they pursue irrational (unwise or immoral) policies. In these respects, even if they provide a government *by* the people, which is questionable, they do not provide a government *for* the people.

On its face, this is a telling indictment. It reminds us (in keeping with a classical tradition) that what counts is not the method—the procedures of democracy—but the results, not how we go about attending to our arrangements but what we do with the arrangements we have. More than that, it invites us to look at those arrangements with a jaundiced eye, to pay due regard to the inequalities that militate against the principle of majority rule and to the vast difference that separates the people who formally participate in elections from those who actually exercise crucial decision-making powers. These and other considerations make it abundantly clear that so-called democratic states but approximate the democratic ideal.

Here is the vital rub. If democracy, like liberty or equality, is an ideal—as it is—then it can *never* describe a particular reality; instead, it provides a goal toward which men should strive to move that reality as well as a standard by which that reality is to be judged. Always, therefore, its realization is a matter of degree. As an ideal, it stipulates what is required for a state to be termed democratic; but always (and necessarily) an actual state is in some respects more and in other respects less democratic than the principle stipulates. And we can know this, we can say that a particular state is more or less democratic, only *because* of the principle, not in spite of it. Hence the principle of democracy is not vitiated by the shortcomings of so-called democratic states; rather, those states are deficient precisely because they fail to meet the requirements of the principle.

To say, moreover, that a state is democratic only if it yields the "right" results is to say that one is willing to play the game only on condition that he wins. And what, indeed, are the "right" results and who is to know them? It is surely an act of moral arrogance—for it is to claim objective truth for one's subjective judgment while denying that claim to others—to profess that one knows better than the people what the people want, or ought to want, on the ground that the people have been conditioned (manipulated?) to want the "wrong" things. More, it is to destroy the vital distinction between dictatorship and democracy, for on these terms a dictator who gives the people what they need (what he thinks they ought to want) even if they say they don't want it, would be more democratic than a so-called democratic government that gives the people what they want even if a superior few insist they ought not to want it.

What defines democracy is indeed its method; it is a way of determining who shall govern, and in determining who shall govern it determines too, though broadly, the policies that the government shall then pursue. Whether those policies are wise or unwise, whether that government is constituted of "right" or "wrong" men, is a matter of the quality of the public opinion that has selected them. And however much we may wish to improve the quality of that opinion, what is decisive in democratic politics (because in conformity with the egalitarian principle) is its quantity. What counts is government *by* the people. While it is hoped (and by some believed) that this will prove to be government *for* the people, at any given historical moment it may or may not prove to be so.

The indictment of democracy thus turns out to be an indictment of the arrangements and policies of particular states, not an indictment of the democratic principle at all. And the appropriate remedy is not the jettisoning but the fulfillment of democracy, not the further manipulation of public opinion but its genuine enlightenment.

One more thing, perhaps, needs to be said. Men whose estimate of themselves and of their ideas exceeds that held by others often tend to impute stupidity or malevolence to their detractors, or to the system which has produced and now sustains them. Thus they say that the governing and leading opposition parties are like peas in a pod but that people don't understand this and therefore don't have a real choice.

But men and women who subscribe to the leading opposition party believe that there are significant differences between their own and the governing party, and in any case they can if they wish—in a democratic polity—elect to support still another opposition party, even one of the extreme Right or extreme Left. It is no argument against the democratic principle to show that socialist or communist or fascist or vegetarian parties are unable to command a majority. Democracy does not stipulate that all opposition parties must some day win, or even that substantial support be given to them. It demands only that opposition parties, whatever their persuasion, be free to organize and to appeal for electoral favor. And if it be said that this is formally but not substantially correct, because the masses of the people have been conditioned to think and to desire only what their masters are willing to accept, the response is surely that Orwell's *1984* is still a utopian nightmare rather than a present reality. A substantial portion of the citizenry has not been successfully manipulated, whether in democratic or in totalitarian states.

In short, democracy does not guarantee that the "right" views will prevail. It provides only that those views, along with others, shall have the opportunity to be heard. And in a world where repression is so much the order of the day, it is no mean achievement for a political system to leave the adherents of diverse views, whether "right" or "wrong," free to press their positions and remain unmolested as they seek popular support. Only those who believe that reason and experience are calculated to ensure the victory of error can repudiate this principled appeal to the free play of conflicting opinions.

So I end where I began: that what is crucial to the principle of democracy is not the practices of particular states, nor the triumph of particular views, but the presence of a constitutionally sanctioned opposition.

On Revolution

What I find strange in history is not that there have been so many revolutions but that there have been so few; for surely the causes that make for revolutions have always been with us. Always men have suffered injustice. Always life has been brutish and in some sense absurd. Always rulers have been insufficiently responsive to justifiable demands for social change. Yet sensitive men aware of these things have more often than not either themselves refused to go to the barricades or found themselves unable to mobilize the masses in support of such an enterprise. Why has it been so?

Paramount among the reasons for this abstention from revolutionary violence I would put not principle but fear—fear of losing even the little that one may have, fear of failure and of the repressive consequences attendant upon that failure, above all fear of death.

Second, and still before principle (some might say even before fear), are inertia and docility. Men at the bottom of the pyramids of power do not commonly resent their fate. They accept it as given by the order of things. Those who would marshal them into battalions consequently encounter resistance; for, it is often believed, what is, is fated or a matter of God's will, and there is salvation only in heaven. So men are placid and docile and inert; and they will not be moved. Or, if they are to be moved, it is primarily in the direction of reform, not revolution. What they want is a bit more, but only of what is immediate and central to their understanding—more money, more leisure—not the distant and incomprehensible ideal of social justice.

What is significant about industrial societies is that, by and large, they have provided this bit more. They have not generated revolutionary sentiments because they have, as it were, delivered the goods. This is not to deny the great element of validity in those terrible indictments of 18th- and 19th-century capitalism drawn by novelists like Dickens and social critics like Marx. There were, there still are, degrading conditions of labor. There was, there still is, shameful exploitation of men, women, and even children. But the list of grievances, long and legitimate as it is, must not be overdrawn. For along with those grievances have come both a real and rising standard of living and (in the democratic states of the Western world) a lessening of political oppression. Marx's great blunder was to believe that the more industrialized a society was to become, the more prone it would be to revolution—even if, as he said of England and the United States, the revolution might be a peaceful one. The facts attest to an opposite truth: that the more industrialized a society becomes, the more it draws the teeth from the resentments that make for revolution.

This leads to a fourth consideration: the effectiveness of partial revolutions, whether evolutionary or sudden. Revolutionaries customarily think and talk in terms of total change, but history is a more mundane procession of trivial spasms and moderate reforms. Women gain the suffrage, or the right to abort unwanted children; labor gains the right of collective bargaining, an improvement in wages and working conditions, even an edge into managerial prerogatives; students and blacks erupt and effect educational and social reforms; but in all these cases the changes are partial and specific, they do not entail a total reconstruction of the political and social order. Even the welfare state is a manifestation of partial rather than of total change. And revolutions themselves, when properly understood, are but a product of and a stage in a slower and more enduring evolutionary process.

In democratic states both the fact and the desirability of limited attainments are institutionalized into a pragmatic principle: the principle of peaceful and continuing partial revolution. Men without substantial power in one field, say the economic, may now exercise effective power in another, the political; the state becomes the instrument through which they can hope to achieve economic and educational and social reforms. And they can do so peacefully, without risk of death or major repression. To the degree that they are able to achieve their limited objectives, it becomes unnecessary to overthrow the political system. Indeed, what would be the purpose in overthrowing democracy when the alternative is a system that would deprive them of the one effective power they have?

There is also a moral deterrent to revolutionary violence: it is not merely inhuman to kill, it is dehumanizing to resort to violence. Violence corrupts both the user and those against whom it is employed. It corrupts the user by making him a different man than he was before: consumed by passion and convinced of the rightness of his cause, he soon loses the capacity to draw distinctions; all who are not with him are against him, all are the enemy; and in the crudity of his monolithic rage he turns into a weapon of destruction. He becomes an extension of his gun, and those who use guns know neither tolerance nor decency. So it is with those who must now unleash their own guns against him. From the civilized world of moral discourse we thus move into the jungle, where beasts, not men, walk the surface of the earth. Revolution, even the "success" of the revolution, destroys both the revolutionaries and the cause for which the revolution was ostensibly begun.

If to all these considerations we add: the terrible power of modern governments, against whose advanced technology and sophisticated weaponry revolutionary movements are unlikely to prevail, whatever current advocates of revolution say to the contrary; the fragmentation of revolutionary movements and their often ineffective leadership; the habit of law-abidingness; and the knowledge that unanticipated consequences will always plague and probably frustrate the best-laid and well-intentioned plans; then we can readily understand the disinclination or inability of most troubled men to resort to revolutionary violence.

Under what circumstances, then, is the appeal to revolution valid, or likely to carry conviction? Historically, the answer has been some variant of the following: when there is great economic discontent (Marx) or psychological resentment (Aristotle) among the people; when there is no real hope or significant possibility of effective change within the system; when the ruling class (or classes) is so stupid or ineffectual as no longer to be able to maintain order and impose its will; when there is ready at hand and actively at work a well-organized, professional cadre of revolutionary leaders to mobilize the masses and lead them in a desired direction (Lenin).

But all this is less a matter of principle than of tactics. It amounts to little more than a cliché: where a grievance (or set of grievances) can be corrected by peaceful means, it is wrong to call for revolutionary action; where a grievance (or set of grievances) cannot be corrected by peaceful means, then there is no recourse but to revolution.

What it overlooks, further, is the difficulty of attributing specific grievances to the character of a regime. If, for example, it can be demonstrated that babies are starving because of the policies of an autocratic regime, and if it can be established that another regime will in fact reduce or eliminate this starvation, then there is a *prima facie* case for revolution. But it is not always the case that such a direct causal relationship can be shown. In contemporary India, for example, infant mortality appears the consequence far more of vast population growth and social and economic backwardness than of oppressive government.

Where, to take another and more general example, the grievance is located in the denial of equality, or of vital liberties, or of some conception of justice, then the case for change is conclusive. But whether or not this change requires revolution is to be determined by the tactical situation—whether, that is to say, a revolution is in fact likely to succeed and whether the consequences are likely to be less disastrous than the situation it is designed to correct.

Finally, it ought never to be forgotten that revolution, even in the name of reason, is *always* an attack upon reason and that one of the terrible consequences of revolution is the inflammation of the passions, the governance of might rather than of right. And who can say whether the might that prevails is truly in the service of the right cause, or whether that right cause will not itself be corrupted by the new strong men who, rather than the revolutionary idealist, come to power and impose repressive policies of their own?

2

Liberalism and Conservatism

I

Political labels may be employed either as general categories or as ideological weapons. As categories, they are models or ideal types, not descriptions of empirical realities. As ideological weapons, they are slogans or epithets that serve, all too commonly, as pigeonholes into which individuals and groups may be squeezed. That very few people fall completely into a single classification matters little to purveyors of political rhetoric or caricature intent on manipulation.

To the extent that we seek understanding, we need, therefore, to guard against the confusions wrought by political slogans. We need to avoid certain other pitfalls as well. Of these, none is more pernicious than the notion that political labels explain the motives of those who embrace them. Motives, even of a single act, are always complex; and when diverse men unite behind a common label or cause, it is generally for a variety of reasons. Some seek to promote their self-interests; others are driven by blind prejudice or idealistic commitment; and still others are there simply because they are there: Prisoners of inertia or of habit, it would no more occur to them to abandon a traditional allegiance than it would to incite a revolution against themselves. Yet all employ the language of high principle; all appeal to justice, or the national interest, or the common good, or the inherent nature and dignity of man. But since the real grounds on which they hold their beliefs are not always the grounds alleged, a refutation of those avowed grounds will not persuade them to abandon their cause. Reasoning alone is but a poor instrument of political conversion, as instance any attempt to argue the biological merit of miscegenation with a Southern racist.

For related reasons, political labels are not to be identified with a particular man or party or position on a specific issue. Men hold different positions, and in

Reprinted, by permission, from Robert A. Goldwin, ed., *Left, Right, and Center,* pp. 18–41. Copyright © 1965 by the Public Affairs Conference Center, Kenyon College, Gambier, Ohio.

different degrees of commitment, depending on the issue at stake. One may be mildly or extremely liberal or conservative; one may be conservative in some-things and liberal in others. When Representative Robert Taft, Jr., was a candidate for the United States Senate in the Ohio election of 1964, he declared that he was a conservative on fiscal matters, a middle-of-the-roader on issues of education, health, and welfare, and a liberal on civil rights. Unkind critics might conclude that he was a sadly disjointed man. But surely the more useful and accurate view is to recognize the need to draw distinctions, and that an apparent inconsistency such as Taft's may be inconsistent in a superficial sense only; for it might reflect significant differences in the character of the conse-quences of those diverse positions and thus be in harmony with a larger purpose. Consistency, moreover, while a necessity in logic, is not a pervasive or characteristic attribute in politics; and it is perhaps as often the case that men are both liberal and conservative as that they are either of these alone.

Positions change. Conservatives who defended and liberals who attacked the Supreme Court in the 1930's have now reversed their roles; for in the earlier period the Court was identified as the protector of property rights and now it is regarded as the protector of human rights.

Political parties change; they also display both internal agreement and diversity on ideolgical questions. On the issue of national power versus states' rights, both of the major American parties have historically committed them-selves to opposing positions, not once but repeatedly, according to whether or not they occupied the seats of national power. In Germany, the Social Demo-cratic party after the First World War was not what it had been before, and the party today is significantly different again. In England, both the Conservative and Labour parties have shifted their positions markedly over time. In Italy, the Communist party after the Second World War even supported the union of Church and State, and more recently mourned the death of a pope. In all these and other democratic states, members of the same political party have often divided on some issues and united on others, and have crossed party lines accordingly.

Political labels do not have the same meaning across national boundaries. To be a Liberal in Italy is to be a member of the Right; in America liberalism is associated with the Left. Conservatives in Britian, while on the Right, are in many respects far to the left of conservatives in the United States.

In short, political labels, by the very fact that they are verbal abridgements of political life, are as mischievous as they are useful. Indeed, if they are to be useful, not merely as ideological weapons but as categories of analysis, they must be employed with extreme caution, and as guides to rather than as specific descriptions of political realities. All this has to be borne in mind when one encounters the use of such labels in contemporary America, nowhere more so than in the case of such terms as liberalism and conservatism. Are these terms, in fact, of any use in describing actual political alignments, or do they belong to the lexicon of political mythology?

II

To the realm of mythology we must, by and large, consign what is perhaps the simplest and most widely-shared view of the distinction between liberalism and conservatism, which turns on their reputed attitudes toward social change. Liberalism, it is said, seeks and promotes change; it is the party of something called progress. Conservatism fears and resists change; it is the party of stability. Where one stands in relation to the status quo is in this view the crux of the matter.

There is much truth in this contention. In every society, it may well be argued, there are two classes: the politically active and the politically apathetic. The active class everywhere divides into two subclasses: the contented and the discontented. The discontented class, precisely because it is the impoverished, the frustrated, the inferior, or otherwise subordinate class, yet is unwilling to remain so, is the primary, though not the sole, proponent of change—through an alteration either of the system or a part of the system. Since change endangers the position of the contented or superior class, this class becomes the primary, though again not the sole, antagonist to change. In societies that resolve disputes through elections or force, both classes need and consequently seek the support of the otherwise apathetic, who are thus mobilized behind the one or the other faction, or, as is most commonly the case, divided in varying proportions among them. It is in this conflict that politics has its beginnings and its abiding character, for it is this conflict that divides men in a struggle for power. And it is because of this conflict that we find, in every society, the use of relevant political labels: liberalism and conservatism, left and right, heresy and orthodoxy, innovation and resistance, modernity and tradition.

But here a word of caution: the labels are not descriptive of the actual spectrum of loyalties. Not all who are contented or discontented are that way with respect to all or the same matters. Some may approve the political system but disapprove the economic system, or approve some aspects of the political and economic systems but disapprove others; some may be satisfied or dissatisfied with both but not with their religion and church, or with the existing patterns of education and of family life. Since a group may thus be both contented and discontented, it may seek change with respect to some things but resist it with respect to others. It may find itself allied with other groups on one issue but opposed to them on another. This being true, it is possible for a particular individual or group to be a partisan of both change and stability; and this, as I have already suggested, is frequently the case.

Not only does our simple and quite elementary distinction thus collapse when applied to individuals and groups in the real world, it tells us nothing of the degree to which different men seek change; nor does it distinguish the direction of the change. Not all who want change even on the same thing want the same degree of change; some desire moderate change, others are extremists. More important, some want to move to a new and hence untried political or economic or social principle or arrangement; others seek to return to that which has allegedly been abandoned. Change in itself tells us nothing of the character and consequences of the change desired—whether it is progressive or retrogressive, whether it furthers the interests of the entire community or of a portion of that community, and if a portion whether of the upper or middle or lower classes, or of the colored or white peoples, or of the urban or rural power groups, and so on. Clearly, it is in these things, not in the mere fact of change itself, that the true issues and divisions of political life reside.

These considerations are underscored by the fact that after a political revolution or orderly reversal of the parties in power, the elements that previously opposed or supported the government now reverse roles. This does not make the Left conservative and the Right liberal. For if it is the Left, say, that is newly come to power in a democratic state, that power may be employed to change not the political system but certain economic and social arrangements, as in Britain after the election of 1945 and in America after the elections of 1932 and 1960. Both Left and Right, then, give their allegiance to a political system that institutionalizes, if not change, at least the peaceful processes by which change may be effected. And the Right, in its turn, may undo what the Left has done or introduce changes of its own, some of which may be resisted by the Left. Not change, then, but the character of the change, is the decisive consideration.

A second and scarcely less prevalent and misleading view of the distinction between liberalism and conservatism derives from their alleged respective attitudes toward property and freedom. In its most popular form, this view holds that conservatives defend the rights of private property and individual freedom while liberals attack private property and urge collectivist controls. Since Communists and fascists also fall into this latter description, it is easy to see why conservatives find this distinction particulary attractive. But if we set such ideological devices aside, the deceptiveness of this formula and alleged cleavage readily becomes apparent.

It is perhaps no more than a commonplace to note that property as such has no rights; only men have rights. Men may claim a right to property, to the exclusive possession and use of whatever it is they desire, but what converts such a claim to a right is its recognition in law or morality; and such recognition is warranted only in terms of its human and social consequences. Hence, when it is said that liberals attack private property, what they actually attack in the first instance is the allocation and use of human and social resources on arbitrary and socially undesirable grounds. The property that is at stake, moreover—not individual dwellings and personal possessions but large-scale industrial, commercial, and agricultural enterprises—is private only in minimal degree. What we are dealing with today, and indeed for some time past, is pre-eminently corporate, not private property; and to vest corporate property with the attributes of private property is a palpable fiction. Surely this is not what writers in the natural law tradition had in mind by the word "property." Most important of all, however, is the fact that property is a form of sovereignty. It divides men into those who have and those who have not, and who are thus dependent on those who have for their very survival. Dependence makes for inequality, inequality begets servility, and servility renders freedom impossible. Property then is government, and because power in such government is most commonly dynastic or oligarchical in form, it denies the principles and aspirations of the democratic creed.

In these terms, conservatives who today defend what they call the rights of property defend neither private property nor the existing economic system nor individual freedom. Not private property, for as even Woodrow Wilson and Herbert Hoover recognized, large-scale corporate property is the denial rather than the realization of individual property and individual enterprise. Not the existing economic system, for throughout this century and especially since the Employment Act of 1946, our political system has taken account of, indeed has been interwoven with, our economic system so as to produce a regulated or mixed economy. Not individual freedom, for when conservatives of this sort speak of freedom they mean freedom from political controls. But controls derive too from sources other than the state. They are imposed by private powers no less than by political governments, thus producing a paradoxical situation in which political restraints, by curbing nonpolitical restraints, may assure freedom to those who would otherwise be controlled by private powers. The freedom of a man to do X, that is to say, may be secured not by the silence of the political government but by its intervention; for in the silence of the government a private power—be it a corporation like General Motors or a voluntary association like the Ku Klux Klan—is free to limit the freedom of men dependent on it or too weak to resist it. Through intervention, the political government can act as a countervailing power and thus liberate those who might otherwise be deprived of certain freedoms.

This is why the liberal plea for collective or state action is not a call for totalitarianism but a call for individual freedom. In an earlier time there may have been some justification for regarding the state as the crucial, even the sole, enemy of man's freedom. But the coming of democracy has converted the state from the agent of a privileged few to the agent of the whole. In such a state, properly actualized, the government is the people's own; it is their instrument, not their master. As such, it can provide men with those conditions that make freedom both possible and meaningful, and that they cannot otherwise attain by themselves, such as education and adequate medical care. The concern of the liberal is not with collectivism but with individuality, the development of personality, to which collective action is but a means. In the modern world it is a necessary means. Hence the issue is not whether collectivist controls shall be employed, but only whether they shall be employed wisely, and in the public interest. The conservative who denounces state intervention also looks to collectivist controls, but to nonpolitical collectives: and these, because they are oligarchic rather than democratic associations, operate to the advantage only of those who sit at the top of private pyramids of power. For these and other reasons, the contention that conservatism is to be distinguished from liberalism by its concern for private property and individual freedom is patently false. Even more misleading, as well as dangerous, is the converse proposition that liberalism, because of its recourse to state action, is hostile to personal freedom and human rights.

The two major misconceptions of liberalism and conservatism dealt with here by no means exhaust the very considerable catalogue of errors, but they are, I think, representative of the more important among them. As such, they may suffice to show the careless and misleading designs to which our political labels are regularly put. But can they be used at all in any meaningful sense?

III

If we are to talk sensibly of liberalism and conservatism, we must probe somehow to a common core of meaning—a core that transcends though it does not obliterate the many diversities and transformations of liberal and conservative doctrine. We may well want to distinguish between, say, classical liberalism and modern liberalism, or between liberalism as a dogma (e.g., the doctrines of John Locke or of Herbert Spencer), liberalism as an ideology (the reflection of a mood or the rationalization of certain economic or political interests), and liberalism as a philosophy (whether skeptical about ultimate values or optimistic about human progress). But inexorably we return to the crucial question: Is there a constellation of policies and attitudes that tend to correspond to and appear concomitantly with the one or the other label? If there is a recurring convergence of such policies and attitudes, then these labels have a viable and abiding significance, and it is possible to speak of them in terms of a tradition or a unity.

I believe that such a unity does exist, even though it is not always described in precisely the same way. Sometimes it is presented as a cleavage between parties or classes. Here liberalism, or the Left, is identified with that party associated with and representative of the interests of the lower classes, while conservatism, or the Right, is the party associated with and representative of the interests of the upper or dominant class. Sometimes this untiy is found at the intellectual or philosophical level. Here liberalism is tied to the principle of experimentalism, to the open-ended negotiation of differences, whether of ideas or of policies, while conservatism bespeaks the cause of absolute truth, of a belief in an objective moral order, of a relatively closed rather than an open society. Both these conceptions of liberalism and conservatism, I think, are broadly correct, but because they do not readily distinguish between or adequately encompass the different spheres of thought and action—the political, the economic, the intellectual or cultural—they need to be incorporated into a larger and multidimensional framework.

In the political sphere, the unity or tradition of liberalism is unambiguous. Its pre-eminent principle is political equality. Whatever the form of state, whatever the historical situation or national character, the liberal has associated himself with the battle against entrenched privilege. Always the liberal has denied that power and station are the appropriate perquisites of lineage, or of the exercise of force, or of something called History or God. Always the liberal has looked to that which is common to men, not to that which divides them. This does not mean that the liberal is oblivious to the fact that men are not identical, that there are indeed differences of religion and race, wealth and power, talent and intelligence. What it does means is that for the liberal such differences, important though they may be for certain purposes, are politically irrelevant. Each man has a life to live, the poorest as well as the richest man. Each man requires freedom—to exercise his reason, to discover and develop his talents, to achieve his full growth and stature as an individual. And each man suffers the consequences of deprivation and injustice, the oppressor no less than the oppressed. Hence each man has a common stake in the conditions, and in the determination of the conditions, under which he lives.

Liberals have no faith in human infallibility, or in the capacity of an allegedly superior few to respect the principle of equality or to withstand the corrupting temptations of power. Hence, while liberals recognize that political decisions taken by the people may be wrong, decisions taken by a self-proclaimed aristocracy are not necessarily right. Indeed, their wrongs have been far more numerous! What is crucial, then, is a political arrangement that makes possible the peaceful and effective correction of error. This dictates democracy, for only democracy provides a constitutional mechanism for the removal of the rulers by the ruled. Whatever its limitations or defects, democracy commends itself to liberals by this one overriding virtue—the principle of responsibility, by which the governed can protect themselves from misgovernment. This is why liberalism has consistently opposed authoritarianism in politics, why it has fought against all forms of oligarchical rule.

Conservatism, in contrast, has traditionally been identified with the impulse to hierarchy, a hierarchy based on the inequality of men. What is impressive to the conservative is that societies are made up of men, not Man, and that men are different. Some men (it is held) are wiser, more intelligent, more talented, better informed, than others. And if some men are superior and others average or inferior, it is the height of folly, conservatives argue, to let the unwise, through their numerical superiority, govern the wise or even themselves. For if they are unwise, they will make wrong decisions and thus defeat the very purposes they seek to accomplish. Indeed, because they are unwise, they cannot, save by accident, know what the right purposes are. It is true that conservatives are not always in agreement as to the character of the superior few. Some believe this superiority derives from race or blood; others, that it is an attribute of wealth or strength; still others, that it is associated with intelligence or virtue. But that there are a superior few, whether determined by nature or nurture, conservatives do not doubt. Hence the right political order is in the conservative view that which in one way or another institutionalizes this crucial fact.

Moreover, when the conservative speaks of order, he has in mind an order that is given, not contrived. Its laws are to be discovered, not created, to be adhered to, not defied. Just as the heavenly bodies have their accustomed place, just as the waters fall and the trees rise, so there is pattern and degree in human communities. Each man, said the ancient philosopher, must be given his due; but no man must seek more than his due. Hence those who are qualified to rule must rule; those who are fit but to obey must obey. And if, at a particular moment, the few who actually occupy the seats of power are not those fitted by reason and nature to rule, if, as Santayana and others of this persuasion sometimes admit, past aristocracies have been artificial rather than natural and just aristocracies, still it is better to have order than disorder. This is why conservatives, despite internal disagreements, have throughout history defended the prevailing aristocratic order, resisted the encroachments of egalitarianism, and associated themselves with the upper or dominant class.

In the economic sphere, this distinction between liberalism as representative of the interests of the lower classes and conservatism as spokesman for the interests of the upper classes is even more clear. There is, however, one crucial exception that must be noted. This is the disjunction among conservatives on the indentification of wealth and virtue. When Socrates asked why it is that philosophers are to be found at the doors of the rich but the rich do not wait at the doors of the philosophers, he expressed in rhetorical form a contempt—shared by liberals and some conservatives alike—for the notion that money means wisdom. For the philosophers attend the rich only because philosophers know what they need; the rich do not. Consequently wealth, far from constituting proof of one's virtue or superiority—unless perhaps we speak here of superiority in chicanery and greed—establishes the reverse. With respect to the things that matter, the wealthy, precisely because they have spent their lives and their thoughts on the acqusition of money and material goods, are essentially philistines.

Yet it is a peculiar fact that even conservatives of this sort, who like to denote themselves "philosophical" conservatives, or even drop the term conservatism completely, tend in their practical conduct to unite with other conservatives who esteem wealth and account it a mark of virtue. When the lines are drawn, conservatives of all persuasions come together, in greater rather than in lesser degree, to defend the interests of the upper classes. In part, this may be because all conservatives revere "order," not any system of order, to be sure, but that order which reflects the tastes and values of men of quality, men who embody the aristocratic spirit, who understand the dictates of nature or of nature's God. In part, therefore, this joint conservative defense of the upper classes is the product of their conviction that, however we conceive the relation between wealth and virtue, the lower classes are the classes of the common man, who is in this view the vulgar, the mass, the inferior man. As such, he is disrespectful of law and order, he lacks knowledge and understanding of the "right" order, he does not—because he cannot—appreciate the need for standards and quality. In part, however, it is also to be explained by the fact that, whatever the grounds on which conservatives arrive at their position, all tend to share the view, even if only the suspicion, that the men at the top of the eonomic ladder are there because they really are men of superior ability. They are, on the whole, educated men. They have nice manners. They exhibit some at least of the outward trappings of "culture." They are, therefore, in certain visible ways superior to the men at the bottom. Above all, they think to themselves as superior men, they act like superior men. By comparison, the poor, the uneducated, the hewers of wood and the drawers of water, are a sad and visibly inferior lot. Economic policies, consequently, should not only be made by those who are competent, who "know" what is right; they should be geared, in the first instance, to the advantage of those superior men, for only that state which uses its political power to secure and further the interests of those who have economic power can hope to achieve that abundance and stability necessary to survival in our troubled world.

The argument, in fact, can be pushed further. As a conservative like Alexander Hamilton fully understood, economic power divorced from and antagonistic to political power makes for an unhealthy, perhaps an impossible, situation. For economic power will not stand idly by and permit itself to be destroyed. On the contrary, because it perceives its interests, because it has the knowledge and skills appropriate to the promotion of those interests, and because, above all, it possesses the means and the will to act in defense of those interests, it will destroy the forces antagonistic to it. If, then, order is to be maintained, it must be an order which unites economic power with political power. And this, in the conservative view, inexorably means an attachment of political power to the interests of the dominant economic class. This is why conservatives defend not simply wealth, but inherited wealth. This is why conservatives oppose tax policies and measures that seek to regulate the conduct of businessmen, that is, to reduce their power and position. This is why conservatives speak little of human or civil rights, but much of property and vested rights.

Liberalism, on the other hand, has always been identified with the interests of the lower classes—not because the lower classes have by some mystery of incarnation been blessed with a monopoly of virtue but because wealth, especially inherited wealth, is not a sufficient test of function or capacity. In the liberal view, all men are equal. Insofar as distinctions of place and power must be admitted, they properly derive only from the freely recorded and continuing consent of the people, not from such arbitrary factors as ancestry or ruthless force. It is hoped, and by some believed, that the people will choose wisely, that they will recognize men on the basis of merit, of demonstrated competence. To discover merit, equality of opportunity is essential. This requires the elimination of hereditary privilege and of unwarranted discriminatory practices, such as those based on race or religion or sex. It requires, even more, reduction of great inequalities of wealth which make equality of opportunity impossible. It requires, from a positive standpoint, the creation of those conditions which assure access to all positions to those who, whatever their origins, demonstrate by their individual qualities and achievements that they merit them. It is thoroughly false and misleading to assert, as some critics of liberalism do, that liberals seek absolute equality of condition, that liberals recognize and respect no differences. On the contrary, what liberals contend is that equality of opportunity is the necessary condition for the rational determination of those qualities in which men are different and truly unequal, and hence in what respects power and position may properly be apportioned. Anything other than this is a defense of artificial and false inequalities.

Liberalism is concerned not only with equality of this sort in the economic sphere; it is concerned also with liberty. Now what is crucial about private ownership of property in the real world is that such ownership confers power without responsibility; those who own property have the legal right to use it to promote their own interests, whatever the consequences of their decisions on the welfare of others. Such ownership divides men into independent and dependent men; by denying some men equal access to the use of the earth—though we have not, curiously, sought to deny them equal access to air and to water, perhaps because this presents certain practical difficulties—such ownership forces some men to become the slaves or servants of others. This enables those who possess property to use, to exploit, other men for their advantage. And it is this fact, that some men can use other men, can treat them as a means to their purposes rather than as ends in themselves, that constitutes in the liberal view a debasement of man.

For this reason, liberals have traditionally supported the efforts of the lower classes, through legislation by government and through the countervailing pressures of economic organizations, e.g., the labor unions, to curb the great economic powers of the owners and managers and to give workers a voice in determining the conditions under which they labor. They have sought to restrain and curtail the growth of corporate monopoly, which destroys individual enterprise and penalizes the consumer. They have sought to introduce into the operation of the giant large-scale enterprises that today constitute the economic-technological system a pattern of controls that mitigate the depersonalizing and dehumanizing effects of a master-servant relationship. They have even urged government to move directly into the economic sphere through the public ownership and operation of certain services and industries, where private ownership either has served the public interest inadequately or has diverted natural and social resources away from this public interest to the promotion of private gain. In diverse ways, including schemes that look to the transformation of the entire system of economic power, liberals have sought to lessen the harsh impact of oligarchical rule in economic life, to introduce a measure of democracy within or democratic controls over the industrial-technological process, to assure freedom from arbitrary command within the economic no less than within the political sphere. For how can a man be equal and free when he is a dependent and servile man? Not the rights of property, then, however these may be defined, but the rights of man are for liberalism the guiding principle of economic organization and action.

We come, finally, to the distinction between liberalism and conservatism in the intellectual or cultural sphere. Here the issue that divides these camps, while not unrelated to social classes, turns primarily on their respective attitudes toward freedom of inquiry and expression.

Conservatism, it is claimed, seeks to conserve not everything but only the Good. But the Good is not self-evident; hence conservatism requires a standard or body of principles by which we can distinguish the good from the bad. It requires, even more, a demonstration that this standard or set of principles is both applicable and right. Conservatives agree that there is, indeed there must be, such a standard or body of principles. It exists because it is inherent in the very nature of things. It needs, then, only to be discovered and, when discovered, to be obeyed. What defines and accounts for the present malaise, the malpractices and discontents of our time, is from this standpoint the fact that men no longer seek or abide by these true principles. They look to opinion rather than to knowledge, and opinion, precisely because it is not knowledge, is an uncertain and puny guide. More than that, opinion in democratic states is formed by average, which means inferior, men. Hence policies based upon public opinion are likely to be wrong. Only if we recapture and adhere to the true principles of political life, conservatives argue, can we hope to achieve right and good government.

It is true that conservatives are in no sense agreed as to what these true principles are, or why they are warranted. Some conservatives believe that these principles are revealed by God, or, in some constructions, by His teachings as these are mediated by and through His One True Church, whichever it might be—for not all conservatives agree as to which God is God and what it is that God says. Others derive these correct principles from history or tradition, but since there are, alas, conflicting traditions or at least diverse readings of the same tradition, this leads to multiple and not always consistent principles. Still others look to nature, to the doctrines of natural law or natural right, but here again there seems to be considerable disagreement as to what it is that nature teaches. And some, finally, appeal to intuition, to a subjective but nontheless (it is said) correct apprehension of what is right as distinct from what is wrong; though here again, since men do not all palpitate in the same way, intuitive judgments do not always coincide. Despite these differences and conflicts, which often divide conservatives into congeries of warring sects, they are all, in one crucial respect at least, still conservatives; for they all believe in the existence of an absolute truth, of an objective moral order, and hence of a political system and body of policies deriving from and corresponding to the principles of this true morality.

This is why Walter Lippmann, for example, seeking to transcend internecine conflicts and to unite conservatives behind a cohesive, if general, body of principles, invokes the Public Philosophy, or the Traditions of Civility, as an appropriate substitute for otherwise diverse conservative labels. This is why, too, he seeks their warrant not in logical or historical demonstration but in need. We must, he says, "repair the capacity to believe"; we must accept as valid those priciples on which sincerely and lucidly rational men, when fully informed and motivated by good will, tend to agree. This is why, finally, conservatives are so partial to religion, though it is curious to note that their defense of religion is often couched not in terms of its truth but in terms of its utility. For conservatives generally, as even for men otherwise so diverse in their outlooks as Hobbes and Rousseau, concerned as they are with stability, it is far more important to have a single religion than to have the "right" religion. A universal or general commitment to the same religion—in contemporary America, according to some conservatives, *any* religion—not only precludes religious, i.e., civil, wars; it also makes for piety, which makes for obedience, which makes for stability and peace.

Whatever the specific formulation of the conservative creed, the fact that it does build throughout on a claimed objective truth produces the same practical consequences. Above all, these include the disparagement of freedom of inquiry and a readiness to limit and control freedom of expression. Since the truth is already known, freedom of inquiry rests in the conservative view on a false premise: that it is proper seriously to entertain error. In fact, because error may appear in attractive and plausible guise, unsophisticated minds may well mistake it for truth. To permit the unrestrained expression of such false-hoods may lead to their widespread acceptance. Then error, not truth, will govern mankind. Since it is the business of government, according to conservatives, to apply justice and achieve virtue, not speech but "good" speech, not conflicting ideas but "right" ideas, should alone be tolerated. The idea of an open society, in which men are free to utter and debate diverse opinions, including the wrong opinions, is from this standpoint both evil and absurd. What is vital is the inculcation of right attitudes, right habits, right conduct; and this can only be achieved if men who know what is right teach and control those who would not otherwise understand or do what is right. Thus conservatism moves toward an authoritarian, conformist society, based upon the rule of allegedly aristocratic minds. This has been its traditional pattern. This is, on the whole, its present practice.

Liberalism differs from conservatism most sharply in its insistence on the value of individual liberty, and concomitantly on the value of freedom of inquiry and of expression. It may, though it need not, deny that absolute truths, at least with respect to the "right" political principles, are known; but whether these truths are known or not, liberalism insists nonetheless on the freedom to examine them, to subject them to empirical and logical criticism, and to expose them to the challenge of conflicting ideas. Skepticism about ultimate values, that is to say, is often associated with the liberal creed; but while it is appropriate to that creed it is not necessary to it. Individual liberty, however, with all that this implies in the way of cultural diversity or nonconformity in cultural and intellectual life, is indispensable to the liberal idea.

Insofar as liberalism repudiates the conservative claim to absolute and infallible truth, it rests on the assumption that man is born not stupid but infinitely ignorant, and that however much he may learn in his very short span of life, the things he learns amount to but a small portion of what there is to be known. Always the things he does not know are greater than the things he does know. Consequently, the beliefs he holds to be true may prove, on the basis of later knowledge, to be erroneous or only partially true. Awareness of this fact makes for a certain measure of humility; it also leads to a commitment to the methods of rational inquiry, rather than to the specific results that may at any one time emerge from such inquiry. The basic value of the liberal is, from this standpoint, the value of free inquiry; his basic attitude, the skeptical, or at least the inquiring, mind.

It follows that when two rational and relatively well-informed men disagree, it is less likely that one has complete possession of the truth and the other error, than that each has a partially valid insight. This is why liberals find so persuasive John Stuart Mill's argument for the toleration of dissenting ideas: The heretical view, Mill pointed out, where right, enables us to abandon error and embrace the more valid doctrine; where wrong, it helps us perceive the wholeness of our truth, indeed, it prevents us by its very challenge from clinging to our accepted truth in the manner of a prejudice or a superstition, without an adequate comprehension of its meaning; and where partly right, it reinforces our own partial truth and helps us correct our partial error. This is why a political liberal (but economic conservative) like Mr. Justice Holmes insisted that "To have doubted one's own first principles is the mark of a civilized man." And why a liberal philosopher like Morris Cohen added: "To refuse to do so is the essence of fanaticism."

Liberalism need not, however, be identified only with this skeptical approach to knowledge. It is altogether possible for one to believe that the truth is known and still hold to a liberal defense of toleration. In part, this rests on the very arguments advanced by Mill. One's confidence in the validity of his position, along with a conviction that opinion should be countered only by opinion, not by force, is alone sufficient to sustain his readiness to entertain dissent. In part, however, it rests on the recognition that in a society constituted of diverse men and groups many may claim to know the truth. Though all cannot be right, the political problem is to deal with a situation in which all believe they are right. Authoritarians provide a simple method of resolving this difficulty: The "right," that is, the most powerful, group suppresses the others. But since force is irrelevant to truth, the most powerful group may not in fact be the group that is right. Hence reason dictates a solution other than force. This solution, for the liberal, is twofold. On the one hand, he would have the state leave these different groups alone. Where it is possible for each group to pursue its own truths, its own values, without infringing upon or denying the values of the other, there is a prima facie case for freedom. To this extent, at least, the state is a limited state. On the other hand, where such differences produce conflicts, the liberal would seek to negotiate these conflicts through free debate and free criticism in the marketplace of opinion. This does not, of course, assure the victory of the "right" view, but it gives the "right" view its maximum opportunity to prevail. And unless one is prepared to maintain that evidence and logic generally lead men to the wrong conclusions, it is difficult for the liberal to understand why so rational and peaceful a method of resolving differences is inappropriate, why it is better, say, to resort to mutual slaughter. Even if the "wrong" view should carry the day, there remains, through this method, full opportunity to continue to criticize and to show, with the added knowledge of experience, that it requires correction.

The ultimate argument of the liberal in this context, however, is his belief that individual liberty is a good in itself. What defines a man, according to an ancient teaching, is his reason. Now for reason to be exercised, a choice must exist. There can be no choices without alternatives, and there can be no alternatives without liberty. To deny individual liberty, either in the presentation of alternatives or the making of choices, is to deny an individual that which constitutes his humanity. Instead of his right to exercise his reason, someone else's reason is exercised for him. He is then not a man but a child. If he is to be a man, he must be free—to inquire, to consider diverse possibilities, to choose among them, and to pursue, so far as he can, his own way or style of life. From these conflicting ideas and practices, liberalism believes, men can learn and mutually aid one another to grow. Without these, there can be only a deadening uniformity. Individual liberty, and its consequent diversities, becomes then a cardinal principle of liberalism.

It is not to be denied that equality and liberty, both central tenets of liberalism, stand at times in a state of tension. Equality of opportunity, for example, may well run into conflict with the liberty of a parent to raise his child with the benefit of whatever advantages he may be able to give him. Then men must choose between equally ultimate values, and this is admittedly not an easy choice. But this is not a problem unique to liberals, and what liberals can well argue is that through freedom of inquiry and expression men can more rationally and peacefully negotiate these conflicts.

In sum, then, what distinguishes liberalism from conservatism is that, politically, liberalism stands for democracy and the equality of men, while conservatism inclines toward oligarchy based on certain alleged inequalities of men; economically, liberalism represents the interests of the lower classes and argues for equality of opportunity and the protection of human rights, while conservatism is associated with the interests of the upper classes and defends vested property rights; intellectually, liberalism is committed to individual liberty and the freedoms of inquiry and expression, while conservatism is far more concerned with the applications of an already existing objective Truth and the consequent curbing of erroneous and pernicious doctrines. It would be misleading to imply that all liberals, much less all so-called liberal states, affirm and consistently practice all these aspects of the liberal creed, or that conservatives do so with respect to their doctrines. But as categories of analysis rather than as descriptions of actual men or groups, the elements that make up this multidimensional understanding of liberalism and conservatism may enable us more easily to comprehend and to identify what it is that men and groups actually do.

IV

I would be disingenuous were I to pretend that I have contented myself to this point with analysis, not evaluation. On the contrary, I have sought here not merely to understand and describe the political labels known as liberalism and conservatism, but also to underscore at least the more obvious of their respective merits and deficiencies. For unless we affirm that the world as it is is the world as it ought to be—and except for a fictional Dr. Pangloss or a real Michael Oakeshott, who would have us believe that this is not only the best of all possible worlds, but that everything in it is a necessary evil, few sensible and sensitive persons, whether liberal or conservative, entertain this view—we must identify and commit ourselves to that course of action we believe to be right. I have no hesitation in asserting that, for me, the correct course is the position of the Left. I am a liberal, not a conservative; and while space precludes a detailed exposition of the reasons for this preference,[1] some of the more important considerations, other than those already articulated in the foregoing discussion, may at least be suggested here.

1. Liberalism provides a reasonable, perhaps the best, answer to the first and most fundamental problem of political theory: whether, and on what terms, men who hold conflicting ideas and pursue diverse interests can live together without slaughtering one another in advocacy or defense of their own values. Conservatism offers neither a unified reply nor specific guides to conduct in concrete cases; surely, to "do good and avoid evil," though an eminently laudatory prescription, is too vague to be meaningful. Conservatism offers, instead, only the authoritarian response that men must submit to authority, to the right principles as these are known by the right men. Liberalism builds, in contrast, on the recognition that in every society men are held together by common interests and set apart by individual or dividing interests. Always men need community, some form of collective endeavor to achieve certain values they cannot secure alone. But always, too, men need solitude, or group autonomy, in order to pursue certain interests that are limited to but a portion of the community, or to themselves alone. To meet this twofold need, liberalism urges that the state establish a system of order that is limited rather

than all-inclusive, that it distinguish those matters that are properly the concern of the state from those that, because they require diversity, are properly left to the individual or group. Since, moreover, threats to individual freedom come from sources other than the state, liberalism is fully prepared to accept even governmental interference in the latter realm—not to curtail those freedoms but, by restraining the restraints of nonpolitical powers, to assure their effective enjoyment. In these ways, men become part of a unity that accomodates rather than destroys their essential diversities.

2. This requires, of course, a rational method of determining the proper line or lines of demarcation, of determining which liberties and which restraints are to be established—for whom, under what conditions and to what degree, and for what purpose. For liberalism, this method is the process of democracy, which resolves differences through free discussion and majority opinion. What is crucial about freedom of inquiry and expression is, in the first instance, that it makes possible both the discovery of truth and the exposure of error; and to the degree that it is a way of revealing error it makes clear the fallacies of suppression to which conservatives are too often prone. For on the historical record, attempts at suppression have generally succeeded both in degrading the suppressor and in strengthening the suppressed by focusing greater attention on the latter's doctrine. No less important, if freedom of inquiry is a way of discovering error, to curb freedom of inquiry is to proclaim heretical not error but a way of discovering error, which is an absurdity. But in the second instance, freedom of inquiry commends itself because it encourages that diversity which makes for the development of individuality. To the liberal, stagnation, not difference, is the overwhelming danger to society; and the inclusion of the infinite varieties that constitute mankind into fixed categories or classes of sameness is both the denial of individual uniqueness and the death knell to social improvement.

It is sometimes argued by conservatives that this method may lead men to arrive at the wrong solutions, to adopt false and pernicious doctrines, to repudiate truth. This is clearly possible. Men are not infallible, and in the effort to mitigate evil and correct injustice, men may well introduce other, if not greater, evils in their stead. But what is the alternative? Surely it is not a fatalistic resignation to already existing injustices. Surely it is not submission to the authoritative declarations of allegedly superior men, those aristocrats and oligarchs whose incompetent and unjust rule over centuries of time has provided the primary reason for the impulse to democracy. On the contrary, liberals argue, it is precisely a recourse to reason and experience that vindicates this method as the best, the preeminently rational method. This does not mean that liberalism alone rests on reason and empiricism. Some conservatives, too, claim to be empirical, and differ from liberals only in their reading of the facts.

Thus, should some conservatives affirm and liberals deny that the Negro is by nature inferior to the white man, the dispute turns not on the question of empiricism but on the correctness of the data. Similarly, conservatives can properly argue that the passion for reason is itself a sentiment, thus disproving the allegation that conservatives are governed by emotion and liberals by reason. Nonetheless, it remains true that for the bulk of the conservatives, the truth—empirical or rational—is (a) already known, and (b) derived from sources other than reason and empiricism alone, e.g., from the revelations of God or the practices of tradition. For the bulk of the liberals, the truth is but tentatively known and remains subject to correction, while arbitrary authority is ruled out of the court of reason. Hence, is it not unfair to say that liberalism rather than conservatism is the more committed to the rational and empirical method. If this is so, it argues that the liberal approach, with its insistence on the toleration of conflicting ideas, is—as Locke and Milton and Mill and others have argued—the more likely to lead men to the right answers.

3. Liberalism minimizes social conflicts and promotes progress. By distinguishing those realms, or more properly those situations, in which political control may appropriately enter from those in which the government should let individuals and groups alone, liberalism minimizes social conflicts. More important, by providing a constitutional framework and mechanism for the resolution of those conflicts that remain, liberalism contains them and prevents them from disrupting the social and political order—all the more so since it attaches the loyalty of men to the process, not the result, to the value of the method by which conflicts are resolved, not to the policies that temporarily emerge out of that method.

The idea of progress is, of course, a tricky one; for progress involves not merely change but a value judgment upon that change. Now, it is often contended by conservatives that liberals are oblivious to the dangers of the wrong change, and hence stand for indiscriminate change. But this is surely as misleading as would be the counter-assertion that conservatives seek to conserve everything, including the things that are evil, like prostitution and murder. Both favor some changes. What distinguishes liberalism from conservatism is, then, not an unawareness of the tragic element in human history but a greater willingness to combat rather than to surrender to it. Evil is real; it exists; it is not easily overcome. To do nothing, as so many conservatives urge, is simply to submit to it. But if man is a rational animal, and if man is also a sensitive and compassionate animal, he can do no other than address himself to the correction of recognizable evils. That some injustices may continue to exist, that new injustices may arise, is not an argument for abject resignation. Consequently, the liberal does believe in the idea of, the very real possibility of, progress; though some liberals, it must be added, because they recognize the pervasiveness of human apathy and the hindrances imposed by specific historical circumstances, are far less optimistic than are others.

4. But when all is said and done, the crucial component of liberalism is that, within this approach, man is the end and political and social arrangements merely the means to individuality. For conservatives, there is glory and honor in such abstractions as the nation or the state, in such concepts as contract and property, in such relationships as custom and usage have rendered traditional. For liberals, these are instruments, not ends. What counts is man, and what defines a good society is not its wealth or power or prestige but the qualities of the men who constitute it. Hence not collectives but persons merit reverence, and what liberalism seeks above all is the removal of those hindrances, whether of institutions or of sentiment, that would bend men to another's purpose, and the creation of those conditions—political, economic, and cultural—that give individuality its greatest opportunities for development. To dedicate oneself to this task is, in the liberal view, the very hallmark of what it means to be a man.

3 Freedom and Individuality:
Mill's *Liberty* in Retrospect

I

It is a truism that much of the confusion in political theory is less the work of political theorists than of their commentators. Ranking high in the list of intellectual victims in this regard, John Stuart Mill is still being belabored today for errors he did not commit, assumptions he did not make, conclusions he did not draw, and confusions he did not originate. This is not to suggest the presence of an ingrained fallibility or ill will in his critics; they have scored frequently, and with telling effect. Yet today, after a century of such criticism, most of it converging on his essay *On Liberty*, his work remains more of a formidable testimony to the spirit of rational liberalism than most of his critics are willing to concede.

Typical of the extremes to which criticism of Mill has gone is the charge leveled by John Plamenatz, who wrote:

> He [Mill] was often bewildered by the intricacies of his own thought, unaware of the implications of what he had said and of what still remained to be proved. He could abandon a doctrine the most completely when he thought he was defending it with the greatest warmth. . . . He was more thoroughly educated than it is good for any man to be and his knowledge had so long a start of his understanding that the latter could never catch up with it.[1]

Lest this be discounted as the product of personal or political bias, it should be pointed out in all fairness that much the same judgment is to be found in Bertrand Russell, certainly not one to disclaim a general kinship with the libertarian spirit of Mill's political philosophy. According to Russell:

> Morals and intellect were perpetually at war in his [Mill's] thought, morals being incarnate in Mrs. Taylor and intellect in his father. . . . The amalgam which resulted was practically beneficent, but theoretically somewhat incoherent.[2]

This essay appeared originally in Carl J. Friedrich, ed., *Liberty: Nomos IV*, Yearbook of the American Society for Legal and Political Philosophy. Copyright © 1962 by Atherton Press, New York. Reprinted by permission of Lieber-Atherton, Inc., New York.

And, finally, we have it on the authority of the best of the present-day histories of political theory that

> His [Mill's] expressly stated theories—of human nature, of morals, of society, and of the part to be played by government in a liberal society—were always inadequate to the load that he made them carry. . . . On nearly every subject he was likely to begin with a general statement of principles which, taken literally and by itself, appeared to be as rigid and as abstract as anything that his father might have written. But having thus declared his allegiance to the ancestral dogmas, Mill proceeded to make concessions and restatements so far-reaching that a critical reader was left in doubt whether the original statement had not been explained away. . . . The importance of Mill's philosophy [thus] consisted of its departures from the system which it still professed to support. . . .[3]

To be sure, Mill has not lacked defenders; from contemporaries like John Morley, who spoke of Mill as "my chief master" and confessed his "young disciple's reverence,"[4] to an occasional appreciation of recent date,[5] Mill's work has come in for some share of applause and admiration. And of those who take a more jaundiced view of his work, many would still agree with Halevy that if Mill was not an eminent thinker, he was "at least eminently useful";[6] or even with Sabine who, having ventilated *On Liberty* for all its deficiencies, still assigns it a place alongside Milton's *Areopagitica* "as one of the classical defences of freedom in the English language."[7]

But, such as they are, these concessions to Mill's place in political thought have been all but muffled in the overwhelming chorus of criticism. Croce, for example, was not far from the general tenor of opinion when he asserted that *On Liberty* is a work of "cheap" and "ignoble arguments" and "wretched and fallacious reasonings."[8] How, then, are we to account for the fact that it still engages the attention of serious thinkers, not merely for reasons of historical interest but on its own ground as well? I venture the answer that it still continues to be read and debated because it deserves to be taken seriously despite all that hostile critics have said against it, and, further, that much of what has been said against the essay is neither relevant nor convincing if one takes the pain to follow Mill's argument in all its dimensions. I shall argue here that after all is said against the essay that can be said—and this is admittedly a good deal—a considerable residue of truth and pertinence remains in *On Liberty* to justify the high regard in which it continues to be held.

II

Let us consider, first, certain criticisms of, or approaches to, Mill's essay that I believe to be fundamentally irrelevant or misleading.

1. *That Mill's ideas are tainted by their source.* It is sometimes asserted that the proper way to understand Mill's essay is in historical, even biographical, terms. In these terms, Mill's argument for religious toleration is explained by saying that, as a freethinker in religion, he personally resented and resisted the pressures of the established Church; his much beleaguered association with Harriet Taylor is cited to account for Mill's attack on conformity in matters of taste and morals; and, similarly, the older Mill's tyrannizing of his son is said to be responsible for Mill's argument in defense of the liberty of the individual to develop freely.[9]

I confess that I find such an approach devoid of merit. The day may well come when meddlers in clinical research will relate—and judge accordingly— passages in *On Liberty* to the accidental burning in Mill's father's house of the first volume of Carlyle's manuscript on the French Revolution, or to Mill's morbid thoughts of suicide as a young man, or to the fact that he was once arrested and imprisoned for distributing birth control literature in the slums of London,[10] or to the startling but absurd "hypothesis" already ventured by Plamenatz that Mill's *On Liberty* was "written by a sick man in his premature old age."[11] There is no need to multiply examples, for they would all turn out to be instances of the genetic fallacy that perennially bedevils discussions of this kind when critics are either unable or unwilling to come to grips with an argument on its own merit.

2. *That Mill's ethics are other than what his critics would like them to be.* On a more sophisticated level, a good many critics have raised loud objection to Mill's essay largely because its ethical assumptions derive from a qualified utilitarianism. This, they have argued, deprives him of any effective case for many of his crucial distinctions, all of which require grounding in absolute moral principle. Because of this alleged "poverty of Mill's ethical end," one critic writes, he cannot really tell us which of many diverse ways of life is truly best, which human behavior is good and which bad, which interests are permanent and which transitory, and so on. In short, he has no way of *really* vindicating his moral distinctions and judgments.[12]

Now, for those who both believe in a deity and "know" what its teachings are, or who are committed to a doctrine of natural right that yields them what they regard as an equally infallible insight into the true nature of things, or who profess to have an intuitive grasp of the human condition that enables them authoritatively to distinguish between right and wrong conduct, Mill's failure to provide an absolutistic ethic grounded on their own particular principle may indeed seem sufficient reason to reject his argument *in toto*. But criticism of this kind misses the very heart of Mill's argument. He wrote his essay not because he lacked an ethical standard—for the principle of utility (and I am not here concerned to argue the rightness or wrongness of this principle), however uncertain and inadequate a moral principle it may appear to be to nonutilitarians, *is* an ethical standard—but because he denied that any man or group of men could ever possess the type of absolute knowledge which would entitle them to suppress ethical standards other than their own. If Mill had thought that he himself possessed this knowledge, or that the keys of truth had by some mysterious alchemy been delivered into his custody, his own case for individual liberty would have been pointless. Not that anyone who professes to be guided by an absolute ethical principle will necessarily try to compel others to live according to its dictates, merely that he is not generally eager to secure for others a liberty to depart from the "right" prescriptions. But Mill valued liberty and diversity precisely because he rejected the possibility of such an absolutistic conception of morality.

3. *That Mill is an extremist in his position.* Mill is frequently taken to task for pushing his argument to absurd extremes. But it turns out in all too many cases that it is the critic who, by failing to note Mill's qualifications or by stretching the plain meaning of his words, makes more of Mill's argument than Mill himself intended.

Thus we find critics representing, or, more strictly, misrepresenting, Mill's concern for individuality and his distaste for the idea of men being governed solely by custom, to mean that Mill had no use for any customs whatever and regarded individuality as the only legitimate value, which would in effect make him out to be a utopian or ultranihilist.[13] But this is not only irrelevant to, it is completely at odds with, Mill's fundamental thoughts on these subjects. This is readily seen if we only look, for example, at the title of the third chapter of the essay *On Liberty*, where Mill speaks "Of Individuality, as *One* of the Elements of Well-Being" (my italics); or at the statement early in his introductory chapter that "some rules of conduct . . . must be imposed . . . ," or at his repeated insistence that individuality should assert itself only "in things which do not primarily concern others."

In a similar farfetched vein, and because Mill included strength of character as one of the essential elements of individuality, it has been argued that Mill is oblivious to qualities in man other than his strength—in the literal sense of "strong characters" who are good simply because they are strong. Hence, Mill would be compelled, according to one critic at least, to endorse a character like Al Capone.[14] And this is said of the same Mill who not only listed strength of character as but *one* of the essential elements of individuality; who not only in his *Utilitarianism* explicitly professed his own fidelity to the Golden Rule, but who also uttered the famous sentence: "It really is of importance, not only what men do, but also what manner of men they are that do it."

Finally, but only because I would not belabor this point, we find critics treating Mill's argument for diversity as if it were a plea for any and all kinds of diversity, including even pathological abnormality, and as though Mill were utterly unconcerned with how much diversity a society can afford. That this is a ludicrous interpretation of Mill is revealed when these very critics triumphantly (as they think) quote Mill against himself as saying: "There is not a more accurate test of the progress of civilization than the progress of the power of co-operation."[15] And what, one might ask, is the point of Mill's entire essay, and in particular of the questions set forth at the beginning of Chapter IV, if it is not only to admit the claims of authority but also to ask what are the rightful or legitimate, as distinct from the illegitimate, exercises of that authority? It is curious, indeed, that this attempt of Mill's critics to turn Mill against himself destroys their own interpretation of Mill, not Mill's position.

4. *That mass tyranny is a myth that happened to suit Mill's partiality for aristocracy*. Many of Mill's critics charge him with an elitist or aristocratic bias; they see him as an apologist for elite minorities against the sweep of democratic majorities, or of what he called the "despotism of a collective mediocrity." They indict him, too, for entertaining what they hold to be a grand illusion, namely, that individuality is in fact being smothered by the pressures of conformity, that we are in danger—to use Tocqueville's phrase—of a tyranny of the majority. The critics insist that there was no such tyranny either then or since: not in the England of Mill's day,[16] not in the America of Tocqueville's day,[17] nor in the America of our own time.[18] His entire essay, therefore, they conclude, is directed against an imaginary evil.

That there is a grain of truth in this line of criticism is undeniable. It is true that Mill displayed a considerable bias in favor of intellectually eminent men; he respected men of superior mental gifts and attainments; he valued genius. It is true, also, that a society capable of producing a Herbert Spencer, a Thomas Carlyle, and a John Stuart Mill is clearly not a society in which *all* individuality is stifled or one in which *all* intellectual superiority goes unrecognized and unrewarded. The very fact, indeed, that men like Mill were free to protest that men were not free, or were in danger of losing their freedom, testifies to what may be called the "openness" of that society. It is true, further, that the social despotism that Mill feared was a pressure of conformity known to every society and every age; it could not, consequently, be attributed simply to the coming of democracy, or to the England of his own time. The problem is not whether such pressure exists, for it always does; the question turns rather, on what forms and degrees of intensity that pressure takes. If it remains no more than censure, the individual subjected to it may well find that he can, nonetheless, go his way. But if that social disapproval is translated into law, or into economic sanctions or physical violence, any or all of which would make it impossible or extraordinarily difficult for him to persist in his heterodoxy, then tyranny enters. It is not the mere existence of an antagonistic public sentiment but the actual exercise of a legal or economic or physical power to enforce that sentiment so as to deprive an individual of his legitimate rights that constitutes oppression.[19]

All this, I think, can properly be said against Mill. Yet it is not enough to dispose of Mill's essential position on these matters. The elements of truth that still remain in Mill's argument far outweigh these misconceptions. It is surely insufficient merely to point to Mill's high regard for intellectual eminence and his concomitant distaste for tyranny by the majority, however this tyranny may be conceived (and I shall argue in a moment that there is a sense in which it is properly conceived by Mill), and conclude from this that Mill is concocting here no more than an aristocratic fable. One would have to show, in addition, that with respect to these matters Mill was both fundamentally wrong and fundamentally at odds with the principle of democracy. And this, I am convinced, cannot be shown. On the contrary, three things at least can and must be said in defense of Mill.

(*a*) To respect and to seek to foster the emergence of intellectual eminence is in no sense inconsistent with democracy. What democracy requires is equality of opportunity; it does not stipulate equality of talent or intelligence or reward. Indeed, to insist upon equality of opportunity is to ask for no more than the first condition for the discovery of true inequality of talent. Only one who emerges first in a fair race can legitimately be termed the winner; and democracy seeks not to stack the cards against the best but to assure him that the race will be run fairly.

What would convert this regard for intellectual eminence into an apologia for aristocracy would be the imputation that such superiority of knowledge and understanding is the peculiar and exclusive attribute of a particular social class or elite, and the insistence, following from this, that such a class or elite is alone entitled to rule. But—and this is crucial—this imputation and insistence can nowhere be found in Mill. To the contrary, he repeatedly and consistently affirms, as did his father before him, that aristocratic rule, with all its deleterious effects on the character of rulers and ruled alike, is the principal barrier to good government. He invariably argues, therefore, that those who govern must, before everything else, be held constitutionally accountable to the ruled. "The honor and glory of the average man," Mill writes, "is that . . . he can respond internally to wise and noble things, and be led to them with his eyes open." But there is never the suggestion in Mill that if the average man does not voluntarily follow the initiative of intellectually eminent men, he must be compelled to do so. Everything that Mill ever wrote, pre-eminently in *On Liberty* and its superb companion volume *Representative Government*, is a flat denial of this aristocratic principle.

It is true that Mill was equally concerned not to have "the opinions of masses of merely average men" dominate and stifle the "individuality of those who stand on the higher eminences of thought." In this respect Mill was indeed opposed to the intolerance of tradition-bound majorities. But here, too, three things need to be said: first, this plea for the right of difference, or even eccentricity, applied to those matters that did not *primarily* affect the interests of others—that is, it applied to the self-regarding rather than to the other-regarding sphere of human conduct;[20] second, although Mill "dreaded the ignorance and especially the selfishness and brutality of the mass," he antici-pated a time when men would no longer need to dread these things; he held it, rather, as a "merely provisional" view warranted only "so long as education continues to be so wretchedly imperfect";[21] and third, Mill was also, and just as strongly, opposed to the intolerance of and consequent tyranny by bureaucrats and officials. Nor was he what one critic has called him—an apologist for intellectual snobs.[22] He pleaded instead, and for a clearly defined area, only the cause of those who are different and who, though despised and rejected, often become the movers and makers of the world.

Unless, then, diversity of character and the possession of superior brains are to be deemed an intrinsic affront to democracy, I think the allegation that Mill was an elitist and an aristocrat is unfounded.

(b) Notwithstanding what I said earlier in criticism of Mill's idea of the tyranny of the majority, I want to argue now that there is a very real sense in which Mill was correct in his apprehension of this danger. I do not see in what other terms we are to account for the treatment of American Indians and Negroes by the dominant white majority; of Jews by Christians; or of Mormons by gentiles; or—but need one canvass the full depth of human experience to make the point?

What all this suggests is that in the world we inhabit, as in the world of John Stuart Mill, there is always a pressure on men to conform. This pressure is manifested in various ways—from statutes that disallow socially disapproved acts, to acts of violence and the imposition of economic sanctions by private groups in an effort to prevent men from pursuing legitimate goals, to acts of social discrimination, including ostracism and disdain. This pressure is also called by various names—from conformity to adjustment to "togetherness." But whatever the technique or the label employed, this essential fact remains: that what every society esteems, and seeks to produce, is the tranquilized, and tranquilizing, man. What is valued is harmony, congeniality; what is expected is a due measure of diffidence, even perhaps of obsequiousness; what is achieved, or at least intended, is the anonymous, not the autonomous, man. And it was to oppose this pressure and this result, this very real "tyranny" of majority opinion that stifles the mind and banishes creative or merely dissident ideas, that Mill entered his plea for diversity and freedom and individuality.

(c) It remains to be added that Mill's opposition to unbridled majority rule, far from being antidemocratic, is of the very essence of democracy (though I am aware that at this point majoritarian theorists of democracy will doubtless disagree with me). But surely I need not here labor the point that one of the essential conditions of a democratic state, as democracy is commonly understood in the Western world, is the free play of conflicting opinions, the right of men freely to disagree and to organize with others in the more effective pursuit of their diverse values. What Mill sought was a principle that would enable men in a democratic state to recognize and respect the line between the legitimate power of the majority and the rights of dissident minorities. Whatever his success or failure in drawing that line—and of this, more later—to term his effort at drawing it a mark of aristocratic bias is to strain all credulity.

5. *That Mill retracted his argument in his later work.* For lack of space I omit here one of the more inexplicable of the many fallacious arguments leveled against *On Liberty*—namely, the contention that although Mill urged that the state *require* an education for every child, he did not favor state support for education and would not permit the state to *provide* it[23]—and turn instead to what shall here be the last of the irrelevant or misleading criticisms of Mill's essay. This is the attempt to play Mill against himself by confronting the doctrines of *On Liberty* with those of his allegedly later and maturer work, the posthumously published essay *On Social Freedom*.[24]

But even if *On Social Freedom* had been written by Mill, it does not necessarily follow that it is more convincing as a criticism of *On Liberty* than any other book critical of *On Liberty* would be; for it might well be that the Mill of *On Liberty* can be shown to have been wiser than the Mill of *On Social Freedom*.[25] I am persuaded by the evidences and argument of J. C. Rees,[26] however, that Mill did not write *On Social Freedom*; hence, it is unnecessary to undertake such an examination.

Finally, a brief digression on the most mindless of all irrelevancies! Some, but happily not all, of Mill's critics think they can refute Mill by quoting, sometimes at length, from an opposing political philosopher or critic of Mill. Bernard Bosanquet[27] and James Fitzjames Stephen are perennial favorites of those invited to sit in judgment—Bosanquet on the ideas of freedom and individuality, Stephen on these and just about everything else in, or allegedly in, Mill's essay. Now, clearly, to quote Bosanquet or Stephen or anyone else proves only that Bosanquet or Stephen or anyone else said what he said, not that he was right or that he proved his case against Mill. Occasionally, however, one encounters the argument that Mill must surely be in the wrong, for the overwhelming bulk of the literature on his essay is adversely critical. But so crudely quantitative an approach ignores the quality both of the respective critics and of their arguments, and is thus unworthy of attention.

III

We come now to the criticisms of Mill's essay that deserve a more respectful hearing, even if they do not always carry conviction. But before scrutinizing them, it might be well to emphasize at the outset two important considerations frequently ignored by his critics. One of these is the simple fact that Mill, model of lucidity though he was, could occasionally slip into an inept phrasing of his ideas.[28] Where such is the case, many a critic has had an easy time of it by rendering Mill's argument in its most vulnerable terms. But Mill, as any other writer of his stature, should be given the benefit of literary doubt; if such a rendering seems egregiously out of line with his obvious intent, there is a prima facie case for challenging its pertinence—particularly where it is possible to construe his argument in terms more in keeping with his general outlook and level of intellectual sophistication.

The second consideration is that even where critics have scored a telling case against this or that element of Mill's essay, they have frequently vitiated their own argument by driving it to extremes. An essay such as Mill's is, in the nature of the case, bound to limp here and there—to do less than full justice to all the pertinent facts, to overlook some and overweigh others, and even to go astray in some of its conclusions. But even when Mill can be shown to founder on some particular point, his critics, too often mistaking the part for the whole, have been curiously myopic about the truly important elements of insight in his argument.

Both of these points will be detailed in the course of our examination of the major criticisms of *On Liberty*. Briefly stated, these criticisms come to the following:

1. *That Mill, in defending freedom of expression, is caught between the conflicting claims of abstract right and utilitarianism.* In raising this objection, Mill's critics are fond of laboring the point that his commitment to the doctrine of abstract or natural right, as he had learned it from Coleridge and Aristotle, cannot be squared with his devotion, however qualified, to the tenets of utilitarianism, as expounded by Jeremy Bentham and his own father.[29] Mill, so the critics urge, argues that there is a sphere of self-regarding conduct which society must respect under any and all circumstances, from which it follows—to Mill's critics at least—that Mill presumably recognizes inviolable or natural rights that inhere in the individual by virtue of his humanity. But if this is so, how, they ask, could Mill reject, as he expressly did, "any advantage which

could be derived to my argument from the idea of abstract right as a thing independent of utility"?

The bearing of this criticism becomes particularly apparent when the critics come to grips with two of Mill's central propositions: on the one hand, his insistence on defending freedom of expression, along with freedom of thought itself, as though it were something in the nature of an absolute and, therefore, inviolable right; and, on the other hand, his recognition, no less emphatic, that society has a right to interfere with an individual's conduct for the sake of its own preservation, a right which comes into play whenever the individual's conduct is bound to affect adversely the interests of others. Plainly, these two propositions cancel each other out; for if, as Mill concedes, *all* expression is by its nature other-regarding, it cannot be defended as an absolute and inviolable right of the individual. Indeed, Mill himself is forced to admit that under certain circumstances—e.g., where unrestrained expression is likely to produce harmful effects—society can properly take steps to curb freedom of expression.[30] But if this is so, the critics continue, what Mill is really defending is not the absolute right of the individual to speak his mind freely, but his right to do so only when, and to the extent that, he does not transgress society's claim to protect itself from harm. The principle at stake, then, becomes one of relative, not absolute, right, or, to put it in terms of practical policy, one of establishing the line at which freedom of expression should be limited. What appeared to be a reliance on the doctrine of abstract right turns out to be merely an application of utilitarian criteria. To be sure, it is still possible to salvage from Mill's argument a defense of the right of freedom of expression on absolute grounds by regarding it, as he does on occasion, to be a form of self-regarding conduct in the sense that it is indispensable to and "practically inseparable from" freedom of thought. But here too the critics think they have the advantage of the argument, for they can then presumably show that in that case it is impaled on the second horn of the contradiction: if freedom of expression is a form of self-regarding conduct, no conceivable ground remains, least of all on Mill's own terms, for political or social action to curb freedom of expression in the interests of collective self-protection.

It is difficult to deny that arguments such as these have a surface plausibility of a kind. Taking the wording of a portion of Mill's essay at its face value, but disregarding all else that he wrote, one can find enough to construct the outlines of the dilemma of which the critics make so much. But if Mill's work as a whole is taken into account, it becomes quite improbable that he was ever an adherent of a natural rights approach to the problems of political life. And if this is true, all criticism on this score becomes quite pointless.

Consider, first, what it is that Mill actually says. He affirms as "the appropriate region of human liberty . . . liberty of conscience in the most comprehensive

sense, liberty of thought and feeling; *absolute* freedom of opinion and sentiment on all subjects, practical or speculative, scientific, moral or theological"
(my italics). Then, after conceding that "the liberty of expressing and pub-
lishing opinions may seem to fall under a different principle, since it belongs to
that part of the conduct of an individual which concerns other people," he
nevertheless seeks to bring it within the protection of the same principle by
contending that freedom of expression, "being almost of as much importance
as the liberty of thought itself and resting in great part on the same reasons, is
practically inseparable from it."

Mill's critics take this to mean that he in effect regards and would treat
freedom of expression on a par with freedom of thought. But this is decidedly
not the case, as a careful reading of the passage in question will readily bear
out. Mill does not say that freedom of expression is of the same importance as
freedom of thought; he says it is *almost* as important. He does not rest its
defense on the same reasons; he would defend it *in great part* on the same
reasons. He does not say that freedom of expression is identical to or inseparable from freedom of thought; he says only that it is *practically* inseparable from
it. Any interpretation of Mill's teaching that ignores these nuances of qualifications and distinction does less than justice to its meaning, and this becomes all
the more certain when we consider the context in which this portion of Mill's
argument occurs. For, as it happens, the very same paragraph which specifies
the various liberties necessary to man is also the paragraph which cautions, in
unmistakable terms, that they are to be exercised only so long as they do not
involve harm to others.

All of which leads to the inescapable conclusion that Mill did not regard
freedom of expression as an absolute or natural right, as something which may
not be curbed under any circumstances. His argument must rather be read to
mean that freedom of expression constitutes a right of the highest priority, a
right which can be justified per se, whereas the right of government or of
society to curb freedom of expression is a subordinate one conditioned on the
first. When, for example, Mill argues at another point in his essay that actions
are never to be accorded the same freedom as opinions, and that "even
opinions lose their immunity when the circumstances in which they are expressed are such as to constitute their expression a positive instigation to some
mischievous act," his qualification would apply *a fortiori* to the alleged absolute
right of freedom of expression whenever a dire emergency requires that it be
curbed. His argument is thus to be understood as a guide to practical conduct,
as a statement of policy which clings to complete freedom of speech as a valid
general rule for "normal" periods and which sanctions restraint for exceptional
or emergency situations only. So understood, the argument is not subject to the
dilemma discerned by Mill's critics; for such a dilemma presupposes that the

two principles—that of freedom of expression and that of self-protection—are on a par with each other, thus making it impossible to distinguish an order of priority between them.

Where the critics have gone astray has been in their failure to take account of the relative and conditional quality of the principles advocated by Mill, however much he may seem to have phrased them in absolute terms for polemical purposes. They formulate the problem as though Mill has assigned equal weights to the principle of freedom of expression for the individual and that of society's right to survival, or self-protection; from their formulation, it would seem to follow that the two cannot be reconciled in principle. But this, I think, is entirely to misread Mill's intent and argument: the first principle, that of freedom of expression, is indeed first; the second, that of society's right to protect itself from harm, is but a qualification, a subordinate principle of limitation. And, as Mill had occasion to write elsewhere, it would indeed be "a strange notion that the acknowledgment of a first principle is inconsistent with the admission of secondary ones."[31] Stated this way—that anyone should be free to say what he likes, provided only that, in doing so, he does not endanger the existence of the group or do harm to others—the problem is not one of reconciling principles at all, but of judging the wisdom of any proposed measure to curb freedom of expression in terms of the relative order of the principle and its qualification. This does not, to be sure, offer a foolproof guarantee against misjudging the relative urgencies of the moment, against suppressing a speech or a book, for example, on the ground that it endangers society or harms others when it does not actually do so; but then, no set of principles, however stated, is immune to this possible abuse.

It turns out, then, that the choice for Mill never devolved on the insoluble problem, of deciding between the conflicting, yet equal, claims of natural or abstract right and utility but, rather, on the eminently utilitarian problem of weighing the relative merits of a prior and a subordinate principle, of qualifying the primary principle of freedom of expression by the practical requirements of the principle of self-protection. I conclude, therefore, that Mill did not in fact abandon his utilitarianism for a principle of abstract right, even if his particular brand of utilitarianism was not in all respects that of Bentham.[32]

2. *That Mill poses a false dichotomy between self-regarding and other-regarding acts.* I think it can properly be said that Mill's attempt to distinguish two types of human conduct, the personal and the social—or what he calls self-regarding and other-regarding acts—entails a number of theoretical and practical difficulties. But here, as elsewhere, critics go much too far when they deny that there is any merit at all in Mill's distinction. Freedom for the individual, they argue, would be little more than a triviality if the distinction had any merit; but since, in their view, it has none, we are left with nothing but a

theoretically unsound argument that does not admit of any clear-cut application in practice. Let us consider these points in turn.

(*a*) When Mill, to take the first line of criticism, singles out the self-regarding type of human conduct as being beyond the jurisdiction of society or the state on the ground that it affects the interests of no one but the agent himself, is he not positing a distinction that is essentially sterile? So, for example, argues Sabine when he objects that "an act that affects no one but a single person probably will not affect him very much."[33] In one sense this is perhaps true, as Mill himself conceded when he observed that "whatever affects himself may affect others through himself." But it does not follow that the distinction is without some vital bearing on the issue; unquestionably, there is a considerable range of conduct, including even deviant conduct, which has at best but an indirect or remote effect on others and which, for that reason, can be construed as *primarily* self-regarding. Consider such well-known cases of idiosyncratic behavior as Vincent van Gogh's mutilation of his own body, or Toulouse-Lautrec's dissipation in drink, or Modigliani's addiction to drugs. Should these be called forms of self-regarding behavior, and, if so, are they indeed trivial, as so many of Mill's critics would insist? To say that they are other-regarding would beg the entire question by implying that these idiosyncracies did in fact affect the interests of others adversely, which they demonstrably did not. One could go even further to argue that in many, if not all, such cases conduct of this kind is indeed self-regarding in the most compelling personal sense if it can be related to the creative gifts of the artist. In that event, freedom to indulge in such conduct is anything but trivial, and the same would apply to far more numerous cases of "normal" personal behavior.

To be sure, the distinction between these and other forms of conduct which have obvious social consequences is frequently blurred. In many cases, however, human actions can be, and are, in fact, sorted out one way or the other, and anyone presuming to say that conduct is trivial merely because it is self-regarding betrays a lack of psychological insight into what it is that constitutes the unique concerns of an individual. To him, in fact, it may be his own "private" life and nothing else—or, as Mill would have put it, his self-regarding conduct—that is the very axis of his claim to personality. And it is no less vital a concern of any society which prizes freedom if we but recall the consequences that have always followed whenever the notion of private conduct was not recognized. The theory and practice of modern totalitarianism speak eloquently on this score.

(*b*) Having convinced themselves that Mill's argument is vitiated by a protean theoretical distinction, critics find it easy to conclude that it is inherently incapable of practical application. Mill puts forward, as the "very simple" yet absolutely governing principle of his essay,

. . . that the sole end for which mankind are warranted, individually or collectively, in interfering with the liberty of action of any of their number is self-protection. That the only purpose for which power can be rightfully exercised over any member of a civilized community, against his will, is to prevent harm to others.

This, of course, is hardly a novel notion. It was said by Rousseau and by others before him; and as Mill's contemporary critics were quick to point out, it constitutes one of the most stale commonplaces in political philosophy. For it still leaves open the questions: What is the meaning of "harm"? Is it *moral* harm or *physical* harm, or both? Moreover, who is to tell, and by what criteria, whether a particular action does or does not cause harm to other people? Is a "village atheist" flaunting his fishing pole on a Sunday morning an offender by Mill's standard? How, by the same standard, is one to judge the practice of birth control, or of polygamy, and the like? The fact of the matter is, as Harold Laski and others have argued, "that we can have no information as to the social relevance of any act until we consider its consequences."[34] But since not all consequence can be anticipated, there is no way of knowing whether an action is self-regarding or other-regarding until those consequences have in fact occurred; which means that we may not be able to tell whether an action does or does not concern or bring harm to others until well after that action has taken place. Thus, Mill's distinction (it is said) is not a guide to practical conduct at all; at best, it can be employed only as a standard for judging an act *post factum*.

But this is only the beginning of the difficulties that Mill's critics have with this argument. Mill, they insist, makes a damaging concession when he seeks to limit the scope of self-regarding conduct to those matters that do not *primarily* concern or affect the interests of others, and introduces the notion of a "distinct and assignable obligation." Who, they object, is to say what *primarily* concerns others? If society can interfere with a man for purposes of self-protection, does it not follow that its right to interfere is limited only by its own judgment of its interests and of those matters that are of primary concern to it? Where, then, does self-regarding conduct begin, and what liberties can the individual claim save those that are given to him by society? Further, to bring in the notion of a distinct and assignable obligation only raises the questions: What is an obligation? Which obligations are assignable? And who is to assign them?

If for example, we take Mill's illustration of drunkenness—that no person should be punished simply for being drunk, but a soldier drunk on duty should be punished—we see the difficulty, if not the impossibility, of applying Mill's principle. All drunkenness clearly involves the risk that some damage might be done; hence, on Mill's own showing, society always has a right to interfere. If it does not, it is presumably because such interference is considered unnecessary or undesirable in the particular instance, not because society lacks the right to do so.

And to the extent that Mill's argument entails the concept of obligation, it is well to remember that obligation is inescapably social in all its ramifications. Whether defined as a moral norm or as a legal prescription, obligation always refers to social rights and duties. It is not the act but the situation in which the act occurs that gives the act its meaning. And an obligation drawn to fit the situation is always social.

These criticisms seem to me largely unexceptionable. Yet their total impact is not quite as paralyzing to Mill's argument as many a critic would have us believe.[35] What robs this line of criticism of much of its force is the qualification, already noted, that the two principles expounded in Mill's work are not coequal but ranked in the order of their urgency. Suppose we grant, for example, that *all* conduct, down to one's deciding what one should eat for dinner, can have social consequences. Does it follow as a matter of principle that *all* conduct ought to be made equally subject to punitive or regulatory action by society or the state? Clearly, we are dealing here with distinctions of degree that cannot be subsumed under general principles but that cannot be disregarded in practice without depriving an individual of all human rights and freedoms. Therefore, when Mill speaks of matters that do not *primarily* concern or adversely affect the interests of others, he is on clearly reasonable ground; for surely one's religion and his sexual practices, his choice of friends and occupation and place of residence, his freedom to decide between reading a book or attending an athletic event, and the like, are not *always* matters of concern to others. All that Mill is arguing here is that so long as one's actions do not injure the legitimate interests of other people, or do not have a deleterious effect on society's welfare, they ought not to be interfered with by society. Thus, for Mill, the self-regarding becomes the primary principle: each man, if he is to realize his potentialities as a man, must be free to do those things that *primarily* concern him and do not adversely affect the interests of others;[36] to that end, the individual needs an area of freedom within which he should be unrestrained from doing those things that are by common-sense standards personal. Where harm is done, the subordinate or other-regarding principle enters to protect society.

Admittedly, this rendering of the problem, valid though I think it is, does not altogether save Mill's formula. It is true, of course, that no general principle can state the conditions of its application in all cases, but Mill's principle is peculiarly liable to this difficulty. It does tell us that it is improper to impose social or legal restraints simply because we may dislike the other man's actions. It suggests, further, that when there is any doubt as to whether an action is self-regarding or other-regarding, the benefit of the doubt should be reserved for the self-regarding side when making the distinction. A principle of measure and appropriateness is thus built into this kind of utilitarian reasoning that should not be depreciated or ignored. Nevertheless, Mill's distinction cannot be maintained in its pristine form, for, because so many human actions are of the mixed type, Mill would have been on sounder ground had he contented himself with pointing out that they embody varying degres of social implication. He could then have argued that it is not the act but the situation in which the act occurs that is crucial, from which it follows that, depending on circumstances, certain acts should be treated *as if* they were private. When society stands to gain by permitting men to act freely, their conduct should be treated accordingly.

It may be useful, perhaps, to add one final note. Too much, I think, has been made of Mill's deficiency in drawing this distinction between self-regarding and other-regarding acts. Even if we concede the validity of *all* the criticisms that have been leveled against his treatment, I do not think—as I shall argue later—that the larger thesis Mill was concerned to defend is thereby destroyed. For if men are to make any claim to liberty at all, it can only be because in some sense they value the right of an individual to act differently from his fellows, to be in some respects a *unique* person. And the fulfillment of such a value, it is clear, can only come about in a society that recognizes, however vaguely and ambiguously, the importance of privacy. But this brings us, in part, to the next major criticism of Mill's essay.

3. *That Mill's conception of individuality amounts to a plea for social irresponsibility*. One major line of attack on Mill has not been a direct challenge to the more immediate political element in his thinking but rather an attempt to point out what are considered to be serious flaws in his sociology and psychology. To be specific, many critics have argued (*a*) that Mill's idea of individuality is altogether ambiguous and unclear—so much so that in one writer's view Mill is identified as "the prophet of individualism . . . the prophet of an empty liberty and an abstract individual,"[37] whereas to another writer the reverse is true, Mill's thoughts being said to move "always on a grand scale, embracing the universal, allowing the individual to slip from notice";[38] (*b*) that what is at fault is not Mill's *definition* of individuality but rather "his psychological and sociological conception of the *conditions* necessary to the development of individuality,"[39] or, more severely, that Mill's attempt to emphasize the importance of the individual to the utmost leads him to forget that there is no such thing as individuality without society;[40] and (*c*) that Mill's effort to relate individuality to a utilitarian ethics "grounded on the permanent interests of man [or a man] as a progressive being"[41] succeeds only in leading him into additional difficulties.

In dealing with these criticisms, it may be useful to consider them at two levels of discourse. I shall ask first, and *in seriatim*, whether and to what extent these interpretations of Mill's doctrine are valid. It will then remain to consider whether their total effect, if valid, would in fact seriously undermine the main burden of Mill's argument.

(a) Consciousness of individuality is a relatively recent phenomenon in human history. Historically, man has been a social animal in the ultraexistential sense. It was only with the Renaissance that the individual and his needs began to move closer to the center of human thought, and Mill was thus in line with a post-medieval tradition which he carried forward when he stressed not merely the reality but the unique importance of the individual. In doing this, he did not mean to imply that the individual was something altogether apart from and unrelated to the society in which he lived and of which he was a product; his point was merely that each individual is a unique constellation of personal qualities significantly different from those of his fellow men—qualities which must be prized and encouraged for their creative potentialities.[42]

From this standpoint, most of the criticisms that are based on an extreme reading of Mill's teachings are, to put it mildly, confusing or wrong. On the one hand, there are those who take this concern with individuality to mean that Mill was a defender of social and economic individualism in the narrower sense, which clearly was not the case; and on the other hand, oddly enough, Mill has also been taken to task by others for losing sight of the individual in a system of abstract and universal truths. Both views can be shown to be utterly without ground. Nevertheless, Mill cannot be absolved from some share of responsibility for confusion on this score; he never tired of emphasizing the crucial importance of individuality of thought and character, but he failed to make clear just what he meant by "individuality." Sometimes he seemed to equate individuality with difference alone, as when he argued for the development of the individual in his richest diversity, thus implying that mere difference in itself is a virtue. At other times, however, he pleaded for the value of originality. Originality, as Mill emphasized in his essay "On Genius," need not be identified with the discovery of new truth; it is enough if the individual discovers truths by himself even if they are truths already known to and accepted by others. Originality, in other words, is a process of discovery, not an attribute of that which is discovered; from which it would seem to follow that originality, though incontestably one of Mill's hallmarks of individuality, need not include eccentricity of conduct or difference of values. Thinking for himself, the original mind might well arrive in fact at conclusions altogether consistent with those current in his society and thus turn out to be a conformist after all. It cannot be argued that conformity on such terms negates the claim to individuality, for as long as a decision is arrived at through autonomous thought, it meets Mill's notion of originality. How, then, one may ask—and this, of course, is what troubles the critics—can Mill continue to identify individuality with difference or self-gratification or eccentricity per se?

The answer, I would suggest, is that Mill's plea for diversity must not be read in psychological terms as an argument for eccentricity in itself. It must rather be understood as a plea for a system of social arrangements which would allow each individual maximum freedom to develop his own bent. Mill viewed the human being as an organism—not as a "machine" or a "sheep" but as "a tree, which requires to grow and develop itself on all sides, according to the tendency of the inward forces which make it a living thing." We do not, therefore, enhance what is best in men by grinding down their unique or individual characteristics into a dead uniformity, but rather by cultivating them. This is why Mill was led to assert that a person's "own mode of laying out his existence is the best, not because it is the best in itself, but because it is his own mode." And this, too, is why, however we define it, individuality cannot be understood save in such terms as incorporate the elements of spontaneity, diversity, and the latitude of choice provided by freedom of expression and mutual criticism.

(b) Surely it is a misreading of Mill to interpret him as believing that the individual is the only reality and that society is purely imaginary. In fact, it is only by recognizing that the reverse is the more true, that it was Mill's very clear awareness of the reality of society and of its pressures upon the individual, that we can understand why Mill was led to write *On Liberty* at all. The one element of plausibility in this criticism of Mill, I think, is the contention that Mill's argument, at least as he develops it in this essay, does not give *sufficient* attention to the fact that the process of individualization is itself a social process, and that, from this standpoint, however much an individual may be at odds with society in a given situation, his individuality—and the very fact that it clashes with the demands of his society—is itself the result of a socializing process. In this sense, individuality is not intrinsically in opposition to sociality but emerges from it. Individualization and socialization, that is to say, always work together to produce a single human entity, even one in rebellion against the accepted norms of his society. He becomes an individual, a total and unique human being, only in and through society, only as a social product. In every aspect of his being, he remains, therefore, a social being at the same time that he is an autonomous and self-legislating person.

I do not mean to overstate this point, for we have ample evidence to show that the processes of modern society, with its increased technology and specialization, its increased alienation of man from himself, from the instruments and products of his labor, and from his human associations, have led to a fragmentation of the individual so serious as to have brought the concepts of alienation and anomy into common currency. Nevertheless, it is perhaps true that Mill's idea of the social and psychological conditions requisite for the formation of individuality focuses in such an extreme way on the one aspect—

the innate qualities—of an integral whole as to split it off from itself and thereby divest it of much of its meaning.

Here again, however, a word of caution must be entered. The fact that one becomes an individual only in and through a social process has little to do with, or at least does not eliminate the problem raised by, the claims of a given society upon a given individual in a concrete situation. We do not normally argue, for example, that because an individual is the child of his parents, and could not have become what he is without the benefit of his parentage, that he has no claims whatever *against* them should they attempt to mold him completely in their image. By the same token, we cannot ignore the claims of individuality when these run counter to social pressures.

(c) One of the lesser joys afforded teachers of logic and moral philosophy is the opportunity to display what they take to be Mill's fallacious argument uniting, or attempting to unite, Bentham's greatest happiness principle as a standard of social good with the desire for one's own greatest pleasure as the individual's only motive. That Mill went on to qualify his hedonism by asserting that pleasures can be graded as superior or inferior in moral quality put him—or so the critics argue—in still further logical difficulty; for then, as Sabine triumphantly notes, he was "in the indefensible logical position of demanding a standard for the measurement of a standard, which is a contradiction in terms, and also reduced his utilitarianism to complete indefiniteness."[43]

If these criticisms are valid, then Mill's further attempt in *On Liberty* to relate his values of freedom and diversity and individuality to the "*permanent* interests of man as a *progressive* being" (my italics), would only compound his difficulties. For what are the permanent, as distinct from the transitory, interests of man, and who is to determine them? What is meant by a progressive as distinct from a nonprogressive being, and who is to establish the criteria for this distinction? Finally, is it necessarily true that the permanent interests of man, however these may be conceived, are in fact furthered only by the self-regarding decisions of individuals and never by the acts of society? Surely compulsory vaccination and compulsory education, not to speak of distasteful tax laws and traffic regulations, may well conduce to the permanent interests of man even though there might be some who are foolish enough to dispute this. Whose judgment, then, shall prevail—the individual's or society's? If Mill's self-protection principle is permitted re-entry here, society's right to control and direct the individual in such matters is beyond disclaimer. Freedom of individuality, of tastes and pursuits, may at times, then, be required to give way to Mill's principle that society has a right to protect itself from harm.

These and similar criticisms are not altogether without validity. They lose much of their force, however, if we recall that Mill's argument, on one possible interpretation, may be taken as a defense of individuality not simply in terms of rationalistic hedonism but also on the ground that individual character has intrinsic value. Like Kant's, Mill's commitment is not really to happiness—as Bentham, for example, conceived this term—but to respect for the moral personality; "he believed," as his ablest biographer put it, "in individuality and self-development as ends in themselves and as the only means to the end of human welfare."[44] For happiness, as Mill was later to argue in his *Autobiography*, eludes men when they seek it as a direct or immediate aim; it is rather a by-product that comes to men in the course of their other activities.

However—to move now to the second level of our discussion—suppose we grant the general validity of these and similar criticisms of Mill's idea of individuality. Does it follow that they effectively undermine Mill's main argument? Do they, for example, demonstrably show that Mill's plea for individuality constitutes nothing less than an argument for social irresponsibility? I think not, and much of what I have already said by way of rejoinder or qualification to some of the specific criticisms in this context also tend to corroborate this judgment. Here I would only add that Mill, understanding as he did the need for social control and political stability, nevertheless pleaded for a society that would give maximum freedom to man to grow according to his own nature and desires because he anticipated that the net income of such an arrangement would be a more harmonious and happier society than one based on the contrary principle. Not all men, to be sure, share this anticipation; and there are others who do what they can to render its achievement impossible. But unless we value a static society inhabited by men of a like mold, we need to develop, even more than we presently have, those diversities of character and temperament that are the indispensable prerequisites of social improvement. To this end, individuality—with all the ambiguities that may attach to its definition—must be furthered rather than denied. Indeed, it is the mark of a civilized man (and of a mature society) that he recognizes and respects the inescapable fact that such ambiguities are inherent in a concept such as individuality; for he knows that to define individuality in a precise and final way is only to destroy it.

4. *That Mill misconceives the nature, and hence the proper limits, of freedom.* Mill's critics assert that Mill is at times confused and imprecise as to the nature and limits of freedom. They argue, among other things, that (*a*) he seems to conceive of liberty primarily, if not solely, in a negative sense, as the absence of restraints; most commonly, therefore, he views law and liberty, or social authority and liberty, as opposing forces, when, in fact, the critics argue, law and liberty always constitute two related aspects of a single whole; that (*b*) Mill speaks of liberty fairly consistently as the freedom of a man to do with himself as he desires; yet, the critics contend, a number of his illustrations can be cited to show that when he speaks of man's freedom to do as he desires, what he

really has in mind is only man's freedom to do as he *ought* to desire; or else these illustrations can be taken as an indication that Mill has no clear understanding of precisely what he means when he speaks of man's desires; and that (*c*) Mill does not, in *On Liberty* at least, give sufficient attention to economic and organizational threats to liberty; or even, for that matter, to legal or political infringements on liberty. Let us consider these several points in turn.

(*a*) For Mill, as for Hobbes, liberty is the absence of restraints; it follows that any interference by society, whether through law or through its moral code, constitutes an invasion of liberty. And so, like Hobbes, Mill is compelled by his own premise to reason that law and liberty necessarily stand in an inverse relationship to each other: the more law, or social authority, the less freedom— and vice versa. It would also seem to follow from this understanding of liberty that only a despot, entirely unfettered by either law or moral rules, can truly be said to possess complete freedom of action. But Mill also argues, in one of his early articles, that measures of political and social reform are not to be rejected merely because they are contrary to liberty; to oppose them for that reason alone, he said, merely "leads to confusion of ideas."[45] This, his critics are quick to point out, testifies to a fundamental confusion in Mill's thinking, a confusion that can only be removed by revising what they regard as his erroneous idea of freedom. He is confused, or at least inconsistent, to the extent that in his earlier essay he recognized freedom as a qualified rather than an absolute social value, whereas in *On Liberty* he affirmed a contrary and extreme view that "all restraint, *qua* restraint, is an evil." Only by redefining his notion of liberty, the critics argue, could Mill have escaped this inconsistency and made political sense.

There is, I believe, a legitimate criticism to be made of Mill's position here, but it happens to be the reverse of that put forward by his critics. They think Mill was wrong in defining freedom as he did in *On Liberty* but right in thinking that political and social measures are not to be condemned even when they run counter to the clear implications of his definition. I would contend, somewhat to the contrary, that Mill is correct in his definition but wrong in some of his inferences with respect to its bearing on the role of law.

As a matter of sheer definition and nothing more, Mill is on unimpeachable ground when he argues that law, being a form of restraint, is necessarily an invasion of liberty. Clearly, to the man who is hindered by the law from doing what he wants to do, there is a denial of freedom. In this purely formal sense of the term, then, I do not see what objection can be taken to Mill's definition or to the implication he drew from it that law and liberty consequently stand in an inverse relationship to each other.

What is at fault here is not the consistency of the argument from definition but Mill's failure to do full justice to the nature and effect of law as such, and, most of all, his neglect of the fact that law may, in a particular situation, operate as a restraint on a restraint: by restraining some, it may give others a degree of freedom they would not otherwise possess. So too with social authority. An employer may impose restraints on his employee, but a labor union which restrains the employer may free the employee from those restraints, or from some of them; as the law in turn by restraining certain practices on the part of the union may free the employee from restraints the union might otherwise impose on him. Freedom, that is to say, is not a fixed whole like an apple pie, into which the law cuts, and with each cut takes a piece away. Freedom in the real world is meaningful only when it is reduced to a complex system of individual liberties and concomitant restraints, each restraint operating to limit an action that someone else might take to deny a particular liberty to another person. The question then is not one of law versus liberty, or social authority versus liberty, but rather one involving a multitude of decisions as to *who* shall enjoy *which* liberties, under *what* circumstances and for *what* purposes, and *which* specific restraints, consequently, need to be imposed to make such enjoyment possible. To say, as Mill does, that "all restraint, *qua* restraint, is an evil," is in these terms misleading, and prevents Mill from emphasizing what he well understands: that a legal restraint may, in a given situation, become the indispensable condition for the exercise of a social freedom.

(*b*) In the history of political thought, two conceptions of liberty have long been opposed to each other. These are the liberty to do as one wants versus the liberty to do as one should. In general, Mill commits himself to the first of these conceptions of liberty. In various ways throughout his essay he repeats the principle, set forth in his introductory chapter, that with respect to self-regarding conduct society cannot rightfully interfere with the freedom of any man:

> His own good, either physical or moral, is not a sufficient warrant. He cannot rightfully be compelled to do or forbear because it will be better for him to do so, because it will make him happier, because, in the opinions of others, to do so would be wise or even right. These are good reasons for remonstrating with him, or reasoning with him, or persuading him, or entreating him, but not for compelling him or visiting him with any evil in case he do otherwise. To justify that, the conduct from which it is desired to deter him must be calculated to produce evil to someone else . . . Over himself, over his own body and mind, the individual is sovereign.

All this seems clear and straightforward enough until Mill seeks to illustrate the application of his principle. He offers, by way of example, the case of a man about to cross an unsafe bridge, and tells us that, if the bridge is known to be unsafe and there is no time to warn the man of his danger, it is proper for a public officer or any one else to seize that man and turn him back, "without any real infringement of his liberty; for liberty consists in doing what one desires, and he does not desire to fall into the river." It is true that Mill distinguishes here between the certainty of his mischief as against its danger and would limit such interference only to those cases where there is absolute certainty of the consequences which would follow if the individual decided to cross the bridge. Clearly, however, this is a secondary matter of application which does not affect the main principle for which Mill is arguing. Lest this example be taken as a single departure from an otherwise steadfast principle, Mill offers still a second illustration to the same effect—namely, that no man has a right to sell himself into slavery:

> His voluntary choice is evidence that what he so chooses is desirable, or at least endurable, to him, and his good is on the whole best provided for by allowing him to take his own means of pursuing it. But by selling himself for a slave, he abdicates his liberty; he foregoes any future use of it beyond that single act. He therefore defeats, in his own case, the very purpose which is the justification of allowing him to dispose of himself. . . . The principle of freedom cannot require that he should be free not to be free. It is not freedom to be allowed to alienate his freedom.

These illustrations have furnished critics of Mill with an argument that he was guilty of a basic intellectual ambiguity when he defined liberty as he did. One line of such criticism can of course be found in representatives of the English idealist school—notably in Bosanquet. They insist that when Mill spoke of "desire" in each of the two illustrations, the term "desire" could only mean man's real or ultimate will as distinct from his actual or momentary will. Otherwise, they contend, Mill's defense of any legal or social action taken in either case would clearly make no sense of his major premise that liberty consists in the absence of all restraint on that which a man desires for himself. Is not such action, the critics ask, an interference with a man for his own good, *both* physical and moral? If this is so, does this not imply, as Bosanquet, for example, insisted, "that it may be right, according to the principle of liberty, to restrain a man, for reasons affecting him alone, from doing what at the moment he proposes to do"? Are we not then "entitled to argue from the essential nature of freedom to what freedom really demands, as opposed to what the man mometarily seems to wish"?[46] So Bosanquet, and so, too, various idealist critics of Mill.

Other critics of Mill who are not committed to the idealist distinction between man's real and his actual will also find Mill's examples confusing, though for other reasons. Ritchie, for example, argues that if we are to take Mill's illustrations as guidelines for the application of his principles, "there is almost no limit to the amount of interference or restraint which would be justified."[47] An interesting variant of Ritchie's argument can be found, more recently, in Lancaster, who raises the following objection:

There are many things which people really do not desire to do, but few of them are as clear as the one suggested. The circumstances surrounding most human choices in a modern society are so numerous and complicated that the individual can scarcely be expected readily to know which one is best for him—*i.e.*, which one he "really" desires. In view of the fact that these complicated situations are the typical ones, Mill's principle is of little or no help.

Even more to the point, and more damaging to the end which Mill obviously had in view, is the fact that his reasoning in the example that he gives may easily be used to justify the most extreme interference with individual liberty. Thus, a religious enthusiast might decide by similar reasoning that, since the heretic really wishes his own salvation, he must be prevented from holding beliefs which, in the opinion of the enthusiast, make salvation impossible. Any individual choice could be interfered with on similar grounds, since those with power to do so can always argue that they are as sure of the result which they would prevent as the man in Mill's example is sure that the bridge is safe.[48]

In brief, whether they hail from the idealist tradition or prefer a more empirical approach, the critics agree that these examples, as well as others that Mill offers in the same vein, defeat the very principle that he was anxious to establish; for his examples suggest, if they suggest anything at all, that Mill would defend legal or social interference with a man for reasons that affect him alone, so as to prevent him from doing what at the moment he proposes to do. To the idealist, such as Bosanquet, this is "in germ the doctrine of the 'real' will, and a conception analogous to that of Rousseau when he speaks of a man 'being forced to be free'";[49] to others, it means merely that Mill denied in his examples what he affirmed in his statement of principle.

It must be conceded, I think, that there is a sense in which much of this criticism is both pertinent and valid. Mill's choice of language is unfortunate; for when he admits that interference with a man seeking to cross an unsafe bridge is an infringement but not a "real" infringement of his liberty, he gives his argument a turn which would seem to identify it with the arguments of the idealist philosophers. Moreover, by failing to anticipate through his examples the whole range of choices open to men, and what their exercise implies for his political principles, he left uncertain, and perhaps rendered unconvincing, the relevance and applicability of those principles to actual social problems.

But here again, it must be insisted, the critics display their habitual itch to overextend themselves; they carry their criticisms to extremes which would nullify any type of political theory, their own included. For what they demand, in effect, is nothing less than a set of political recipes, a set of specific instruc-tions for this or that particular problem. And this, of course, cannot be supplied. Mill, like any other political philosopher, is writing a book of political principles, not a catalogue of *do's* and *don'ts*. As such, his book cannot anticipate all contingencies, nor can his examples do more than *illustrate* his meaning. Consider, for example, what is involved in his argument granting society, or the state, the right to prevent a man from selling himself into slavery. Is Mill saying anything more here than that, on any sane reading of human history, we are entitled to make certain assumptions about human nature, specifically in this case that no man *wants* to be a slave, that no human being—unless he is a child, or momentarily delirious, or so agitated as to be unable to govern his actions by reflective thought—would *voluntarily* sell himself into slavery? If, therefore, a man were actually to express a willingness to contract himself into slavery, it could only be because the circumstances which surround him are such as to "force" him into this action; seeing no feasible alternative, he finds himself compelled to become a slave. What Mill sought to protect was man's *permanent* freedom of voluntary choice, a freedom which is irretrievably taken from him by the one act of selling himself into slavery; for, says Mill, he is then "in a position which has no longer the presumption in its favor that would be afforded by his voluntarily remaining in [a state of freedom]."

If it is correct to assume that slavery is contrary to man's actual desires, and that society or the state may therefore properly interfere with an individual's momentary willingness to sell himself into slavery, how much more correct is it to assume that no rational man desires to commit suicide, and to infer from this that it is right for society or the state to prevent a man from committing suicide? In the absence of information to the contrary, are we not entitled to assume that he is being forced to take this drastic step only by the pressure of momen-tary circumstances?

This reading of Mill, of course, does not altogether confute Bosanquet's insistence that in all this Mill is really adverting to the essential nature of human freedom and human will, building not on what an actual man says he wants but on what a rational man would really want. However, it seems to me to go a long way toward reconciling Mill's own definition of freedom with the requirements of human survival—at least as Mill understands those requirements. And since there is no political theory that does not rest on *some* assumptions, whether stated or unstated, about the nature of man and of the human condition, Mill's argument is no more subject to criticism in this respect than is any other political theory. Moreover, the idealist objection here is quite beside the point. As an empiricist, Mill did not have to make a distinciton between a real and an actual will to vindicate his principle; it was enough for his purpose to recognize that man is a bundle of conflicting desires and to distinguish between those which are grounded permanently in man's make-up and those which may sway him from time to time; it does not speak against this empirical approach to say that man's desires fall into some kind of hierarchical order.

Similar considerations apply to Lancaster's critique of Mill on this point. Where the range and complexity of alternatives open to an individual are so bewildering that he cannot make a well-defined choice one way or the other, where the situation is so blurred and the conflict of choices so great as to leave the individual thoroughly confused and unable to decide, then the state, regardless of how it acts, cannot be said to be interfering with him in any sense which violates Mill's teaching; for whether it pushes him in one direction or the other, it does not violate his desires. Moreover, although such ambiguities of choice unquestionably bedevil much of human life, they do not govern all of it; and when Lancaster argues that the individual cannot be expected to know which of the many and complex choices open to him is "best," it does not follow that he cannot decide which of them he actually wants. He chooses what he desires, as a hungry man confronted with an enticing array of foods at a *smörgosbord* chooses, however falteringly, what he desires; and to say, with the idealist philosophers, that he does not choose what he "really" desires, or even, with a gastronomical empiricist, what is "best" for him, is in no sense to prove that he is unable to exercise effective choice of some kind.

(c) One of the most glaring faults for which Mill's essay can properly be taken to task is its curious failure to deal with what was then, and remains now, one of the greatest sources of danger to individual freedom—the power of social and economic organizations. One need not subscribe to Harold Laski's extreme view that ". . .it is upon the issue of property that the whole problem of liberty hinges today, as it has always done in the past,"[50] to recognize that individual liberties have not always found their maximum security under the hegemony of near-dynastic economic empires like the Ford and Du Pont and Rockefeller enterprises, or within the near-feudal world of the modern corporations, or in the petty domains of lesser landlords and businessmen. Certainly, Mill himself was fully aware of this problem in certain of his other writings.[51] Yet, oddly enough, he gives all too little attention to this vital aspect of his problem in *On Liberty*, contenting himself with but a few short pasages on free trade and on the limits of governmental interference with economic activity.

Similarly, in what is perhaps one of his more startling sins of omission, Mill fails here, though not in other writings, to explore the role of organization as a countervailing power. If individual liberties are threatened, as they are, by great economic and social organizations; or if power has passed, as Mill believes it has, "more and more from individuals, and small knots of individuals, to masses [so] that the importance of the masses become constantly greater, [and] that of individuals less," until we have arrived at the point where "the individual is lost and becomes impotent in the crowd"; it may well be that individual liberties and the recovery of individuality can effectively be secured only through "greater and more perfect combination among individuals." No single individual, that is to say, can hope successfully to resist the tides and tendencies of public opinion or of the great organizations. But if individuals were to band together in the common pursuit of their common interests, they might through such combination significantly influence the course of events. That "such a spirit of combination is most of all wanted among the intellectual classes and professions," was, for Mill, a ludicrous spectacle and lamentable in its consequences.[52] What is crucial for us, however, is the fact that although Mill elsewhere appreciated the importance of voluntary association as a means of protecting the individual from economic exploitation and intellectual subjection, he did not incorporate this insight into his discussion here.

It is curious, finally, that whereas Mill in *On Liberty* did appreciate and dwell upon the evils of bureaucracy, he did not somehow realize that the translation of social prejudice into law, and into actions taken by police and administrative officials, might well constitute a more important threat to liberty than would mere manifestations of social disapproval and disesteem. I think Russell has unnecessarily overstated a good point when he argues that in our day the police constitute the most serious danger to liberty "in most civilized countries";[53] for, although it cannot be denied that even in the Western democracies the police are guilty of many crimes of omission and commission, there is a considerable distance to be traveled before one can equate the malpractices of some police officers or police systems with "the police," or to hold that the police are, in fact, more the invaders than they are the defenders of freedom, or more of a menace to individual liberties than are the great economic and religious power organizations or the bands of self-appointed vigilantes who harass racial and religious minority groups and political nonconformists. Nevertheless, the petty tyrannies of the police, as of bureaucrats and political office holders generally, constitute a major and continuing affront to the democratic idea of free men in a free society. More than this, the laws enacted in response to the demands of powerful interest groups demonstrate only too well that liberty is endangered not so much by man's capacity to dislike other men as by his capacity to injure them.

Still, it should be borne in mind, in extenuation of Mill, that *On Liberty* is an essay, not a treatise, and as such need not, and could not, cope with all contingencies or possibilities. In so far as such criticisms focus on Mill's *omissions*, they do not argue against his larger thesis; they merely indicate further avenues of exploration and application to extend the scope of his thesis to what Mill called man's other-regarding conduct.

IV

If what I have said thus far is at all justified, the numerous criticisms leveled against Mill's essay, whether taken singly or in combination, neither destroy nor seriously impair the validity of its central argument, however much they may qualify it in some respects. This, to say the least, is a far cry from the intemperate judgment of the more extreme of Mill's critics who dismiss his essay as a good illustration of how a book in political theory ought *not* to be written or, worse still, as the product of a sentimental moralist venting his personal prejudices and idiosyncrasies, and doing so in a rhetoric which bemuses only literary connoisseurs or those already committed to his views.[54] As against these and other dim judgments of Mill's performance, I would argue that Lord Morley was far closer to a just appraisal of its qualities when he said of *On Liberty* that "The little volume belongs to the rare books that after hostile criticism has done its best are still found to have somehow added a cubit to man's stature."[55]

What, then, are the positive contributions of *On Liberty* that still make it a landmark in the history of political thought? If these came to nothing more than establishing the essential impregnability of Mill's major principles to the assaults considered heretofore, they would constitute enough of a formidable claim to that distinction. But the essay, I would urge, has other claims to our critical esteem as well. Of these, it may be enough here to mention only two.

1. *Mill reformulated the problem of freedom so as to give it contemporary relevance and application.* The issue that Mill raised with regard to the problem of freedom was in many respects a different one, and certainly more important in its implications, from that generally allowed him, or even from what he himself considered to be the central question of his essay. That issue, simply put, is whether, and how, conflicting interests can be reconciled in a modern democratic state without victimizing the individual either in his relations to the institutions of government or in his personal claims against the pressures of mass sentiment.

To appreciate the essential modernity of this question, one has only to recall that, with the qualified exception of Tocqueville, political thinkers before Mill had explored almost every other major aspect of political freedom without seriously coming to grips with the second—and, in Mill's judgment, the more significant— dimension of that problem, namely, that of respecting the requirements of individuality as against the demands of a controlling majority opinion.

To take a diametrically opposed conception of freedom, when the Greeks talked of liberty, they had in mind, primarily, the liberty of a whole people, of the *polis* or community-state, as against the tyrant or foreign oppressor.

Liberty to them was the liberty of a commonwealth. The people were thought of as a homogeneous unit—a body of men who shared the same values and pursued a common way of life and who consequently sought their fulfillment as men not in the relative privacy of their homes or of their "self-regarding" activities, as Mill would have put it, but in the life of the *polis* itself. To be a man was pre-eminently to be a social or political animal. Hence the classical conception of liberty did not recognize, much less focus on, the right of an individual (or group) to do as he (or it) might choose; it built instead on the right of the people as a whole to follow their own ways. This is why Greek thinkers could identify the community with the state and liberty with a particular way of life.[56] This is why Socrates could properly be charged with a crime for teaching disrespect of the gods, and why Socrates in turn, in the *Republic*, could urge that all those who did not conform to the common ways and teach the "right" things should be sent into exile.

Even Hobbes and Locke, though they broke in important respects from the classical tradition, bypassed the problem of mass tyranny in complete silence. To Hobbes, the problem of liberty was one involving the relations between the individual and his "alien" government; and because Hobbes feared the possible consequences of an individual's unrestrained actions, liberty to him was largely a matter of how far the law lets people alone. To Locke, who viewed the problem from the standpoint of the relations between the individual and his "own" government, and who feared the possible consequences of actions taken by a government separated from the people, liberty was primarily conceived of as the right to cherish one's own property and to have one's own government. Moreover, Locke—like Milton before him—excluded a portion of the community, e.g., Catholics, atheists, and other blasphemers, from the protection of civil society. For all three, further, the people were still seen as a relatively homogeneous entity; consequently the problem of freedom still turned, as with the classical political philosophers, on the relations between the people and the government. To be sure, the authors of the American Constitution, and later of *The Federalist,* introduced an innovation when they made greater allowance for a truth stated but not developed by Aristotle—that a political society rests in some respects on a heterogeneous and divided people—and when they squarely confronted the possibility of a majority using the leverage of government to tyrannize; but they, too, limited themselves to the relations between the individual or the group and the government. It remained for Tocqueville, in his celebrated *Democracy in America*, to point out that the problem goes beyond the mere relationship between the individual and government to embrace all other relations which may affect the freedom of the individual. But whereas Tocqueville saw and brilliantly expounded this new dimension of the problem of liberty, he confined himself largely to a description of its actual operation and effects, and of its tendencies and potential dangers, although he was not unaware of certain forces that might mitigate the gravity of conformist pressures. And yet, for all his perspicacity, he did not ask the question Mill was later to raise: What is the principle or principles that a democratic society *ought* to observe so as to make it possible for diverse groups and conflicting creeds to function within a livable framework of government? What is more, Mill went beyond Milton and Locke to extend the scope of freedom to include all men and not merely those who have, broadly speaking, the "right" faith. The holders of power, he cautioned, are not always identical with those over whom it is exercised, so that "self-government" is "not the government of each by himself, but of each by all the rest." Hence it follows that individual liberty might well be endangered even by a government chosen by and responsible to the people, or by the people themselves acting directly.

It is true of course, as I noted earlier, that Mill neglected to consider in any detail the nature and implications of political interferences with individual freedom and, hence, did not see that in a democracy some political interference may actually curb acts of private interference with individual freedom, and thus serve to enhance, rather than to curtail, some freedoms for some men; but this neglect is to be accounted for by Mill's belief that such political invasions were more a potential than an actual danger, more a threat to the future than to the society of his own day:

> The majority have not yet learned to feel the power of the govern-
> ment their power, or its opinions their opinions. When they do so, indi-
> vidual liberty will probably be as much exposed to invasion from the
> government as it already is from public opinion.

Believing as he did, then, that the immediate threat to individuality derived not from the mandates of law but from the pressures of public sentiment, Mill sought throughout his life, and increasingly in his later years, to emphasize his conviction that intellectual stagnation was the real ultimate threat to democracy. It is not surprising, therefore, to find in his essay strong and repeated expressions of concern for the nonlegal restraints that seemed to him, as to Tocqueville, to vitiate or endanger individual and group liberties—restraints imposed by physical violence, economic sanctions, and most of all by the play of public sentiment or, as he and Tocqueville called it, the tyranny of the majority. I think Mill's case would have been stronger had he seen that it is not so much the play of public sentiment as the actual exercise of coercive power to enforce that sentiment that constitutes tyranny. But who in contemporary America can seriously deny that Mill was eminently correct in his terrible account of the blights of conformity?[57]

The danger which threatens human nature [wrote Mill] is not the excess, but the deficiency, of personal impulses and preferences. . . . In our times, from the highest class of society down to the lowest, everyone lives as under the eye of a hostile and dreaded censorship. Not only in what concerns others, but in what concerns only themselves, the individual or the family do not ask themselves, what do I prefer? or, what would suit my character and disposition? or, what would allow the best and highest in me to have fair play and enable it to grow and thrive? They ask themselves, what is suitable to my position? what is usually done by persons of my station and pecuniary circumstances? or (worse still) what is usually done by persons of a station and circumstances superior to mine? I do not mean that they choose what is customary in preference to what suits their own inclination. It does not occur to them to have any inclination except for what is customary. Thus the mind itself is bowed to the yoke: even in what people do for pleasure, conformity is the first thing thought of; they like in crowds; they exercise choice only among things commonly done; peculiarity of taste, eccentricity of conduct are shunned equally with crimes, until by dint of not following their own nature they have no nature to follow: their human capacities are withered and starved; they become incapable of any strong wishes or native pleasures, and are generally without either opinions or feelings of home growth, or properly their own. Now is this, or is it not, the desirable condition of human nature?

In this, as in so many things, Mill closely anticipated what later writers have seized upon and exploited as a fundamental insight. For in his discussion of conformity, Mill accurately and concisely set forth the theme and central hypothesis of David Riesman's recent and popular book *The Lonely Crowd*—from the expression in Mill's *Liberty* that "At present individuals are lost in the crowd," to the basic distinction that Riesman draws between inner-directed and other- or tradition-directed men.[58] What, after all, is Mill decrying in the lengthy passage I have quoted if not the emergence into undue prominence of the other-directed individual? What is he pleading if not the cause of the inner-directed man? And to the extent that Mill in the middle of the nineteenth century was able to see a tendency that has since become a central characteristic of our own society, he can hardly be dismissed as a man without relevance and vision. I suppose that some of Mill's detractors would quickly remind us that in this respect Mill has but aligned himself with his usual lost cause; but I hardly think this historical judgment impairs the validity of his argument. On the contrary, I think it makes his plea only the more urgent.

What is important in Mill, then, is that he did understand and systematically treat the hitherto neglected problem of the relations between individuals and groups within a single political and social system, seeking in the process not merely to describe what men actually did but *to discover and prescribe a principle* by which they might test the propriety or impropriety of both governmental and social interferences with individual behavior. In this respect his essay, for all its shortcomings, represents a major advance in the literature of political thought.

2. *Mill propounded the essential elements of the liberal case for freedom of expression.* "Many things," said the Greek sophist Protagoras, "hinder certainty—the obscurity of the matter and the shortness of man's life." Because Mill respected this judgment, claiming no final certainty for himself and refusing to concede it in others, he put the case for freedom of expression on different, and broader, grounds than Milton had done before him. He urged it not only on behalf of truth itself, though he insisted that freedom of opinion and expression is a necessary condition for the discovery of truth, but also for the sake of the individual and of society. He recognized full well, as MacIver expressed it, that "the right of the majority is not the rightness of the majority";[59] and he understood, to quote Morley again, that "repression, whether by public opinion or in any other way, may be the means of untold waste of gifts that might have conferred on mankind unspeakable benefits."[60] Hence Mill insisted that man must be free to think, to choose, and to learn from his own mistakes both for the sake of truth and for his capacity to mature as a self-directed being. To do so does not mean that men need *reject* all received doctrines as untrue, merely that they be free to *test* such doctrines by all the resources of reason.[61] And this was what Mill reaffirmed in *On Liberty*, with the added emphasis that it was indispensable to any society if it is to avert stagnation. What is more, a society faces precisely the same choice between progress and stagnation when it is confronted by the challenge of new ideas; for here, too, it is only by man's free exercise of reason that truth can be distinguished from falsehood.

All of which is enough to indicate how ludicrous some of Mill's critics make themselves when they go off on an epistemological deep end to argue that Mill is here denying the possibility of attaining truth or, worse still, to indulge themselves in the grand *non sequitur* that, for Mill, the test of truth is nothing more than its historical success in winning acceptance in the free competition of the market. The confusion here between the epistemological problem and Mill's concern with the social conditions making for, or discouraging, the exercise of reason is too obvious to need elaboration. Nor, save for the thought processes of Dostoevsky's Grand Inquisitor, is it possible to say, with one of Mill's critics, that the unrestricted competition of ideas should be discouraged for fear that falsehood might then prevail over truth and thus destroy the moral basis of society.[62] One who feels himself sufficiently omniscient to urge that what is needed is "a firm official stand for what is known as right, true, and good,"[63] can well dismiss Mill's case without further ado; but for those of us who lack such self-assurance, there is no evading the choice as Mill sees it. What disturbs critics of this stripe, I suspect, is not that Mill was opposed to truth but that, as an admirer of Mill once put it, Mill wished men "not to take authority for truth but truth for authority."[64]

It was anything but a spirit of jest, therefore, that inspired Mill to urge that, in the absence of an opposing idea, it might be well to contrive one. A contemporary reviewer of Mill's essay—sharing, one might add, the phobias of the aforementioned critics—reacted to this proposal with horror:

> Toleration of devil's advocates is a different thing from institution of them. Would Mr. Mill conceive it to be advantageous to the formation of his maid-servant's enlightened opinion upon the excellence of chastity, that she should be invited to spend her Sunday afternoon in earnest controversy upon the matter with a profligate dragoon from Kensington barracks . . .?[65]

To which Mill's rejoinder, needless to say, would have been distinctly in the affirmative—except that, as a prudent man, he would also have insisted on the proviso that the afternoon be restricted to "earnest controversy." Indeed, he might have added that, in expressing horror at the prospect of an afternoon so spent, the critic himself betrayed a lack of firm conviction about "the excellence of chastity." And the same, *mutatis mutandis,* may be said today of those who denounce Mill's argument "in the name of a higher morality."[66]

What is fundamental to Mill's whole approach, of course, is the altogether salutary reminder that we are not infallible creatures; that truth cannot be attained in any complete and final sense; that what we take to be truth must therefore be held tentatively and undogmatically; and that we must always be prepared, as rational men, to subject the beliefs we hold to be true to the test of new data and new experiences. This reflection, if I understand Mill correctly, is his essential case for liberalism; and it is still very much the case a century later, made all the more compelling by the cumulative pressures which society today exerts upon the individual.

4

Pure Tolerance:
A Critique of Criticisms

Ever since men climbed down from the trees and found it necessary to establish ground rules, they have fought over what those rules shall be. They have fought longest, and perhaps most bitterly, over the most fundamental rule of all—the rule by which the ground rules themselves shall be determined. For he who controls the ground rules is in a position to control the game.

That the rule of tolerance is this fundamental rule is revealed by the fact that dictatorships exclude it and democratic states make it central to their enterprise. Only in democratic states are governments established and changed in response to the free play of conflicting opinions.

This—the securing of responsible government—is not of course the only reason for supporting tolerance. Those who defend it also contend that tolerance makes for diversity, which is essential to progress and the development of individuality, and thus to the common good. They also believe that tolerance, at least in a pluralist society, is the only principle under which diverse groups can live together without resorting either to mutual slaughter or to an authoritarian regime that will impose one group's creed on others.

The argument for intolerance, in contrast, is generally put forward by men who mean to have their way but fear that free discussion will "mislead" other men—either because those others are less wise or virtuous than they or because conditions are such as a favor the false doctrine.

I

Now, the classic case for tolerance has been set forth in John Stuart Mill's celebrated essay *On Liberty*. Consequently, ever since Mill published that essay in 1859, the critics of tolerance have been diligently at work refuting him. It needs to be said, if unkindly, that one obvious reason for this is that later critics have recognized the difficulties that earlier critics have had with him. It is

Reprinted, by permission, from *Dissent* 13 (1966): 510–25.

a mark of no mean significance that this process still continues; indeed, it has become the foundation of a flourishing industry.

As a part-time member of this guild (though one essentially in sympathy with Mill), I can do no other than commend it to the newcomers. I ask only that they first familiarize themselves with already-existing products. Then they might spare their readers, if not themselves, the labor of reencountering ancient formulations under the guise of a new suit of phrases; and in doing so they might also learn to distinguish reputable from shoddy merchandise. For it needs also to be said that much of what is produced by this industry today is neither novel nor imaginative nor important. That, regrettably, is the judgment I must propose in regard to *A Critique of Pure Tolerance,* co-authored by Herbert Marcuse, Barrington Moore, and Robert Wolff.[1]

What distinguishes the three essays that constitute this book is *not* an awareness, and hence transcendence, of these elementary considerations. It is rather the marshalling and occasionally the revision of old arguments to attack Mill from what might (for the moment) be called radical perspectives. Traditionally, Mill has been identified with the Left and his critics with the Right. This ideological cleavage by no means accounts for all of Mill's critics; some of them—Dorothy Fosdick, J.C. Rees, and Isaiah Berlin, for example—have dealt with Mill and his arguments in terms divorced from such partisanship. But it accounts for a good many of them, including, I venture to think, the three critics who here attack Mill's plea for complete freedom of thought and expression on the ground, so they say, that it prevents, or at the very least militates against, the supremacy of "correct" ideas, that is, "their" ideas. And because they profess to be of the radical Left, Mill stands condemned (in their eyes) as a protagonist of the "wrong" ideas, as a purveyor of a political philosophy that safeguards the *status quo.*

The keynote of their argument—on which, despite other differences, they are agreed—is contained in this introductory sentence: "For each of us the prevailing theory and practice of tolerance turned out on examination to be in varying degrees hypocritical masks to cover appalling political realities." And here I must begin with a confession of inadequacy: I have tried, but I am unable to make sense of this statement. What, apart from its strident terminology, does it mean? Is the theory referred to one that accounts for the practice or one that articulates an ideal to which that practice should conform? If it accounts for the practice, then the theory is not a mask but a revelation of the realities. If it articulates an ideal, then the theory stands not as a description of what is but as a prescriptive norm, and hence as a criterion of judgment by which those realities are to be judged. If it is replied that theory here means what people say, then we are simply confronted by the usual dichotomy between rhetoric and performance, between espoused or intended conduct and actual behavior.

But a theory is never this; it is always an attempt to describe the true reality—
our function, Klee somewhere said, is "not to reveal the visible but to make
visible the real"—or to prescribe the proper conduct. Then, if we omit the word
"theory" and look only at the word "practice," all that the statement seems to
mean is that people do not behave very nicely, which is hardly a piercing
insight.

In what sense, then, can the theory or practice of tolerance be termed
hypocritical? Presumably in the sense that the theory is at odds with, and a
rationalization of, the practice. But this means only that the theory (as explanation rather than as prescription) is deficient, that in fact it is not a theory at all
but an ideology.

What, finally, is meant by the phrase "prevailing theory"? Is it Mill's theory
of liberty, or what the writers call the doctrine of "pure tolerance"? If so, there
is obviously a considerable gap not only between Mill's teaching and current
(e.g., American) practice, but also, I think, between that teaching and whatever may be said to be the dominant legal and political view (or views) of
liberty. Is it some other theory, a doctrine more in keeping with what our three
writers are pleased to call the realities of an industrial democracy? If so, this is
not identified. What they attack, then, is not *the* prevailing doctrine of liberty,
and not always, as will become clear, Mill's doctrine, but doctrines and conditions imputed to Mill and which, in their view, constitute the hallmark of a
sorry liberalism.

Let us consider the contentions of our three critics.

II

Take, first, the argument of Robert Paul Wolff. I am not altogether sure
whether he misunderstands Mill or intends his readers to misunderstand Mill,
but to the extent that I may read him correctly he depicts Mill at one point as an
exponent of psychological egoism and at another as an advocate of individual
liberty free of all social restraints. Neither of these characterizations accurately
describes Mill. He also asserts that Mill defended the freedoms of thought and
of action so long as these did not harm others. But Mill clearly and explicitly
distinguished his defense of freedom of thought, which he made an absolute,
from freedom of action, which was conditioned by its consequences. Wolff
makes the important point that tolerance should not be confused with neutral-
ity or condescension but should be recognized as a positive good; however,
though Wolff does not mention it, this is also central to Mill's thought.

What is of interest, then, is not Wolff's critique of Mill—which is, strictly
speaking, essentially irrelevant—but the fact that his essay, though it is entitled
"Beyond Tolerance," deals less with tolerance than with the conditions that

make it ineffective. Wolff believes that tolerance is a doctrine that has emerged from and is only appropriate to a particular stage of historical development, namely, the stage of democratic pluralism. But—and this is what he is most concerned to show—democratic pluralism is no longer adequate to the so-called stage of modernity in which we now find ourselves, and for two reasons primarily: it discriminates against certain disadvantaged social groups or interests—those that are outside the Establishment, that lack "legitimate representation," and that are not consequently given a place or a voice in society—and it discriminates against certain social policies, most directly those that look to the promotion of the common good rather than to the satisfaction of diverse particular interests or claims. As a result, democratic pluralism in its concrete application—though not, Wolff adds, in its theory—supports inequality, maintains the *status quo*, blocks social change. What is required, Wolff concludes, is a new philosophy of community, of the common good, one that goes "beyond pluralism and beyond tolerance."

Now it is curious that one who, like Wolff, relates ideas in near-deterministic fashion to particular stages of historical development—and I must bypass here the familiar and age-old controversy over this asserted but still unproved thesis—should ignore the fact that earlier theories of tolerance, those of Locke and Milton, for example, and perhaps even of Socrates in the *Apology* before them, were not merely arguments for a *qualified* tolerance, but were in a very real sense also arguments consistent with a kind of homogeneous, or largely homogeneous, society. To go beyond pluralism is presumably to plead for a new type of homogeneity, and hence for the new kind of orthodoxy; for from what individuals or groups, and for what purpose, will new and diverse ideas then emerge?

What makes Mill distinctive, and vitally important, is that while he recognized and even pleaded for a sense of national cohesion and for the pursuit of the public interest, he insisted along with this that it was necessary to respect and to build upon a certain heterogeneity, that progress required *both* the promotion of the common good and the furtherance of individual and group differences. Consequently, in line with his utilitarian philosophy, he argued for the absolute toleration of ideas and for the maximum toleration of variety in practices. He sought a unity that would contain rather than eliminate diversity. In these terms, to argue against pluralism and for the idea of a common good, as if these were opposing and mutually exclusive principles, is to argue for a self-defeating proposition; for it may well be—and I am convinced it is—that democratic pluralism, properly understood and properly institutionalized, is precisely what defines or constitutes the core of the common good.

It is noteworthy that Wolff nowhere defines or articulates the nature of his common good; nor does he set out a program for its realization. Were he to attempt to do so, he might find, as many another writer has found, that in a multi-group society the common good requires not the rejection of pluralism but the determination of the appropriate kinds and degrees of pluralism compatible with a political goal. Otherwise there can emerge only a deadening, even if new, conformity. However this may be, if it is true, as Wolff admits, that the fault is not in the theory of pluralism, or of tolerance, but in the shortcomings of its practice, why does he attack the theory of pure tolerance? Why does he not focus instead on the conditions—whether of structure, institutions, attitudes, or all of these combined—that hinder its attainment and impair or delimit its free exercise, and on measures calculated to redress those deficiencies? For it is not Mill and his theory of liberty but the arrangements and practices of modern industrial society that are clearly the issues at stake.

III

Barrington Moore's essay, "Tolerance and the Scientific Outlook," is a more sophisticated and relevant effort. In part, this is because Moore is aware of many of the foregoing considerations and avoids certain elementary confusions. In part, it is because Moore restates and builds upon a number of Mill's arguments—though he does not, curiously, acknowledge this indebtedness. In part, finally, it is because Moore advances an interesting argument of his own.

With respect to Mill, the most important of Moore's restatements is the proposition that the intellectual's task is not to agitate or fight for a particular doctrine or ideal "but to find and speak the truth, whatever the political consequences may be." The latter part of this proposition is, of course, standard Millian doctrine, as may be evidenced by Mill's familiar plea (in his essay "On Civilization") that the very cornerstone and object of education "is to call forth the greatest possible quantity of intellectual *power*, and to inspire the intense *love of truth*; and this without a particle of regard to the results to which the exercise of that power may lead. . . ." But the first part of Moore's statement does not, alas, confront the obvious question: What if one's discovery of the truth is at the same time the discovery of a correct doctrine or ideal? Does his commitment to the truth not require him then to advocate, even agitate for, that doctrine? Does the intellectual not then become a partisan *malgré lui*? If I am to infer Moore's answer from the content of this essay, it is clearly positive. But Moore does not explicitly say so; nor does he pursue the implications of that conclusion. Mill, of course, essayed both roles, precisely because he saw no necessary incompatibility between them.

Moore properly maintains that historical disputes can often be settled by an appeal to the evidence. But does it follow that "tolerance for different 'interpretations' based on different *Weltanschauungen* merely befuddles the issue"?

Or that "a scientific attitude toward human society [does not] necessarily induce a conservative tolerance of the existing order"? Clearly, what constitutes relevant evidence is itself a matter of interpretation; and the issue is not whether tolerance or a scientific attitude implies acceptance (or, for that matter, rejection) of a particular interpretation or social order—it does not— but whether it implies acceptance of one's right to entertain and advance *ideas* that defend (or reject) a particular interpretation or social order. When Moore says, as he does, that tolerance of conflicting interpretations befuddles the issue, does he mean to suggest that the natural consequences of a serious examination of alternative doctrines will always, or mostly, lead to the adoption of the wrong doctrine? This, I think, can only be affirmed by repudiating the value of reason itself, which Moore does not and of course will not do. But if reason itself is not at fault, the rational examination of alternatives cannot lead to befuddlement. What makes for confusion, instead, is the intrusion of unreason, of prejudices or interests or the operation of weighted conditions that militate against the free play of intellect. But then Moore's indictment should turn not on the principle of tolerance but (as with Wolff) on the social conditions in which tolerance is practiced—conditions that deny reason its day in court or that perpetuate the deficiencies of reasoners. All of which would seem to be confirmed by Moore himself when he says that "every idea, including the most dangerous and apparently absurd ones, deserves to have its credentials examined."

This, however, is not the message that Moore is most anxious to communicate. He is concerned rather to argue three things: (a) that the secular and rational (i.e., scientific) outlook, by which he means neither "technicist science" nor "academic humanism" but a conception of science that embraces "whatever is established by sound reasoning and evidence," is adequate both for understanding and evaluating human affairs; (b) that this outlook is able, in principle, to yield clear-cut answers to important questions, including the question of "when to be tolerant and when tolerance becomes intellectual cowardice and evasion"; and (c) finally, and most importantly, that in the present historical moment it may well behoove us to abandon the "nauseating hypocrisy" of "liberal rhetoric," to refuse to work under the prevailing system, and to consider "the conditions under which the resort to violence is justified in the name of freedom."

This is a hard teaching, but not for that reason to be avoided. We must first ask, however, whether it is also true. And here, it seems to me, the answer is by no means as simple as Moore takes it to be.

Consider Moore's claim—(a) and (b)—that objective knowledge and objective evaluation of human institutions are possible, thereby yielding correct and unambiguous answers, independent of individual whims and preferences. If Moore really admires Morris R. Cohen, whom he cites approvingly, he should have borne in mind Cohen's important distinction between the meaning of what is asserted in verified scientific theory and the degree of certainty of its verification. This certainty is always a matter of degree; it is never absolute; for what is verified is the theorems, not the postulates, of the theory. This is why Cohen, like Mill, believed that scientific *method* encourages toleration even as it enables us to differentiate beliefs and opinions which have been confirmed from those which have not.

Now Moore avows his commitment to scientific method. He recognizes that as a method it is a procedure for the testing of ideas, from which it follows that no conclusion, including the contents and very conception of science itself, is permanently above and beyond criticism and, possibly, fundamental change. How, then, can he confuse the principle of tolerance, which at one point he explicitly equates with this scientific procedure, with the acceptance of a particular doctrine or system of order, or assert the possibility not merely of objective knowledge but of objective evaluation, of correct answers to human problems? This is not to deny the relevance and utility of scientific method in the evaluation and solution of such problems; it is only to suggest that the most scientific evaluation, along with its alleged clear-cut answers, is still but tentative rather than absolute, relative to our assumptions and values, and always subject to revision.

Moore, however, confident of his "truths," seems prepared to reject the prevailing system and to adopt a revolutionary attitude. So long as three conditions are met—that the prevailing regime is unnecessarily repressive, that a revolutionary situation is in fact ripening, and that through a rough calculus of revolutionary violence one can reasonably believe that the costs in human suffering inherent in the continuation of the *status quo* outweigh those to be incurred in the revolution and its aftermath—the resort to violence, Moore holds, is justified in the name of freedom.

It is not easy for one who views the prevailing regime (or regimes) with considerable unhappiness, and who would consequently welcome certain fundamental changes in the social order, to cavil at Moore's revolutionary posture. Clearly, unless one is prepared to say that under no circumstances may men rebel, that men must remain always at the base of even the most burdensome pyramids of unjust power, there are moments in history when the resort to violence is fully warranted. That many contemporary nations, including the United States, celebrate their own past revolutions is only the more obvious of many instances in point. Thus, as an abstract statement of conditions that require and justify violence to overturn an indecent social order, Moore's argument merits respect. (Though it should not go unnoted that he here goes counter to his own earlier contention that the intellectual is not to be a partisan in the cause of this, or any other, ideal.)

Nevertheless, if we apply his (very far from precise) conditions to the modern industrial societies of the Western world, his argument becomes less than conclusive. For one thing, it is not at all clear that Western industrial societies are so oppressive that violent overthrow of the entire system is justified. For another, it is questionable that the cultural and human drabness to which Moore presumably objects is, in fact, amenable to correction through political action. For still another, the applicability of his second and third conditions is more than problematical. Nor do his conditions take into account certain useful and perhaps necessary distinctions: those, for example, between a class and a national revolution, or between a revolution initiated to seize power and a revolution, like the National Socialist Revolution, imposed after power has been effectively seized. Finally, his argument either neglects or gives insufficient weight to certain risks attendant upon all revolutionary efforts. Of these inconvenient but ever-present risks, I have space here to note only two.

One is the corrupting effects of the revolution itself, which often degrade and alter the characters and principles of the revolutionaries themselves, so that men who emerge at the top after a successful revolution are rarely the same men (even if they retain the same names and carry the same bodies) as those who made the revolution, with all that this implies in the way of altered ends, new hatreds and antagonisms, and new repressions. To be sure, some consequences of a successful revolution may be praiseworthy, e.g., the institution of certain reforms designed to eliminate or abate injustices and discontents. But other consequences are more than likely to be catastrophic. Of these the most immediately probable is the suppression of freedom of speech and political opposition. For it is not uncommon that governments which have survived revolutionary attempts, or which have come to power through revolution, seek with grim determination to eliminate the possibility of further revolutionary efforts. This, certainly, would seem to be one of the more evident lessons of revolutionary movements that have come to power since, say, the Second World War. Thus the appeal to revolution often invites the destruction of the very principle that makes the revolution possible—the principle of tolerance.

The second dangerous risk is the high improbability of success. Paul Kecs-kemeti has called attention to the striking fact that, despite all the revolutionary talk of the past century, if we except the Iberian peninsula, there have been no serious attempts at internal revolution in peacetime Europe since 1848–49; and if we consider the abortive Hungarian Revolution of 1956 (which took place after Kecskemeti wrote), the point is underscored that in the modern industrial state, with its specialized technology and advanced systems of weaponry, and with the support of powerful external armies and governments, civil revolt is in the ordinary course of events most unlikely to succeed. In fact, the normal complement of apathy, contentment, and especially fear—not of sporadic outbreaks but of wholesale violence and disorder—makes it more than unlikely that the masses will venture to disrupt the prevailing system of order by revolutionary means. It is, then, one thing to call for a revolutionary attitude, quite another to call for and expect revolutionary action. (I speak, let it be emphasized again, not of primitive or developing societies, but only of modern industrial societies; for it is only to such states that our authors apply their arguments.)

Once again, therefore, we are back to the central confusion inherent in this criticism: that which equates the principle of tolerance with the restrictive practices of states avowedly committed to that principle. The criticism actually testifies only to the limitations of those practices, and thus leaves untouched— at least at this level of argument—Mill's plea for freedom of thought and expression.

IV

We come now to the most extreme and convoluted, yet in some ways the most intriguing, of our three indictments of pure tolerance: Herbert Marcuse's essay "Repressive Tolerance." It may seem outrageous to suggest that this very title is a contradiction in terms, as are also other phrases employed by Marcuse, for example "totalitarian democracy" and "the democratic educational dicta-torship of free men"; but I shall make this suggestion nonetheless. I am aware that Marcuse, as a neo-Hegelian (also a neo-Marxist and neo-Freudian), prides himself on his dialectical thinking. But the dialectic—or, as Marcuse likes to say, the negation of the negation—aims to produce not a conjunction of two opposites but a synthesis which is different from either of them. And expres-sions like "repressive tolerance," "totalitarian democracy," and "democratic dictatorship," because they mismate rather than synthesize opposites, are self-contradictory and therefore meaningless. They should be banished from the literature. It is necessary to say this at the outset because Marcuse has dwelt harshly and at length on the inadequacies, even the Orwellian evils, of ordinary language, yet has also condemned philosophers who employ linguistic analysis in an effort to avoid the pitfalls of meaninglessness. Why, then, does he himself foster rather than transcend obscurity?

I will have occasion to return to this problem. Let me first, however, try to state the essentials of Marcuse's argument. Briefly, for it is a reiteration and extension of his argument in *One-Dimensional* Man, it comes to this: We—and by "we" Marcuse means the peoples of *all* modern industrial societies, whether "democratic" or otherwise—live today in a totalitarian system. It is totalitarian because, with the concentration of economic and political power and the use of technology as an instrument of domination, and under the rule of monopolistic media, "a mentality is created for which right and wrong, true and false are predefined wherever they affect the vital interests of the society." Rational persuasion is thus all but precluded. In such a situation tolerance "is administered to manipulated and indoctrinated individuals who parrot, as their own, the opinion of their masters." It is a tolerance abstractly "pure" but concretely "partisan," for "it actually protects the already established machinery of discrimination." It is thus repressive rather than true tolerance. For tolerance to be real, it must discriminate instead against falsehood and evil; it must cancel the liberal creed of free and equal discussion; it must preclude harmful ideas and harmful behavior. It must in fact encourage subversion of the existing order, even if this requires "apparently undemocratic means."

Marcuse articulates these "apparently undemocratic means" as follows:

They would include the withdrawal of toleration of speech and assembly from groups and movements which promote aggressive policies, armament, chauvinism, discrimination on the grounds of race and religion, or which oppose the extension of public services, social security, medical care, etc. Moreover, the restoration of freedom of thought may necessitate new and rigid restrictions on teachings and practices in the educational institutions which, by their very methods and concepts, serve to enclose the mind within the established universe of discourse and behavior—thereby precluding a priori a rational evaluation of the alternatives.

All this, Marcuse admits, is censorship, "even precensorship," but warranted because the distinction between liberating and repressive teachings and practices "is not a matter of value-preference but of rational criteria"; and these, Marcuse insists, are empirical in nature, turning on the real possibilities of attaining human freedom in a particular stage of civilization. To the question: Who is to draw these distinctions and make these decisions?—the answer (and here Marcuse mistakenly believes he is following Mill) is: Everyone in the maturity of his faculties as a human being, that is, "everyone who has learned to think rationally and autonomously." To be sure, such men will constitute a minority, but since all systems—even "democratic democracies"—are in fact controlled by a few, the only questions are whether they are the correct few and whether they act in the interests of the many, in short, whether they are qualified to exercise Marcuse's "democratic educational dictatorship of free men." Such free men are not to be identified with any social class; they are rather "fighting minorities and isolated groups . . . hopelessly dispersed throughout the society." To liberate these few, and through them the society as a whole, it is necessary "officially" to practice intolerance—both in speech and in action—against movements from the Right and to be tolerant only of movements from the Left. Through such "repressive tolerance" alone, Marcuse concludes, we can hope to realize the objective of "true tolerance."

Of the many things that might be said by way of analysis of or in reply to this argument, I shall limit myself here to three points: (1) Marcuse confuses the meaning of freedom with its conditions and consequences and hence misunderstands tolerance. (2) Marcuse's argument is essentially, though in reverse, the argument of Dostoevsky's Grand Inquisitor, of the Right. (3) Marcuse's solution is contradicted and rendered impossible of attainment by his own analysis.

1. Freedom is not, as Marcuse variously affirms it to be, "self-determination, autonomy" or "a specific historical process." It is rather, as Hobbes properly said, the absence of chains. Since in the real world men who are unrestrained come into collision with one another, societies have always and everywhere confronted—and each in its own way resolved—the problem of determining which liberties are worth protecting, for whom, under what conditions, and to what degree, and, as a necessary consequence, which restraints must be imposed. Freedom then becomes an ordered system of liberties and restraints. Men may differ as to the right order of priorities with respect to such liberties, but some order of priorities there must be. Thus, in democratic states a high value is given to freedom of political opposition; in dictatorships it is not. But to assure and protect this freedom, restraints must be imposed on those men (and practices) who would interfere with it. This is one, though not the only, function of law; but it is not, of course, merely a matter of law, for it involves a complex set of attitudes and appropriate behavior in other realms of social life as well.

Now Marcuse may deplore the particular freedoms granted in a specific society. He may properly object that a formal or legal freedom is in fact negated by informal or social pressures. But freedom as a principle is always a matter of specific liberties and concomitant restraints. It is not self-determination, though a measure of self-determination may be achieved through a particular combination of liberties and restraints. Nor is it a specific historical process, though the specific combination of liberties and restraints may be conditioned by and reflect the values of a particular historical period. Nor, again, is freedom limited to rational and autonomous men. While Mill clearly preferred a society made up of such men, he was realistic enough to recognize that this could not be a necessary condition of freedom. Thus, while he would not apply his principle of liberty to children and immature peoples, i.e., those not capable of improvement by free and equal discussion, he would and did apply it to all mature (not necessarily "autonomous") men, and not simply to Marcuse's elites. Nor, finally, is freedom vindicated only by "good" results, or rightfully "confined by truth." Freedom is in part a value in itself, in part an instrument of individual development, in part a necessary means of social change. That men and societies might make the "wrong" or "false" choices is clearly possible, but this too is an essential aspect of freedom. Otherwise a select group of allegedly wise men will make these choices for them, and this, by whatever name it may be called, is not freedom.

From all of which it follows that tolerance is not the freedom to express only the right ideas, but the freedom to express even stupid or loathsome ideas. The results may improve or depress the lot of men or societies, but the results are distinct from the principle of tolerance itself. And those who argue for tolerance, even absolute tolerance of ideas, do so because they believe that reason and experience are not calculated to lead men to the wrong decisions. Marcuse's rejection of pure tolerance is in these terms either a distrust of reason itself or a belief that the conditions under which reason operates today are such as to vitiate the process of reason, and probably both. But to the extent that it is the second, his attack is properly directed to those conditions and not to the principle of tolerance. Clearly, the "tolerance" he espouses is intolerance, and so it should be called, lest we abandon all semblance of meaning in our ordinary use of terms.

2. Those who believe not merely that there is an objective truth but that, by some mystery of incarnation, it has been given to them to know it, have rarely been willing to respect the claim to such knowledge by others. For such True Believers, allowing others to disseminate what is believed to be true, but what in fact is false, is to make possible the adoption of error. For error, seductively presented, may prevail over truth even in free and equal discussion. How much more likely is it to prevail when the conditions are not free and equal, when those who propound the error (because it gratifies their passions or promotes their conceived interests) also control the sources of information and media of communication, and where the objects of the debate are neither rational nor autonomous but "conditioned" men! In such circumstances to trust to an abstract but spurious toleration is to yield the cause. For truth to prevail, the "right" men must impose it—either by altering the conditions or directing otherwise irrational men, and generally both. In this way men will be governed by truth, and thus, even though forced, they will also be free.

This, it is clear, is the argument of Socrates in the *Republic*. It is the argument of Rousseau in the *Social Contract*. It is the argument of the Grand Inquisitor, both of the Roman Catholic Church and of Stalin's Russia. It is the traditional argument of the Right, of all who would usurp the gates of heaven and in the name of a higher morality insist, as with Gerhart Niemeyer, upon "a firm official stand for what is known as right, true, and good." And it is, in all essentials, the argument of Marcuse. But it is not the argument of John Stuart Mill.

For Mill, as for all democrats committed to the liberal idea of freedom, to believe in Man is not to dispel one's doubts about men. Men are fallible and cannot presume to know the whole truth. Room must therefore be left for the rectification of error and the discovery of additional knowledge. This requires tolerance, the free exploration and articulation of ideas. It may well be that there are deficiencies in the intellectual marketplace, but the remedy is not to mistake Marcuse's authority for truth; it is rather to correct those deficiencies. To substitute one allegedly right authority for another, to compel or manipulate men to do what Marcuse (or anyone else) is convinced it is proper for them to do is not to force them to be free. It is simply to subject them to Marcuse's (or another's) will. This, by any name, is coercion. It ill accords with the purposes of one who professes to respect humanity.

3. Finally, and briefly, Marcuse's argument collapses because the reality he portrays renders unattainable, and is in turn contradicted by, the proposals he recommends. If it is true that we live "in a democracy with totalitarian organization" and that this "coordinated society" rests on "firm foundations," how is it humanly possible to change it? Surely not by election, for the "conditioned" masses will simply acquiesce in the opinions of their masters. Surely not by education, for the rulers control both the educators and their media of communication. Surely not by revolution, for who will revolt but "hopelessly dispersed" minorities? It may well be, as Marcuse thinks, that in such a situation the alienated man is the "essential" rather than the sick man, and that rebellious men merit applause rather than condemnation. But such men, however viewed, cannot overturn a firmly established order. Then to whom, and for what purpose, does Marcuse speak? Is his message really more than a tocsin of futility, a summons to surrender?

If, on the other hand, we are to take seriously his plea for fundamental social and political change, for the establishment of "real" tolerance (or, as he says, "official" intolerance), it can only mean that the society is less than totalitarian, that its foundations are not altogether firm, that there are chinks in the monopolistic concentration of power.

Marcuse cannot have it both ways: either his analysis is correct and his recommendations are unrealizable, or his recommendations are meaningful and appropriate, in which case his analysis cannot stand.

V

It would be less than just to conclude these remarks without noting the deep anguish and high moral commitment that animate all three of our critics. They are disturbed, and properly so, by the injustices that disfigure modern societies. They are distressed by the realization that these injustices are maintained by an indifferent, because unseeing, or acquiescent public opinion. Consequently they probe to the roots in an effort to uncover the sources and the interests that mold that opinion. And they have found, as every sensitive observer of human societies has always found, that within our cities there are still two cities—the city of the rich and the city of the poor, with all that this implies in inequalities of power, of access to privileges, and of opportunities. One need not accept everything that A. J. Liebling has written in *The Press*, or that C. Wright Mills has written in *The Power Elite*, to recognize that freedom of speech, for example, has a different meaning for those wealthy enough to buy a newspaper or to purchase time on radio or television, than it has for the masses of individuals who may wish to express their thoughts but have no effective access to the various media of communication. Nor does it require undue imagination to note that men cannot choose what they do not know exists, or will not choose what they have been taught to believe is evil. For these and other reasons, it is less than convincing to argue that the principle of equality accurately characterizes the world of public opinion, or that the free play of ideas does in fact afford people a full range of alternatives.

In underscoring these objectionable features of contemporary life and in urging their correction, our three critics manifest a concern for Man rather than for rich or powerful or prestigious men. Further, in their readiness to foster even revolutionary social and political change in an effort to elevate Man from what he presently is to what he ought to be, to what he *can* be, they identify themselves with an abiding radical tradition. They are legitimately of the Left.

But a wise radicalism seeks to overturn not all things, only unjust and harmful things; and not everything that men have thought and done in the course of human history demands repudiation. There have been achievements, too, and of these not the least noble has been the slow and painful liberation of the human mind. Whatever the merits or demerits of liberalism as a political and economic doctrine, in the realm of the intellect it should command our supreme allegiance: for it has freed reason from the chains of dogma and superstition; it has broken the back of orthodoxy; it has given us a method by which we may continue to correct our errors and improve our understanding. And whatever the merits or demerits of a particular social system in observing, or failing to observe, the principle of liberalism in the intellectual sphere, it is necessary—and I believe that even under circumstances that most humanly approximate the ideal, it will remain necessary—always to distinguish the fact of public opinion, what may be called the will of the people, from the motives and influences that elicit it. Democracies rest on the volume, not on the quality, of that will; and though no one would contend that it is better to have a stupid

or misguided will, what distinguishes democratic from nondemocratic governments is that the former rest upon that will even though oligarchic or pluto-
cratic influences may have been powerful in creating it, while the latter reject
that will, or at most seek to mold it in support of their policies; it is not, as in
democratic states, an initiating and controlling will. To render that will a purer
or wiser will is surely a proper concern of democratic (whether liberal or
radical) theorists, but this means that they must look not to the removal of that
will, or of the process that alone gives it the opportunity to be formed after a
consideration of alternatives, but to the correction of those conditions that
limit or block the introduction of new and conflicting ideas. In any case, the fact
of will and not its purity or disinterestedness remains the foundation of the
democratic state.

Those who, therefore, in the name of a social revolution, would destroy not
merely the conditions that still constrain reason but the principle of tolerance
that alone gives reason its chance to prevail, defy the grim lessons of history.
What, then, can one say of those who, like Marcuse, seek to reverse history by
substituting for even the imperfect democracies of our day an intellectual and
political authoritarianism that would allegedly act *for* the people, on the
ground that a government that really acts in the interests of the people is better
(and more democratic) than a government *by* the people that may, through
ignorance or irrationality, act contrary to those best interests? Such men are
neither radical nor liberal but, let us use the cruel word, reactionary. This is
why, despite all the legitimate criticisms that might be (and in the course of the
past century have been) made of Mill's philosophy, or of his political and
economic teachings, or even of the subsidiary doctrines and incidental observations in his essay *On Liberty*, the central argument of that essay remains
fundamentally unimpaired.

Not Mill's theory of pure tolerance but the repressive intolerance of our
critics is, then, to be condemned.

5

The Pleasures of Misunderstanding Freedom

Definitions, whether of liberty or of other political terms, are neither true nor false. They are useful or mischievous, and in any case they change over time. They are useful, ordinarily, when they enable people to communicate, i.e., to understand each other, or when they open concepts to further (and mutual) exploration. They are sometimes useful, at least to some men, when by failing to communicate, they enable a man or a group of men to achieve ends that otherwise might not be attained.

Definitions change because new circumstances often require new terms and instead of inventing such terms, men attribute new meanings to old words. They change also because new or derived languages, like English (or the American), borrow multiple terms that describe the same phenomenon, e.g., freedom from *Freiheit* and liberty from *liberté*. Hence, where the Germans and the French have but a single term the Americans have two or more, and this may lead to confusion, especially where some men use the two terms interchangeably while others give a special meaning to each of them, as in the distinction between "liberty to" and "freedom from."

I mention these elementary considerations only because they are often overlooked or disregarded in contemporary discussions of liberty, and this failing—from which Michael Walzer is not, I fear, altogether exempt—leads both to serious misunderstandings and untoward consequences.

II

Consider first the striking difference between what may be called, broadly, the classical and modern definitions (or contexts) of freedom. To the Greeks, liberty meant not the freedom of the individual from encroachments by the state, but rather the freedom of a whole people, of the *polis*, from the rule of a tyrant or foreign oppressor. They conceived of the people—by which of course

Reprinted, by permission, from *Dissent* 13 (1966): 729–39.

they meant only that small portion of the people who qualified as citizens—as a homogeneous unit, as a body of men who shared the same values and pursued a common way of life, and who therefore sought their fulfillment as men not in their private and diverse activities but in the life of the *polis* itself. To be a man, as Aristotle said, was preeminently to be a social or political animal. Hence the classical conception of liberty did not recognize, much less focus on, the right of an individual or group to do as he or it might choose; it built instead on the right of the people as a whole to follow its own ways. This is why Greek thinkers could identify the community with the state—the social and the cultural with the political—and liberty with a particular way of life. This is why Socrates could properly be charged with a crime for teaching disrespect for the gods, corrupting the youth, and why in turn Socrates in the *Republic* could urge that all those who did not conform to the established ways and teach the "right" things should be sent into exile.

With Hobbes and Locke and their successors we move to a quite different conception of liberty. Now the problem of liberty is focused inward, on the relationship between the individual and his government, whether that government be an "alien" power (as in Hobbes's *Leviathan*) or the people's own creature. With the authors of *The Federalist* we move a step further, for now it is seen that "the people" constitute not a homogeneous and monolithic force but a heterogeneous and divided society, and that a majority within that society may well utilize the powers of government to tyrannize over the minority (or minorities). But it remained for Tocqueville and John Stuart Mill to point out that the problem of liberty has still deeper and greater dimensions, that it goes beyond the mere relationship between the individual (or group) and the government to embrace all other relations which may affect the freedom of the individual. In particular, they called attention to the deprivations of liberty imposed by non-governmental powers—by majorities in the realm of custom and opinion, and by social and economic power blocs. The problem of freedom, then, is only at the outset a question of the liberty of a nation to live its life without interference from external powers. It is, not less importantly—but perhaps more importantly—also the problem of controlling internal powers, both governmental and non-governmental; of organizing the society so as to enable diverse individuals and groups with different and often conflicting creeds to live together without constant recourse to force and the authoritarian imposition of one group's creed upon others.

It was this problem that Mill—quite properly, I believe—conceived to be the crucial problem for the society of his day. And it remains, all too unhappily, the problem that bedevils us today. This is why Mill is still the seminal figure, and provides the indispensable key, to the understanding of the problem of liberty in our time.

Now Michael Walzer would have us look not to Mill but to Rousseau for this key. But how does Rousseau resolve this problem? The answer is simplicity itself: *by eliminating the diversities, and with them the freedoms that have created and if unimpeded would continue to create those diversities.* For Rousseau, it is impossible to live at peace with those we believe to be damned, i.e., those who hold different creeds from our own. Hence (he tells us) there must be a single religion, a civil religion, whose articles should be fixed by the sovereign, and disobedience to which should be punished by banishment or death. To be sure, tolerance is to be given to all religions that tolerate others, but only so long as their dogmas contain nothing contrary to the duties of citizenship. And those duties require, above everything else, compliance with the laws.

Now, when Rousseau talks of the sovereign he means not the will of all but the *general will*, which is the will for the general good. This will can be known, and in practice is generally to be determined, by the will of the majority. But it is possible, Rousseau admits, that the general will may on occasion be known better by a single individual than by the rest of the community. In any case, the general will—however determined—remains sovereign, inalienable, and above all infallible. From all of which it follows, according to Rousseau, that the citizen in obeying the laws is doing precisely what he ought to do, what he himself "really" wants to do, for he is then doing what is "right." And if the citizen is too blind to see or too weak to do what is "right," if he is so foolish or wicked to wish to disobey the laws, or a particular law, he is clearly wrong; for he then erroneously supposes that he knows better than the sovereign—whose will, let it be remembered, is an infallible will—what is good and just, not merely for the society but also for him. For what is the citizen apart from society? Opposition to the laws, then, is never warranted, for the laws call upon the citizen to do only what he would himself choose to do if he were more enlightened than he is.

Under such circumstances, to permit him to act contrary to the laws is to permit him to act against his own true interests, and this (in Rousseau's view) is an absurdity. This is why, Rousseau emphasizes, he must be compelled to obey, and why such compulsion is not "really" coercion but rather freedom; for it only forces him to be free, that is, to be himself, to realize his own true interests. But this is also why, despite all his democratic preachments about equality and the common good, Rousseau is properly viewed—at least with respect to this portion of his teaching, accompanied as it is with a defense of censorship—as the godfather of modern totalitarianism.

We can now see why Marcuse finds Rousseau rather than Mill companionable. But why Walzer who professes a commitment to *democratic* socialism should also look to Rousseau passes my comprehension. Walzer says: ". . . a free man shares in the making of the laws which he subsequently obeys or evades." But no such evasion is countenanced by Rousseau. And what Walzer mistakes is precisely what Mill perceived: that men who share in the making of the laws do not necessarily get the laws they want, that government even by the people is not miraculously transformed into a government of each by himself but remains in all essentials a government by some over others. Thus, to share in the process of law-making is only to share—and in practice always unequally, for all democratic states are disfigured by inequities in their systems of representation and political structure—in the choice of a government; but a government so chosen may reflect not the will of all, not even the general will, but the will of a majority that may be selfish, iniquitous, perhaps tyrannical, and certainly sometimes wrong. To plead, then, as Walzer does, for the communal autonomy that he associates with Athenian citizenship and with the doctrine of Rousseau is to argue for a freedom indistinguishable from conformity; it militates against the very self-determination that Walzer also values.

These reflections are not put forward to speak against the idea of community, or the obvious fact that self-determination, however, construed, can take place only with and through participation in a communal life. Man and society are always, to use the commonplace phrase, inextricably intertwined. But to recognize that an individual man is an issue of his society in much the same way that a child is an issue of his parents is not necessarily to conclude that the interests of the man are identical in all respects to the interests of his society, any more than the interests of the child may be said to be always identical to those of his parents. Men have separate and dividing as well as common interests, and a wise political philosophy will seek not only to assure the bonds of community but to provide for the cultivation of differences as well. I know of nothing in Mill, or in socialist writers generally, that militates against this awareness. Indeed, if we are to take seriously the humanistic stress that Marx gave to individuality in his *Economic and Philosophic Manuscripts* and other writings, it becomes a matter of more than ordinary importance that socialists should look first to the defense and promotion of what little individuality still resists the conformist pressures of our time.

III

Walzer, like many others, supposes that the problem of freedom is by and large the problem of positive versus negative liberty. But while these are convenient polar extremes—and like Walzer I shall treat them, at least initially, as such—it is important to remember that they do not displace the many variations that occupy the vast middle ground; nor do they account for a wide range of meanings outside the spectrum embraced by the positive-negative dichotomy. Of these and other meanings, one is so widely held and frequently repeated—even by Walzer himself—that it is necessary to touch upon it here, if only briefly.

This is the notion that freedom is something that one either has or has not. It is a totality, so that one is either a free man (or a member of a free society), or a slave. So we and generations of schoolchildren were taught when we were told of Patrick Henry's celebrated plea: "Give me liberty or give me death." And so President Eisenhower reaffirmed, discussing the conflict between America and the Soviet Union, when he said (in his first Inaugural Address): "Freedom is pitted against slavery; light against dark."

But whatever the emotive pleasures produced by these words, they are literally absurd. The choice before Patrick Henry was never that of liberty or death. Henry was not a slave. He had "liberty"—certainly the liberty to enter a church of his own choosing, to utter words of defiance to his parliament and king, to do the many things that slaves and men in prison were not free to do, even to use the Negro slaves who waited outside the Virginia church to serve as stepping-blocks for their freedom-demanding white masters to mount their horses. What disturbed Patrick Henry was the denial of a particular liberty, the liberty to choose representatives to his governing body. This may well have been a vital liberty, but it was not the whole of liberty. Other liberties still remained.

So too with President Eisenhower's dictum. Surely it cannot be maintained that ours is a system of total freedom, a political and social order devoid of restraints—without laws and police and prisons. Nor can it be said that the Soviet system is simply one of slavery, without even such elemental liberties as the freedom to choose one's spouse, or one's food and drink, or one's clothes. Even in the most tyrannical government there are some who support it and who consequently think themselves free, and others who are in some respects free. What the President undoubtedly meant but did not say was that the freedoms secured in the American democracy are in his judgment more significant than the freedoms provided by the Soviet dictatorship. Had he said this, he would have been literally correct but rhetorically less impressive. For the choice before us would have been less stark, and to the people (and perhaps himself) less clear.

Hence, even though many of the decisive cultural and political liberties are present in the American system, but not in the Soviet system, it remains true that in both systems there are some freedoms, and in both systems those freedoms are secured by the imposition of restraints on those persons or groups who might otherwise interfere with them. The real issue, accordingly, does not emerge from a simple (and false) dichotomy between freedom and unfreedom—whatever the latter might be—but from alternative and always complex systems of freedoms and restraints. And the problem of freedom, otherwise conveniently obscured, is the difficult determination of a standard or value that will enable us to distinguish the more from the less important freedoms. It is also the problem of determining *who* shall enjoy the vital freedoms, under what conditions or circumstances, and to what degree. Not all freedoms can be simultaneously secured, and not all men can enjoy the freedoms provided. The delineation of *which freedoms for whom* remains the fundamental task of any intelligible theory of liberty.

We can now see more clearly the essential misunderstanding, and consequent fallacy, in Walzer's appeal to Athenian as distinct from Persian freedom, or to the freedom of democratic as distinct from authoritarian polities. By the standard of communal autonomy, all these systems are free, for all govern themselves free from external control. By the standard of self-determination, none is completely free (or unfree), for in all of these systems men enjoy some liberties and suffer some restraints—restraints which are in some measure not of their own making or desire.

Moreover, to recognize, as Walzer does, that there is a necessary conflict between citizenship and individuality, is to admit the one point that sufficiently destroys his argument. For it is to admit, with Aristotle—and, may I dare add, with Mill—that the problem of freedom is always to distinguish, in one way or another, the realm that is Caesar's from that which is man's; for it is not always the same thing to be both a good citizen and a good man. What Mill tried to formulate as a matter of principle is what every democratic state tries to achieve as a matter of practice—namely, to distinguish those areas or activities in which men are properly to be left alone from those in which they are properly subject to coercion, to distinguish the community (and its cultural life) from the state (and its coercive order). And however difficult the drawing of such a line may be, the refusal to attempt it, the denial that it needs to be drawn, is precisely what characterizes a totalitarian, as distinct from a democratic, state. This is indeed why I shudder at Walzer's equation of freedom with citizenship rather than with man.

IV

We come now to the question of positive versus negative freedom. In a sense, this is a false or misleading question, for liberty is neither the one nor the other but simply the state of being free; and being free means that a man is left alone to do what he wants to do. But men like to play with words, and the word "wants" was quickly redefined to become the term "really wants." For (in this ploy), what a man thinks he wants, and even says he wants, is not necessarily what he "really wants." This can only be determined, it is said, by one able to distinguish between the apparent and the real, or between that which is

immediately or momentarily desired (a particular apple) and that more ultimate end for the sake of which he desires it (e.g., good health); for what is
thought to be a man's interest (eating the particular apple) may actually be
harmful (if the apple is unripe or poisoned) and contrary to his real or true
interest. Mere or negative freedom, then, is in this view not only an empty
freedom but a dangerous freedom. Santayana likes to use the term "vacant
freedom"; other philosophers have indulged in more derogatory language.
Indeed, it is not freedom at all, for while freedom implies the right to choose,
rational men choose (or mean to choose) only what is good; and if what they
"think" is good is not "really" good, why then they will not choose it. From all
this it follows that knowledge—of what is good and right and just—is indispensable to "true" liberty; that without this knowledge men cannot make the
"right" choices and be "truly" free.

Such knowledge, however, is not given to all men. This would seem to
suggest that not all men can be free, and such would indeed be the case were it
not for a saving factor—those who have such knowledge can and do make it
available to others. And those others, by acting in accord with that knowledge,
can also be free.

The crucial question then is: how and by whom is that right knowledge to be
revealed? The answers are multiple, but I shall consider only two here. First
and most immediately, that knowledge (it is said) is incorporated in the laws.
The state (Hegel) or the sovereign (Rousseau) being rational and right, the
laws proclaimed by the state are also right. Hence freedom consists in obedience to the laws; at the very least, it is, as Montesquieu said, "a right of doing
whatever the laws permit."

Now clearly, if men are to avoid legal punishments, if they are to stay out of
prison, it will behoove them to obey the law. In this limited sense, freedom
does indeed entail obedience to the law. But it is surely evident that to secure
this freedom, it is necessary first to surrender the liberty of doing whatever the
laws do not permit; it is necessary first to submit to the restraints of the law.
Thus men are free to do only some things, not all things; they are not completely free. Rousseau and Hegel and their disciples, however, deny this
conclusion. They affirm, to the contrary, that even submission to the law is
freedom. The law, they say, does not "really" impose a restraint; rather,
because it expresses one's "real" rather than actual will, it truly enables a man
to realize himself, to attain what he "really" wants. This is what Rousseau
means when he advances the paradox that men shall be forced to be free.

But this is to remove all semblance of meaning from our ordinary language.
For in this conception, whether a state restrains men, or restrains a restraint on
men, they are in every case free. What then does the word restraint mean? And
how can any law, since it embodies our "real" will—if we but knew this as our

rulers know it—be anything but an act of freedom? To speak properly, we should rather have to say that the law that imposes a restraint is a just law, that the restraint is warranted, but it is still a restraint. Moreover, is it always the case that the law embodies the real will or real purpose of the individual who is compelled to obey? The state or sovereign, despite Hegel and Rousseau, can err. The individual, not the state, may be right. In that case, the law by forbidding a man to do what he wants to do, or by compelling him to do what he does not want to do, is invading his freedom. And surely, if we survey the laws enacted by various states, even democratic states, we cannot but conclude that many of those laws are harmful and unjust. They may satisfy the interests of some men, but not of all men. Hence obedience to the laws may assure freedom for some men but not for others.

This brings us to the second major group that believes in obedience as freedom. They agree that such freedom is not to be found in mere obedience to the law, for the law may be wrong, and in any case there is a morality above the law. They argue instead that men must obey what is "right," that freedom consists in obedience to the truth, to the good, to the right morality, to the will of God. Since no man seeks to do evil, but every man seeks to do what is good, freedom (in their view) is not the right to choose wrongly, to do whatever one might please; it rather is, as Fulton Sheen said, "the right to do what you *ought*," to go back to a "Truth which is inseparable from the purpose of man; namely union with his final end, who is God. As man corresponds in his thinking and in his actions with that purpose, he is free because he is true." And so John Winthrop instructed the Puritans of Massachusetts Bay. Explaining that true liberty is always maintained and exercised through subjection to authority, Winthrop employed the analogy of a woman choosing her husband, "yet being so chosen, he is her lord, and she is to be subject to him, yet in a way of liberty, not of bondage; and a true wife accounts her subjection her honor and freedom, and would not think her condition safe and free, but in her subjection to her husband's authority."

Now there is doubtless a sense in which this argument may be made to appear a plausible one; for if one freely chooses to enter a contract he cannot be said to have lost his freedom by being bound to its terms. Consequently a wife, or a citizen, can be free though bound. But the restrictions imposed by that contract do not cease to be restrictions, and even though they may provide safety and honor they do not in themselves provide freedom. One who freely chooses to be a wife, or a student, or a soldier, or a citizen, does not thereby continue to be wholly free. Even if such a person *felt* free, it does not follow that he *is* free; for there is a vast difference between *feeling* free and *being* free. To act, therefore, according to the truth, or to the good, or to the right morality, or to the will of God, may afford great comfort and pleasure, but only if the person committing the required action does so as a result of a choice freely made can he be said also to be free.

Moreover, to argue that some one other than himself—be that Some One a person or a church or a state—knows better than he does what is "right," is to argue a great deal. It is of course sometimes true, for not every man's opinion is always as good as every other man's. But it is surely the magic of government—political or otherwise—that men rule who are often less knowing, less wise, less just, than some of those who are ruled. And even where the ruled are wrong, is it not the meaning of freedom that men have a right to make mistakes, that self-realization consists not in doing what another requires you to do but in doing what you, fallible and imperfect though you may be, want to do? If freedom implies choice—and this Walzer concedes—it entails the right to choose rightly or wrongly, and not merely to choose what another affirms to be right.

The quest for self-realization, then, if it is also the quest for freedom, must be sought outside the realm of positive liberty; for this is no more than a semantic device to obscure a brutal and demeaning reality—that so to realize oneself one must in fact abandon that self and must submit to another person's will.

V

The virtue of negative freedom is that it recognizes, with Kant, the obvious truth that "out of the crooked timber of humanity no straight thing was ever made." Whatever the respects in which men are equal, whatever their common interests or common stakes, they remain in some measure different men; each is an *individual*, a unique person. Consequently each has a somewhat different road to follow, a different "nature" to fulfill, a different "self" to realize. Society enacts rules, in the form of laws and social sanctions, that are universal in character. They apply to all men in the same way. But the individual, if he is to realize himself as a unique person, needs room for his own development, his own differentiation. Hence the problem of freedom, for him, reduces itself to the broad question: How much will he be left alone?

This does not make him an enemy of others; only a primitive mind can say: who is not like me is against me. Nor does it remove him from the fellowship or society of others; to be different in some things is not to be different in all things. The issue is never, as Walzer puts it, "man-by-himself" versus "man-with-the-others." Rather is it the question how man can be himself at the same time that he is a man among others: how he can be both an individual and a social animal.

It is unfortunately true that some men have falsified the question of negative freedom. Believing, for example that law is a restraint and that all restraints are

chains, they have leaped, with Hobbes, from the correct understanding of
liberty as the absence of chains to the incorrect conclusion that liberty is
consequently to be found only in the silence or interstices of the law. ". . . the
laws being removed," wrote Hobbes, "our liberty is absolute. . . . For law is a
fetter, right is freedom, and they differ like contraries." Or they have
erroneously supposed, with Bentham, that "every law is an evil for every law is
an infraction of liberty." That men are free only when they are unrestrained is
true, and to the degree that Hobbes and Bentham grasped this truth they were
eminently correct. But it does not follow that all laws are merely restraints.
Some laws restrain restraints—or, as T. H. Green liked to say, hinder hindrances—and thereby free men from the restrictions to which they would
otherwise be subjected. This function of law—to block or prevent interferences
with freedom—derives from the necessary fact that men who are unrestrained
inevitably collide with one another; some resolution, some adjustment, must
consequently be made. That Hobbes and Bentham, for all their learning and
insight, failed adequately to perceive that law then becomes not merely a
restraint but a restraint on a restraint—for how else is the weaker to be
protected from the stronger?—is not a reason for our failing fully to apprehend
it. And if to this we add the recognition that freedom is not a totality but a
complex of many particular freedoms, the enjoyment of which may (and
generally does) require the imposition of corresponding restraints, then we can
appreciate the true problem and multiple dimensions of freedom—which is the
ordering and selection from among the many (and some equally ultimate)
liberties those that are most highly prized, and the imposition of concomitant
restraints that will prevent others from impairing these prized liberties.

So to arrange and protect liberties is to assure men certain areas in which
they will be left alone—perhaps only in some measure or for a limited time,
perhaps only under certain conditions. But however qualified those areas of
liberty may be, it is within and only within those areas that men find their
freedom. For to be free is still no more than to be left alone, and what a man
does when he is left alone is for him alone to decide. Perhaps he wants only to
breathe the clean air, to step outside the prison walls. That is enough for
liberty, for that at the moment is enough for him. And no one who has yearned
for that fresh air of freedom can doubt that such negative freedom, while not
assuredly *the* end of life, is one of the essential and really meaningful ends of
life. At the very least, it is the prerequisite to a human existence.

To say that negative freedom so construed is the prerequisite to a human
existence is to say only that without such freedom man is less than human; he is
not a man. But this is to say a good deal. For what is a man if, as Aristotle
insisted, he is not distinguished from the other animals by his reason, or by his
potential for intellectual growth? And how can he be that man if he is not

permitted to exercise his reason? To exercise one's reason means that he must be free to choose; and to choose freely means that he may choose rightly or wrongly. To have another make that choice for him, on the ground that that other knows better what the right choice should be than the person restrained, is to deny him his identity as a rational creature, as a man. It is to refuse him the right to self-realization. It is rather to make him realize another's conception of his self. And this is to keep him forever as a child, as a less than complete human being.

This is why, when all is said and done, one who believes in the autonomy of the individual, who pleads for the principle of self-realization, must opt for negative as distinct from positive freedom.

VI

But liberty, I have said, is properly to be understood neither as negative nor as positive freedom. It is simply the state of being free. And being free means that one has areas of choice within an ordered system of particular liberties and concomitant restraints.

Hence there is no such thing as a completely free and autonomous man. From the moment he is born into the world the individual is subjected to prohibitions and commands, to rules laid down first by his parents and then by his friends, his church, his school, his state, and his several voluntary (and perhaps involuntary) associations. To seek his self-realization in the face of these external pressures is to seek it, and perhaps to find it, only as a member of society. He remains always a social animal even as he pursues and affirms his individuality.

It serves no useful purpose to close one's eyes to this reality. If democratic socialism is to make its way, it must do so not by rejecting this reality but by accepting it. The task then is to determine which elements in that complex reality hinder or obstruct one's quest for individuality—what shortcomings exist in educational and economic opportunities, what deficiencies characterize the social and political structure, and what changes, radical or otherwise, are consequently required if individuality is to be secured meaningfully. That the value of individuality does not, and indeed cannot, displace the value of community, goes almost without saying. For no man can find himself apart from his membership in society. He is still a social animal. As such, he remains concerned to satisfy both his common and his particular interests. If socialism is, as I believe, a moral and not merely an economic principle, then no socialist theory worthy of the name can neglect either of these elements of man's nature. That Mill, among others, perceived this truth and endeavored to build upon it, is surely of greater moment than the work of those who foolishly seek to resolve the problem by wiping out half of it.

Not only is Marcuse's antidote, then, no antidote at all. Not only is his cure worse than our disease. He is a bad doctor, because he neither knows what it means to be healthy nor how to approach the problem so as to make the patient well.

VII

I would add but one last comment. It is that, throughout the history of freedom, men have sought to identify the meaning of the word freedom with the things they hold to be good. It is easy to understand why this should be so. The word freedom has an honorific glow. The things men hold to be good have not always seemed to be good to others. To make those things *appear* to be good, whether or not they really are good, was the almost natural consequence. Since the ultimate object sought or thus secured was deemed to be good, the deception was judged useful and proper and the gain pleasurable. In time the pleasures of misunderstanding freedom proved so rewarding that men ceased to think of it as a misunderstanding and identified that misunderstanding with the very meaning of the word. Thus it is that the term freedom today carries a variety of meanings, some visibly at odds with the ordinary understanding of the term.

But if men are to communicate with each other, if men are to be honest with each other, it is surely time to use the word properly. The pleasures of misunderstanding freedom are trivial when compared to the pleasures of pursuing truth.

6 A Grammar of Equality

Equality, wrote Alexandre Dumas the younger, brought kings to the guillotine and the people to the throne.

Like most felicitous phrases, this is no more than a partial truth. New tyrants rather than "the people" often ascended to the momentarily vacated throne; and not simply equality but the stupidity and malevolence of kings,[1] the ambitions of lesser but avaricious mortals, and the effects of changing economic and social systems brought tyrannical rulers to their deserved end. Yet who can deny that the passion for equality played a stirring and vital role?

Whether it *should* have played that role is the contested and more intriguing question; for the case against equality, though it runs counter to the spirit of the democratic age, remains a formidable one. Consider the following:

● Equality requires us to count heads as if each were made out of wood, when in fact some are made of precious metals and others of lesser or even base materials. Still others seem to be no more than empty carcasses held together by tissue and bone. If intelligence and virtue adhere to the normal distribution curve—if, that is to say, in a random group of ten one or two are "brighter" or "better" than the others—it follows that there are few wise and many unwise, or at least less wise. Since in democratic states the quantity rather than quality of minds is politically decisive, it follows too that the less wise will govern the wise. What saves communities from this appalling consequence—if indeed they are saved—is that the wise, precisely because they possess superior intelligence and wisdom, are able to outwit the unwise and persuade them to do the bidding of their betters. But why impose so time-consuming and needless a distraction on the wise? And what if passion so overwhelms the crowd as to render it incorrigible?

● Equality calls upon men and women to do what is psychologically impossible—to love their own children no more than they love the children of a neighbor, to do for their own parents no more than they would for the parents

Reprinted, by permission, from *Dissent* 21 (1974): 63–78.

of others, to treat friends no differently than strangers. Ordinary experience attests to the stubborn truth that men and women give preferential treatment to those with whom they have had the closest personal ties; it is "unnatural" for them to do otherwise.

As with persons, so with ideas. No man or community will accept the notion that all doctrines are equal, that some doctrines are not to be more favored than others, and that we should "love" or at least tolerate even the most loathsome ideas, e.g., the advocacy of cannibalism or human sacrifice. Is it not, indeed, the very meaning of community that it binds persons together precisely because they share certain values and exclude others?

• Equality is incompatible with the necessary arrangements for organizational efficiency, which demand that some sit at the top of the pyramids of power, others at the bottom, and still others at various levels between. Hierarchy is not merely a concomitant of modern technology; it is a principle indispensable to almost every realm of social life, e.g., an army, a university, a hospital, a political system. In our complex world, administration, whether of men or of things, requires organization (or, as Engels put it in 1874, in an essay attempting to discredit the anarchists, "the principle of authority"); which entails ranking; which means inequality (even if not, as Michels argued, oligarchy). It was not without reason that Shakespeare had the Prince of Ithaca say:

> Take but degree away, untune that string,
> And, hark, what discord follows!

• Equality drives us into an insoluble moral dilemma, and therefore into practices that contradict what we preach. In a world of unequal talents (or diligence, or commitment), equality of opportunity is but a device, though more meritorious than some others, for achieving inequality of results—in power, position, prestige, wealth. To impose equality of results—which is possible in some things, e.g., wealth or income, but not in all things, e.g., status and power, is to limit equality of opportunity. We cannot have both equalities simultaneously, and to opt for equality of opportunity, as in democratic states we purportedly do, is to indulge in open hypocrisy; for we clearly do not intend to follow Socrates' inescapable prescription that children be removed from their parents immediately after birth so that all may be raised alike (by identical nurses and tutors?) and given equal (identical?) chances.

• Equality thus entails a commitment to impossible, certainly wrong values. If we were true egalitarians, we would have to remove the distinctions among people by imposing equality of condition, or at least recognition. Yet we do not really intend to denigrate wisdom, virtue and beauty, achievement and success, by withholding appropriate recognition and applause. We do not really mean to admire stupid or wicked persons, or to esteem failure. At best, we speak of a limited equality, e.g., equality of reward in proportion to one's work or (in some ideal versions) need. We do not seek to treat everyone as if they were the same; for as Hobbes said: If all things are equal in all men, nothing would be prized. Hence we recognize that in certain important respects people are remarkably unlike each other, except perhaps (but only perhaps) at moments of birth and death.

● Moreover, by making equality the ultimate end, when it can never be more than but one among many ends, we make it impossible to come seriously to terms with the problem of conflicting ends, of the need at times to subordinate equality to another value, such as liberty or merit, which in a specific context may impose a higher claim on our loyalty. Thus, it is at least doubtful that Western educators will accept the justification of cheating on an examination recently put forward by a group of students in China: that since knowledge is to be shared, it matters not how this is done.

● To these objections we must add a crucial fact: wherever equality has been proclaimed as an operating principle, it has been subverted by the very people who avowedly espoused it. Thus, despite the American commitment to equality before the law, the rich continue to enjoy marked advantages over the poor, the whites over the blacks. Despite the Christian commitment to the brotherhood of man, most Christians leave fraternal and egalitarian practices to heaven and pursue other practices on earth. Such subversion is deliberate, not accidental. People want it that way. They admire superiority in others; they seek it for themselves; they dream of it for their children. The bitch goddess is sometimes money, but always success; and success means getting ahead of the other, who remains of course—in rhetoric—his brother, his equal.

For these and other reasons, equality (it is still argued) cannot command our exclusive or highest allegiance; perhaps it ought not commend itself at all.

II

On what grounds, then, can the principle of equality be reasonably warranted?

I would argue that there are at least four such grounds:

1. Equality is not what its detractors generally take it to be.
2. Equality has an important *negative* function as a protest-ideal as well as a positive content that properly enlists the loyalty of men.
3. It is a mistake to identify the problems of equality with fatal deficiencies of the principle.
4. When all is said and done, equality remains an essential ingredient of justice.

Let us consider these in turn.

If equality is not what its detractors take it to be, their criticisms are misdirected; they are launched against an erroneous conception or conceptions of equality. For example:

• Equality does not mean sameness or identity. In Plato's *Republic*, Socrates indicts democracy for "dispensing a sort of equality to equals and unequals alike," fathers descending to the level of their sons, and sons standing on a level with their fathers. But this is a caricature as well as a confusion. Fathers and sons do not stand on the same level, not at least while they relate to each other as fathers and sons, though they might well stand on the same level as citizens in a polling booth or in a court of law. For they are not merely fathers and sons; they are also persons, with rights and interests outside the parent-child relationship. They both need food, but if one is a mountain-climber and the other a scientist they do not require the same kinds or amounts of food. They both think, but not necessarily in the same way; nor do they necessarily share the same opinions. They may resemble each other physically, yet they are different. To say that men are equal is not to say they are identical—in these or other respects, like cleverness or temperament or wit or character. It is rather to say that behind all these differences there is some common substance of humanity that marks them as men, and in terms of which they are truly equal. They are not equal in all respects, only in all *relevant* respects. What these relevant respects are, I shall explore in a moment. Here it is enough to note that equality does not imply or entail identity in all things.

Nor, by the same token, is difference to be identified with inequality. An apple and an orange are different, but they are equally pieces of fruit. Two people may differ from each other in sex or race or religious affiliation or physical strength, but these connote nothing concerning intellectual or moral capacity; nor do they touch the fact that both people, despite these differences, are still human beings.

• Equality is not liberty, though certain kinds of *inequality* may well deprive men of important liberties. To require all persons to work one day each week at menial labor, or to attend religious services on the Sabbath, or to serve in the armed forces is to treat them equally but to deprive them of corresponding liberties. To allow inequality of wealth or power is to allow some men to live well but others meagerly. To permit racial or religious or sexual discrimination is to provide a favored group the liberty to deny equivalent rights to the disadvantaged.

• To treat all men equally is not always the same as to treat all cases equally. It may in fact result in treating those very men unequally. Thus, to give all men the same income is to favor the unmarried man and disadvantage the man with a family. To fine all men the same amount for the same offense is to treat the wealthy man lightly and the poor man heavily. To send each person to the doctor once a year, but no more than once a year, is to care for the healthy but not for those who are ill.

● Equality, while essential to justice, is not identical with justice. It is possible to treat everyone equally yet unfairly, e.g., to give all students an unfair examination, to pay all workers an inadequate wage, to compel all persons to worship in the same faith. It may be just to require that all children be sent to school; it would be unjust to require that all be given the same grade, yet to do the latter might (in some curious constructions) accord with equal treatment.

● Equality does not demand that I love my neighbor as myself. To the egalitarian love is not *eros* but *agape*, not carnal or sensual love, not even filial love, but rather charity and respect. Hence I am not asked to *love* or admire him; I am asked only to recognize and respect him as a human being like myself. He is unlike me in many ways; he may be better or less worthy than I in many ways; but in certain relevant ways he remains a person no less than myself.

● Nor does equality require the abolition of hierarchy. If organizational and technological imperatives demand that certain individuals sit at the controls while others do their bidding, it does not follow that (say) accident of birth rather than equality of opportunity should be the governing principle to determine who should sit at those controls. Equality is opposed not to hierarchy but to the unjust distribution of place and power within hierarchy. It seeks to contain the range of that distribution and to base it on agreement (and perhaps merit) rather than on ascription.

● Finally, equality, while an ultimate value, is not the only ultimate and therefore not always the overriding value. Life is not a monolithic or unified whole; there are disharmonies and contradictions, diverse needs and strivings that come into collision, tensions between specific equalities (such as equality of opportunity versus equality of result) and between equality and other values (such as liberty). To press for equality in some things is not to press for equality in all things. To contend for equality does not exclude our contending at the same time for other ends too, which is merely to say that this is what it means to be human, that we want many things but cannot simultaneously obtain all of them, so we must choose. To this problem too I shall return.

III

What, then, is equality? To answer this question adequately it is necessary to consider equality both in its negative significance as a protest-ideal and in its positive content as an ultimate value. This last, in turn, must be grasped both as a general concept and as a system (however disharmonious and changing) of specific equalities and corresponding inequalities. I do not apologize for the complexity of such treatment; for equality, like most political concepts, defies simplistic understanding.

The fundamental and perhaps only legitimate defense of inequality is that it is not conventional but natural; it accords with the nature of men, who differ profoundly in intelligence, talent, and virtue; and it accords with the nature of things, which require hierarchy and degree. Hence the principle: the right man in the right place. However, this, as Giovanni Sartori properly notes,

> is an ideal that is never realized, since in its stead what we find only too often is the privileged man in a privileged place. And this is where the demand for equality actually and rightly starts. The claim for equality is a protest against unjust, undeserved, and unjustified inequalities. For hierarchies of worth and ability never satisfactorily correspond to effective hierarchies of power. . . . Equality is thus a *protest-ideal*, a symbol of man's revolt against chance, fortuitous disparity, unjust power, crystallized privilege.[2]

If the rich and well-born were also the able, if the powerful were also the virtuous and wise, if, that is to say, actual aristocracies were truly natural aristocracies, based solely on merit; or if, to reverse the terms, the able were made rich, the virtuous made powerful, and the naturally best made the actual best, then the demand for equality might lose much of its force and justification. But history gives an emphatic denial to any such shabby claim. Even Santayana, who argued that it is "a benefit and a joy to a man, being what he is, to know that many are, have been, and will be better than he," felt constrained to attack actual "aristocracies" for their artificial rather than natural eminence. And what did Ortega y Gasset mean by the revolt of the masses if not primarily the domination in our time by men of wealth and power but without taste or standards?

It is no easy matter, moreover, to determine who are the naturally best and to devise a method that will accurately select them and elevate them to power. On these questions political writers have been eloquent but also at odds with one another. Blood and race, wealth and power, education and intelligence, strength (especially as demonstrated in military conquest) and athletic prowess, even piety and the mysticism of charisma, even (it must now be said) attainment of celebrity status, whether of the jet set or the Hollywood screen— all these have been put forward as attributes making for *political* virtue and wisdom. But surely not all these define the best. Nor have those who have come to power through these means remained the best—if initially they were the best—very long. Nor do we have gods to decide these matters. If to all this we add, with Edward Bellamy, that what any one man is and does is in large

measure the consequence of what society and past generations have be-
queathed to him and now, by providing conditions and opportunities, make it
possible for him to do, we see that the very notion of merit or achievement is
social and not simply personal. In what sense, then, is any man's superiority
"natural"?

To raise this question is to challenge the most venerable and established
commonplace in writings on equality. Political and social theorists from Plato
through Hume and Rousseau to a host of contemporary thinkers have drawn a
distinction between two sorts of inequality: natural (consisting, for example, in
differences of age, sex, strength, and what Rousseau called "qualities of mind
or soul") and conventional (consisting of differences in wealth, power, and
honor, all of which emerge from the consent of men). We have already noted
that the first rarely leads to or corresponds with the second. What now needs to
be remarked is that what have been called inequalities by nature are often
revealed, on examination and by experience, to be inequalities by convention.
I do not seek to deny that there are some natural inequalities. I only argue that
many inequalities that have been called natural in the past are not in fact so.
Some people still believe women are by nature morally and intellectually
inferior to men, blacks to whites (in Uganda, Asians to blacks), a defeated
people to a conquering nation. This tells us a great deal about those who hold
such beliefs; it does not alter the objective reality. Individuals vary, but why
they do so—whether this is the result of an unalterable heredity or a changeable
environment, for example—is not altogether clear. Nor can it be said that
virtue and wisdom (Rousseau's qualities of mind or soul) owe nothing to
society, or, since they conform to certain standards of behavior which are social
norms or rules, are natural rather than conventional. Much remains to be done
before we can assert with confidence that a particular inequality is natural and
hence, presumably, unalterable.[3]

What is fatal to any justification of inequality, whether natural or conventional, however, is the fact that inequalities are cumulative and self-
reinforcing. Inequality in wealth, for example, leads to inequalities in education, housing, medical care, travel, and the like, and, most important, to
inequalities in power. To alter unjustifiable inequalities in the face of this
"natural" aggrandizement of inequalities is most difficult, and in some measure
impossible. Hence equality as a protest-ideal applies not simply to conventional or unjust inequalities but to inequality as a cumulative and self-
reinforcing system of inequalities, both natural and conventional.

In turning to equality as a positive ideal, we must make a final point about
differences, or inequalities. We must ask: Which differences or inequalities are
relevant, and relevant to what? Inequalities are specific, not general. The

strongest man may not be the swiftest runner, the gifted violinist may be a poor mathematician, the great scientist a bumbling statesman. To be different or unequal in some things is not necessarily to be different or unequal in the important things, least of all in the single most important thing: to be, to live like a man; to seek one's self-development; to be a rational, free, and relatively autonomous human being.

Here we come to the heart of the principle of equality: *in the things that count men are not, and ought not to be, so much different from each other as to matter.* But what are the things that count?

Hobbes, with his usual felicity, answered the question this way:

> Nature hath made men so equall, in the faculties of body, and mind; as that though there bee found one man sometimes manifestly stronger in body, or of quicker mind than another; yet when all is reckoned together, the difference between man, and man, is not so considerable, as that one man can thereupon claim to himselfe any benefit, to which another may not pretend, as well as he. For as to the strength of body, the weakest has strength enough to kill the strongest, either by secret machination, or by confederacy with others, that are in the same danger with himselfe.
>
> And as to the faculties of the mind, (setting aside the arts grounded upon words, and especially that skill of procceding upon generall, and infallible rules, called Science; which very few have, and but in few things; as being not a native faculty, born with us; nor attained, (as Prudence,) while we look after somewhat els,) I find yet a greater equality amongst men, than that of strength. For Prudence, is but Experience; which equall time, equally bestowes on all men, in those things they equally apply themselves unto. That which may perhaps make such equality incredible, is but a vain conceipt of ones owne wisdome, which almost all men think they have in a greater degree, than the Vulgar; that is, than all men but themselves, and a few others, whom by Fame, or for concurring with themselves, they approve. For such is the nature of men, that howsoever they may acknowledge many others to be more witty, or more eloquent, or more learned; Yet they will hardly believe there be many so wise as themselves: For they see their own wit at hand, and other mens at a distance. But this proveth rather that men are in that point equall, than unequall. For there is not ordinarily a greater signe of the equall distribution of any thing, than that every man is contented with his share.[4]

It is important not to slight Hobbes's teaching here. Hobbes advances as an empirical fact—against classical and Christian thought—what I take to be a first principle of politics: that men must sleep, and when a strong man sleeps his life is in danger; hence to protect himself from weaker men he needs either their assurance that he will be left to awake or protection against them, and prefer-ably both; hence government, which involves (rests upon) both force and consent. But to establish and maintain a government, the strong must persuade the others that it is also good for them. The appeal must be to the general interest, the common good. And since the weak are also in danger, what is common to them all is the fear of death, hence a love of peace, and a desire for a system of order that will enable them all to live and to pursue a commodious life. This, whatever their differences of mind, they can all grasp. To this they can all agree. From all of which it follows that what is common to men is more important than what differentiates or divides them. Inequalities of body or mind are thus (in Hobbes's view) trivial, not politically relevant, because not relevant to their survival as men.

It is true that survival without regard to the purposes for which men sur-vive—e.g., to live "virtuously"—is not an acceptable end for a classical or idealist philosopher; but since, for Hobbes, "there is no such *Finus ultimus* (utmost ayme,) nor *Summum Bonum* (greatest Good,) as is spoken of in the Books of the old Morall Philosophers," this is not a fatal objection. It is enough that men should be protected against an untimely death and be given an equal chance to attain their ends.

So too with Rousseau, who in pressing the case for equality differs from Hobbes in but two respects: he looks to other, conventional rather than natural, attributes of men; and he does so in normative rather than descriptive terms. Here is the relevant passage:

> By equality, we should understand, not that the degrees of power and riches are to be absolutely identical for everybody; but that power shall never be great enough for violence, and shall always be exercised by vir-tue of rank and law; and that, in respect of riches, no citizen shall ever be wealthy enough to buy another, and none poor enough to be forced to sell himself.[5]

Clearly, equality does not entail identity, at least not (for Rousseau) in power and wealth. What it does require is moderation—"on the part of the great, moderation in goods and position, and, on the side of the common sort, moderation in avarice and covetousness." It requires that the *range* of differ-ences be contained: that inequality of power shall never enable one man to dominate another, to force him to act against his will; and that inequality of wealth shall similarly be limited to prevent any man from becoming master or slave. Neither a master nor a slave, neither to demean nor to be demeaned—this (for Rousseau) is the essence of equality.

Given these equalities—of ability and of rank—it follows, to invoke Hobbes again, that men may properly have equality of hope in attaining their ends.

And if, to return once more to Rousseau, we are told that such equality is an unpractical ideal that cannot actually exist, that its abuse is inevitable, it does not follow that we should not at least make regulations concerning it. Indeed, Rousseau argues, "it is precisely because the force of circumstances tends continually to destroy equality that the force of legislation should always tend to its maintenance."

Central as these considerations are, it is not enough to rest with them. We must go back, if briefly, to Aristotle and forward to John Stuart Mill. I think of Aristotle here not for his distinction between numerical equality and equality proportionate to desert (of this, more later), but for his discussion of the general causes of revolution. What concerns Aristotle is the state of mind which leads to sedition. Here he makes principal the passions for equality and inequality.

> There are some [he says] who stir up sedition because their minds are filled by a passion for equality, which arises from their thinking that they have the worst of the bargain in spite of being the equals of those who have got the advantage. There are others who do it because their minds are filled with a passion for inequality (i.e. superiority), which arises from their conceiving that they get no advantage over others (but only an equal amount, or even a smaller amount) although they are really more than equal to others. . . . Thus inferiors become revolutionaries in order to be equals, and equals in order to be superiors.[6]

If, then, we are to assure stability in a society, we must take account of the attitudes and opinions of men. Whatever the justification or lack of justification for particular views, a polity that ignores what men think or believe runs the risk of disruption. For men fight for what they want or think they want, and they frequently want what they think they are entitled to have. If ordinary men regard themselves as politically competent (as equal), as they do, they will fight, as they have fought, to obtain an equal voice and an equal position. To deny them that voice is to assure conflict and perhaps revolution. Similarly, if men strive for inequality (i.e., superiority), this too will make for disorder. Moderation in men is then essential for social and political stability, and such moderation can only be achieved where the range of differences does not exceed the boundaries of what is tolerable. Which returns us, inescapably, to equality.

We come, finally, to John Stuart Mill and the liberal conception of man. Here the meaning of (and case for) equality may be briefly stated, for it turns primarily on but two notions: the rationality of man and the importance of individuality.[7] If man—each man—has a mind, he must be free to use it. This entails the right to choose, to decide between alternatives, to determine one's own way of life. It is true that he may choose wrongly, i.e., contrary to what another thinks. But to let that other choose for him makes it unnecessary for him to have, as Mill put it, "any other faculty than the apelike one of imitation." By surrendering his mind, he surrenders himself; he remains a child. If he is to realize (or retain) his stature as a man, he must be equal in his right to decide for himself. And that he may choose differently from other men is not a risk but a virtue, the indispensable condition for the pursuit of self-development, identity, individuality. Without individuality, in all its rich diversity, what is society but a drab, uniform, and static collection of robot-like beings?

It is true also that, because man lives in society, he cannot be free to make *all* decisions for himself. No society can allow him to decide that he will drive on the left side of the road when others are required to drive on the right, or to kill or steal or otherwise injure his fellowmen at his pleasure. But being in society need not deprive him of the right to share equally in making such decisions. In the language of Thomas Rainborough, a spokesman for the Levellers, "the poorest he that is in England hath a life to live, as the greatest he"; hence the poorest and the richest should share equally in determining the conditions under which they are to live. Every man is to count for one; no one is to count for more than one.

IV

I have spoken thus far of equality as a general concept. In the real world, however, we are confronted not by "equality" but by many diverse and not always compatible equalities. Not all of course simultaneously press for our attention; not all are equally relevant to or applicable in a given situation. But it is sometimes the case that two or more equalities collide; then in choosing one we necessarily limit or curtail another. To which specific equality shall we give priority in a particular case, and why? Moreover, to choose among equalities—to treat men equally in some things (say voting) but unequally in others (say income)—requires a principle or principles of justification other then equality itself. To the extent that this choice between two kinds of equality is derived from other considerations, equality becomes a derivative value. But it is still a choice between two equalities in their own right, and in this respect equality remains an ultimate value. Beyond this, it is also often the case that there are ambiguities and tensions both within a particular equality (say equality of opportunity) and between equality however conceived and other values. We do not live in a tidy world. We are constantly jarred and tormented by incompatible, yet mutually commanding, ideals: honesty and kindness, love and obligations, equality and liberty, or excellence, or heroic achievement. These are the problems—to some the deficiencies—of equality, to which I now turn.

Let us begin with Aristotle's distinction between numerical equality and equality proportionate to desert, for in one form or another this remains perhaps the central problem of equality. According to the first sort of equality, all shall be treated alike; hence a sales tax or uniform wage or price or rent or bus fare is just, and a graduated income tax or differential wage or price or rent is not. According to the second, each shall be treated according to his merit; hence the reverse of the first set of practices would apply; for in these terms to give to the superior no more than is given to the inferior, or to extract from the poor man with a family of four the same rent or tax or price as the unmarried rich but not more meritorious man, is manifestly wrong.

In Yugoslavia some years ago, workers in a factory were bitterly divided over the question whether the same wage was to be given to each worker, on the principle that all stomachs are equal, or apportioned according to each person's contribution, on the principle that some did more, or better, or more important work than others. Apart from the not inconsiderable difficulty in defining each man's "desert," or determining the right proportion, which of the two notions of equality is correct? Why? (It ought to be noted, if only parenthetically, that a further inconvenient problem attaches to the numerical conception of equality here. For in the absence of strict controls over spending, providing for equality of wages or income may soon lead to inequalities of wealth—given the fairly evident fact that some men are frugal and save while others quickly rid themselves of all that they receive.)

Or take the idea that each member of an orchestra shall be rewarded equally for a fine performance. Does this mean giving each player his favorite instrument, in which case one may get a pair of cymbals and another a grand piano, or does it entail giving each player the same instrument (say a violin) or a ten-dollar bill?

Consider the socialist principle of equality: from each according to his ability, to each according to his need. The one place where this principle is almost universally found is, paradoxically, in the family, perhaps the least egalitarian of human associations. Shall we now apply it in the realm of work? If so, what shall we say to the women's liberation movement when a wife demands "appropriate" payment for her labor even though her husband may already earn a sum sufficient to provide for both their material needs? Shall we diminish his (or her) earnings proportionately, or insist that she (or he) work without pay?

And what of the venerable adage, Let the punishment fit the crime? Should it not rather be, Let the punishment fit the criminal, thereby taking into account such factors as age, motive, circumstance, and frequency (or infrequency) of offense? Shall the figure of justice really be blindfolded, or should she (or he) look at each case with clear and searching eyes?

To these and similar questions Aristotle, though he understood the problem, offered no satisfactory answer. With his customary prudence he observed:

> Some take the line that if men are equal in one respect, they may consider themselves equal in all: others take the line that if they are superior in one respect, they may claim superiority all round. . . . The right course is (not to pursue either conception exclusively, but) to use in some cases the principle of numerical equality, and in others that of equality proportionate to desert.

The difficulty of course is that such a formulation does not tell us which cases properly fall under the one, and which under the other category. But then, no general principle can decide each concrete case; always secondary principles and special circumstances enter into consideration.

Most decisively, these conflicting notions of equality entail a perennial, because irresolvable, paradox: namely, that to treat different (unequal) people equally (the same way) is often to achieve unequal results— e.g., to give a sickly person no more medical care than is required by a robust person is not to produce equally healthy individuals; while to treat different people differently (unequally) may be precisely what is required (as in the given example) to produce an equal result.

From all of which it follows that not mathematics or formal logic but experience, circumstance, and the shared values of a particular people at a particular time will variously determine the outcome. But whether that determination is the "right" outcome remains an open question.

Let us turn now to certain difficulties inherent in a seemingly simple and widely accepted principle: equality of opportunity. Surely if a society is to have hierarchies or pyramids of power—and what society can avoid this?—it is proper that movement up and down the ladder accord with competence or merit. But (and this indeed is a very large but), as already noted: (1) the equal opportunity principle requires conditions that neither our own nor any other society outside the visions of utopian thinkers is willing to provide, e.g., removing children from their parents immediately after birth and raising them in common. Moreover, every actual society is disfigured by discriminatory practices and unjust arrangements that limit or vitiate equality of opportunity. Hence, whatever the rhetoric, the principle is at best approximated but nowhere fully observed. And (2) even if the principle were to be realized, it would lead, paradoxically, to a nonegalitarian result; for in a differentiated and hierarchical society equality of opportunity is but another mode—even if the "best" mode—of arriving at inequalities of condition, notably of power, status, and (commonly) wealth.

These considerations are alone sufficient to render the principle suspect. But there is, in the view of some critics (oddly enough, critics of the Left rather than the Right), an even more fatal objection to the equal opportunity principle: namely, that it converts life from a cooperative adventure of equal human beings into a competitive struggle of unequal talents, in the course of which not individuals but aspects of individuals are prized, and as a consequence of which losers, who are the bulk of the human race, are denigrated and demeaned.

Consider the following statements:

When you think of equality of opportunity as the career open to talents, you cease to think of the man who is untalented. . . . The newer conception of merit is not talent but personality, creativity, which includes talent but sets it in its rightful place. Justice consists not in seeing that all start from the same line, permitting all to race, and awarding prizes to the winners, but rather, abandoning the whole idea of a race with prizes, in seeing that each is as far as possible given space, scope, room, and encouragement to employ his free powers in the building of a human life.[8]

Striving is not for equality nor for superiority; it is for the enhancement of uniqueness. . . . When it is being itself which is valued, then none can be inferior, or superior. . . . People are not [to be] valued in terms of achievement. People are [to be] valued for what they are. . . .[9]

Now in one sense—a very profound sense—these contentions are surely unassailable, for they ask no more than that we recognize and respect the reality (and the rights) of each individual as a living presence. They ask us to set aside the vexing problem of determining the value of a man's talents—often by arbitrary if socially approved standards—and thereby to avoid the consequential division of men into higher and lower orders, into various strata of inequalities. Far more, they ask us to cease judging men as fragmented beings, in terms of their functional roles, and to look at *who* they are rather than at *what* they do. Then it matters not whether a man is a butcher or a doctor, a garbage collector or an engineer. What matters is that he is a man, who happens to perform a certain task for some portion of his time, but who is also a husband and a father, a friend and a neighbor, perhaps a churchgoer and a participant in certain communal activities, but always a total person and a full-time member of the same human race. He is with us, of us, in us. And he counts, not because he is different, but because he is the same.

In these terms the equal opportunity principle, because it leads to and emphasizes differences, inequalities, is destructive of what is most essential to the human enterprise—respect for that which is common to all men, their humanity.

Yet, when all this has been said, can we really abandon the equal opportunity principle? Can we really ignore talent and dispense not simply with differences but with the esteem we attach to differences? In so far as a man is a teacher, or an artist, or a statesman, do we not wish him to be a *good* teacher or artist or statesman? And shall we not esteem the *better* rather than the poorer teacher? Moreover, if in the modern world specialization of function is unavoidable, if organization and consequently hierarchy are *necessary*, then how except through the equal opportunity principle can we assure a just determination of place? It is true, as Michels argued, that organization and hierarchy carry with them a tendency to oligarchy, but the task then is surely to guard against the conversion of that tendency into a reality; it is not to abandon organization and hierarchy, which is in any case impossible. It is also true that the esteem we generally attach to differences and inequalities may often exaggerate (or diminish) the worth of the individual as a total being; but the problem then is not that men are functionally different, and behave toward each other as superiors or inferiors in certain roles, but that *we* (or society) impute a certain value to such differences, and *that* plainly is a matter of reeducation.[10]

The greater difficulty seems to me to lie in another direction. For if deficiencies in existing arrangements and practices militate against the proper functioning of the equal opportunity principle, it follows that those who stand at various levels in the pyramids of position and power do not necessarily belong there. It is then necessary either to correct those deficiencies or, if that is not possible, to shift our attention away from the principle of equality of opportunity to the alternative, perhaps complementary, principle of equality of result. Thus, it was not the doyens of the New Left but a moderate liberal, Franklin D. Roosevelt, who in 1932 proclaimed that "equality of opportunity as we have known it no longer exists," called for "a re-appraisal of values," and set as our task "distributing wealth and products more equitably." In the same vein, in his address on the State of the Union in January 1944 he articulated what he called "a second Bill of Rights," including the right to a useful job, an adequate income, a decent home, adequate medical care, a good education, and other components of what we now associate with the welfare state.

What is of interest here is the notion that a man's success or failure is not simply the consequence of his innate ability but, in some measure, of the system—its practices, arrangements, and (let it be said) its derangements. Hence equality of result—meaning by equality not identity but the tolerable range of which Aristotle and Rousseau spoke—is the necessary and altogether proper mode of redress. Then, paradoxically, equalization of results provides the conditions that make possible a greater measure of equality of opportunity.

So the two principles, far from being intrinsically in opposition, come together as alternative or complementary means to the same end—the achievement of justice in determining fitness and place.

In short, despite all its admitted difficulties, the equal opportunity principle, whether as a working standard to be approximated or an ideal by which a people shall be judged, remains an essential element of any right ordering of social life.

I turn briefly now to the familiar yet still vexing question: Does a commitment to equality endanger other ultimate and equally prized ends, in particular liberty?[11]

This of course is the problem that agitated Alexis de Tocqueville and John Stuart Mill and that concerns not merely conservatives but traditional liberals today. For at one level the answer to the question is surely affirmative. To say that all persons shall behave, or not behave, in a certain way—pay taxes, observe the traffic laws, send children to school, abstain from polygamy or trespass—is to deprive them of corresponding liberties. In this obvious sense *every* law or custom that imposes a uniform requirement is an interference with liberty.

But liberty, like equality, is not a simple entity, like an apple pie, out of which each law cuts an irretrievable piece. Nor is government, through law, the only source of interference with liberty; other men and groups, through force or economic sanctions or other forms of pressure, also interfere with human freedom. To assure a particular liberty, such as freedom of expression, it is then necessary to restrain those nonpolitical powers who might otherwise limit it—on the alleged ground that the speech in question is (say) obscene or subversive or otherwise harmful. Law in that case enters not simply as a restraint but as a restraint on a restraint. All of which is to say that liberty, properly understood, is a complex of particular liberties—of speech, religion, travel, and the like—and of concomitant restraints.

To determine whether the law should restrain or tolerate a social restraint, and thereby secure a particular liberty for some (perhaps only under certain circumstances) but not an apposite liberty for others, is merely to recognize that not all liberties are equally important, or equally desirable. Liberties, like equalities, must be ranked hierarchically; and when we give primacy to one we may well have to surrender another.

In the same way we must choose between conflicting liberties and equalities: between the liberty of parents to raise their children as they see fit, giving them what advantages they can, and equality of opportunity, which requires that all children be treated alike, that no child receive less (or more) than another, and hence that all children be raised in common; between the liberty of an employer to hire whomever he pleases (say only red-haired, white-skinned females) and antidiscrimination laws which in the service of equality require him to employ qualified persons of whatever sex and color; between the liberty of man to live among "his own kind" and the egalitarian requirement that residential areas be open to all; and so on.

It is not always the case that equality will, or should, prevail over liberty. In the name of individuality, we deny the right of egalitarians to compel hippies to dress and behave as others do. In the name of religious freedom, we deny the right of egalitarians to require all children, including the children of atheists and agnostics, to take religious education in the schools, or, in the case of children whose parents are members of Jehovah's Witnesses, to salute the flag.

Nor is it always the case that liberty will, or should, prevail over equality—witness our antidiscrimination laws.

So when we confront the diverse issues that bedevil us today, whether it be equality versus inequality of result, or conformity versus diversity, we must understand that there is no simple and final resolution. Both liberty and equality, while in one sense ultimate values, are also derivative values; for when there are conflicts among or between them, it is only with reference to another and presumably higher principle that they can be handled. This higher principle is sometimes stability, but since stability is itself justified only when the system is worth preserving, it is generally some conception of justice or the common good.

V

Now every theory of justice—whether it looks to God or nature or tradition or utility or an initial (actual or hypothetical) social contract—is vulnerable to serious criticism; and none, it seems hardly necessary to add, is universally accepted. If we forgo mutual slaughter or the authoritarian imposition of a particular creed, and turn instead to a democratic resolution of this disagreement, we build once again on the principle of equality.

For what counts in democratic states is not the putative truth or falsity of a theory but a majority acceptance or belief, and this is the outcome of a process of negotiation, bargaining, compromise, and voting. What is crucial to this process is the question: Who shall participate? If the democratic response is, as it must be, *all*, then all must be equally free to articulate, assess, and judge among alternative policies. Equality and liberty thus again come together in a common cause.

From this standpoint, equality is not, as Isaiah Berlin would have it, simply an ultimate principle that "cannot itself be defended or justified, for it is itself that which justifies other acts—means taken towards its realization."[12] It is rather an instrumental principle that cannot be other than defended and justified, for it is indispensable to the realization of something other than itself—namely, democracy. Those who, for whatever reason, opt for democracy must opt too for at least those equalities essential to democracy. And if among the diverse forms of state democracy is a just regime, perhaps—though I cannot argue this here—the *best* regime, it follows that those equalities (and liberties) appropriate or necessary to democracy are warranted; for to will the end is also to will the means.

But democracy, it may fairly be contended, is itself not an end but a means, a political principle or set of arrangements that must be defended or justified in terms of what democracy does for man. To the extent that this is true, it only reinforces the justice of equality. For what democracy does, as John Stuart Mill so ably argued, is to enable each man both to protect himself and to elevate himself. To protect himself against misgovernment, not by entrusting another with his guardianship but by himself standing up for his rights and interests, by himself exercising his power—of opinion and of political participation, not merely through the suffrage but also by taking an actual part in the government—and thereby sharing, as far as any one individual can, in the making of decisions that govern his life. To elevate himself morally and intellectually, by that very participation, acquiring through discussion and ensuing enlightenment a concern not only for his own selfish interests but for the general good.

Thus democracy, whether as end or as means, vindicates the egalitarian claim.

The case for the justice of equality of course does not rest here. If the end is man, then equality—even if by equality we mean treating different people in the same way—is essential to the very life of man. For however different people may be, in some respects they are the same. They all want to live, and all societies—despite wars and other forms of senseless killings—respect this as a fundamental right. This is why we have traffic regulations and laws against murder, hospitals and safety devices in automobiles and industrial plants, lifeguards on bathing beaches, and the like—all without regard to sex, race, religion, intelligence, and other matters that differentiate persons from one another. Given this equal right to life, it follows that all men are equally entitled to whatever is necessary to sustain and protect life. At a minimum, this means that no man can legitimately be denied adequate food, clothing, housing, medical care, etc. Beyond that minimum, decent and rational men may disagree as to what is required. In most societies today, for example, education—though not of course at the same level in all societies—is recognized as such a necessity.

What is entailed here is the notion of need. Obviously, different people need different things. But just as obviously, *all* people need the same, or the same sorts of things. Equality thus builds on what is common to men, on what is necessary, perhaps even on what is good, for all men. To exclude any individual or group from these rights—to life and the things essential to life—is to deny their humanity. Possibly there are good reasons for denying these rights, or some of them, to particular persons or groups under special circumstances; but in such cases the burden of proof is surely on those who would argue for those exceptions. And exceptions they must remain. No principle is absolute, automatically binding in all cases without regard to circumstances; but without the principle of equality it is difficult to see what sense can be made of "the common" that is at the very heart of what it means to be a man.[13]

Men want not merely to live but to live well. From a moral point of view, this means that they wish to live, if not nobly, at least justly; to do good rather than evil, to act rightly rather than wrongly. It cannot be said that everyone understands precisely the same things by "the right" and "the good." What can be said is that they are generally agreed on at least one principle appropriate to the determination of what is right and good. This is the principle of fairness.

We do not call a race fair when one runner is hobbled by a ball and chain and another is mounted on a horse. We do not call a fight fair when one pugilist's hands are encased in armor and the other in foampadded gloves. We insist in both cases that those who enter the contest do so on the same terms. We do not recognize as fair a trial where only one party is represented by adequate counsel, safeguarded by the rules of evidence, and given an opportunity to testify in his behalf. We do not call a social order fair that gives only some people the liberty to criticize the government and to pursue their own lifestyles. Nor do we consider fair an arrangement that stacks the conditions behind these procedures to the advantage of one party: e.g., where one pugilist is considerably taller and heavier than the other, or where parental wealth is distributed so unevenly that the rich child but not the poor can satisfy his desires or alone have the power to qualify himself so that he may earn them.

From this perspective, fairness as a principle of justice dictates equality.[14] Fairness does not prescribe the "right" result; it requires us to treat people equally in order to arrive at the right result. Or, conversely, it stipulates that no person shall be treated differently from another without just cause; and by just cause I mean not simply reasons—there are always "reasons"—but arguments and justifications that make sense and carry conviction on logical, empirical, and moral grounds. Thus, to say that there shall be no cruelty without just cause is not to preclude (say) punishment for heinous crimes, but to prohibit the arbitrary imprisonment or debasement of "inferior" by "superior" peoples.

This sort of equality—what may be called equality of consideration—is an ultimate end in that it affirms that intrinsic value of every human being. It does not deny that there are differences (inequalities?) among men. It rather insists that such differences do not justify—except for good and sufficient reasons—the withdrawal from some men of those conditions which are required for the development of their varying individualities. It insists that no man is fully human who must bend his knee to a master, who is cast into secondary importance and subjected as a consequence of that label to unjustifiable inequalities. It insists that, whatever the differences among men, what is common to them all is the desire to lead the kind of life each wants to lead; and that, from this standpoint, it does not matter that one is wealthier or more powerful or more prestigious than another; what matters is that each should be equally free, and reasonably able, to be himself, to live as he wishes to live, and not as another wants him to live.[15] Not merely equality in this kind of freedom, but also respect. It is fashionable in certain quarters today to disparage the value of tolerance; but surely tolerance—of each man's rationality, of his right to be different, to live as he thinks best—is essential to his humanity. In this at least all must be equal. And since it is obvious that some limits must always be placed on individual action, those limits too must emerge only from an equal consideration of each man's rights and interests.

In the wisdom of the classical philosophers, justice consists in giving each man his due. This has generally meant treating unequal men unequally, according to their differences. But in another, and I think greater wisdom, justice consists not in looking at what divides men but at what unites them, what is common to them all. And what is common to them all is their equal integrity as human beings. It may well be that a full theory of justice must attend not to one or the other of these conceptions but to both. In that case all must still be treated equally in those respects in which they are equal. Equality does not require more.

VI

We can now see where the newer critics of equality—Daniel Bell and Irving Kristol,[16] among others—have gone wrong. They are of course much too sophisticated and insightful not to have dwelt on legitimate concerns or not to have taken account of some of the more obvious objections to their positions. Nevertheless, it remains the case that they have not come adequately to grips with the nature and complexities of the specific equalities they treat; they have tended to confuse the specific equality they condemn with the whole of equality; and, most important, because they have sought to build on what divides rather than on what unites men, they have not understood the necessity of equality for the maintenance of community.

Thus, when Bell pleads the cause of meritocracy, he does not fully face up to the deficiencies of the equal opportunity principle in actual societies, and the implications of such deficiencies for the notion of personal achievement. When Kristol worries about the nature and implications of a greater measure of equality in income, and of the costs entailed by a redistributive policy, he neglects the costs entailed by the maintenance of existing, unjust practices and confuses this particular equality with the whole of equality. When they both, along with many others, argue against equality of result, they do not confront the fact that inequalities of result create privileges that vitiate equality of opportunity and thereby render inequitable the results that have in fact emerged and will continue to emerge, and that society must then intervene to redress or even (perhaps) cancel out those privileges so as to restore—or newly establish—an initial equality of opportunity.

All too often these newer critics contest not equality but a caricature of equality. No serious liberal or socialist thinker has ever held to a notion of absolute equality. None, to my knowledge, has ever maintained that equality must apply to all things—to cards in a deck, pictures in an exhibition, ideas in the marketplace. None, to my knowledge, has ever maintained that equality precludes our distinguishing old from young men, or young men from children, when drafting soldiers into the army. Nor has any serious liberal or socialist thinker failed to recognize the tensions and conflicts among equalities, or between equality and other values, such that choices must be made and some equalities set aside. This is precisely why, for liberals and socialists, equality is so important; for in making those choices all men must equally share.

All men must share, for all are members of the community. Now a community embraces partial associations, like a university or a corporation, but it transcends them. For it builds not on those aspects of the individual relevant to the association—his special aptitudes and talents—but on his wholeness as a person. A community, unlike a corporation but like a family, does not recognize degrees of membership; it does not value an individual only as a means, as an instrument to the fulfillment of the association's purpose; it values him as an end. Consequently it respects and cares for him as an end. As such, he is equal—equal in his humanity, and in the rights and freedoms appropriate to that humanity.

Whatever the limits of equality, whatever its difficulties, this then remains true: without equality properly understood and constantly held in view as *a* (but not of course *the*) first principle, there can be no community, and hence no individuality. And without these there can be no just society.

7 Black Rights and Judicial Wrongs

> Whoever hath an absolute authority to interpret
> any written or spoken laws, it is he who is truly
> the lawgiver, to all intents and purposes, and not
> the person who first wrote or spoke them.
>
> BISHOP HOADLY, March 1717

I

Three problems continue to haunt democratic theory.

One is that the right method does not always produce the right results. Majorities, even when properly counted, are sometimes wrong. Governments, even when representative and accountable, are sometimes oppressive or unwise. Justice requires both the right method and enlightened judgments; but a people and its governments are not always enlightened.

Hence the precarious status of human rights. To ensure certain right results, a society may articulate and define rights, and even incorporate them in a constitution so as to put them beyond the reach of ordinary decision-making processes. But rights always require redefinition, for new circumstances produce new claims. And no rights are inviolable: freedom of speech does not embrace libel or slander; freedom of religion does not sanction human sacrifice or polygamy. The struggle for human rights is a permanent war.

Finally, who is to resolve the tension between majority rule and constitutionally stipulated or newly asserted rights? Who shall determine, in concrete cases, what those rights are, who shall possess them, and what is required to enforce them? In democratic theory this determination, along with positive social action, is the business of legislative bodies, constitutional interpretation the province of the courts. But interpretation entails remedies, for courts cannot explain and apply a right without also indicating an appropriate—or barring an inappropriate—course of action. Judicial legislation is thus unavoidable. What then becomes of the separation-of-powers doctrine? Where then does sovereignty reside?

These problems come together on the issue of racism in America. Blacks (and other racial or ethnic minorities) claim an equal entitlement to the rights of citizens. But many groups, and sometimes majorities, do not fully respect that claim, and legislative bodies have not provided effective and sufficient

Reprinted, by permission, from *Dissent* 26 (Spring 1979).

means to remedy that denial. In consequence blacks have turned to the courts. Federal judges have responded not only by disallowing certain practices and arrangements that infringe upon those rights but also by prescribing positive actions to enforce them. How else, those judges argue, can they protect the rights of schoolchildren, prisoners, the mentally retarded, and others in situations where their violation is beyond dispute? If they do not enforce those rights—which is what they are required to do—who will?

But this enforcement has led the courts into an activist role seemingly outside their traditional jurisdiction and professional competence. Once judges limited themselves to a largely negative function, setting standards to which governments were expected to adhere, and articulating basic rights and freedoms with whose exercise governments were not to interfere. Now they essay the positive direction of social policy, transforming themselves in the process into sociologists, social workers, penologists, educational and hospital administrators, fiscal managers, and the like.

In school desegregation cases, for example, judges have redrawn district lines and ordered that children be assigned and transported to schools on the basis of race—to some critics a violation of the principle, asserted in *Brown v. Board of Education* (1954), that the Constitution is color-blind. They have specified the manner in which teachers shall be selected, which schools shall be closed, where new schools shall be built, and even what sums shall be expended (thereby in effect dictating in some cases that additional taxes shall be imposed). They have mandated time schedules and stages of implementation, established review boards with considerable powers, and otherwise involved themselves in administrative minutiae. In these ways, and with respect to other institutions and practices as well—apportionment, prisons, mental hospitals, even systems of local government—they have determined configurations of power and the distribution of resources; and whether, and how, and in what order of priority, one social ill rather than another shall be treated.

The issue is not whether the judges are doing these things badly or well, but whether they should be doing them at all.[1] If they should do them at all, does it follow that they should do all of them all the way? What indeed are the standards or guidelines that demarcate the areas or situations in which judges may properly assume an activist role, and that govern the range and degree of such interventionism?

II

In his recent book, Raoul Berger addresses some but not all of these questions, particularly not the last, for his book is a wholesale indictment of judicial interventionism.[2] He is concerned not with black rights but with alleged judicial wrongs. He contends that blacks are not legally entitled to many of the rights they now claim—e.g., suffrage, reapportionment, school desegregation, miscegenation—for those rights are not in the Constitution. Judges, without warrant, have put them there. This is not only a judicial usurpation and prolonged misuse of legislative power, but also a violation of democratic principle; for in a democracy judges should only apply, not make, the law. To the degree that they are called upon to interpret the law, such interpretation should be limited by the intent of the legislature that enacted it. Blacks should, he avows, have the rights they claim; but they must seek them in the legislative arena, not in the courts. Their remedy is political, not judicial.

To establish this case, Berger focuses on the Fourteenth Amendment, the heart of the constitutional struggle for human rights. The vital sentence in that Amendment is the following:

> No State shall make or enforce any law which shall abridge the *privileges or immunities* of citizens of the United States; nor shall any State deprive any person of *life, liberty, or property,* without *due process of law;* nor deny to any person within its jurisdiction the *equal protection of the laws.*

Each of the phrases I have underscored may appear to the ordinary reader as somewhat vague and ambiguous, requiring judicial explication. But for Berger this is not so; as it would not be, he argues, for anyone familiar with the common uses of language and with the explicit statements of the leading protagonists in the debates—both in the 39th Congress and the states.

Thus, he says, "privileges and immunities" included only those rights previously set forth in the Civil Rights Act of 1866: personal security, freedom of movement, the ownership and disposition of property, and access to the courts—not "political rights" or "unlimited equality across the board." "Life, liberty or property" referred simply to auxiliary rights pertaining to those "fundamental" rights. "Due process of law" meant only ordinary legislative procedures, not the substantive doctrine that a statute is invalid if it is "arbitrary, capricious, or unreasonable," and did not incorporate the Bill of Rights. "Equal protection of the laws" sought only to bar statutory discrimination with respect to those rights protected by the privileges and immunities clause, and did not shift their protection from the states to the federal government.

Far from ensuring the inviolability of what the Supreme Court and "liberal thinkers" have held to be the civil rights of blacks, Berger continues, the Amendment itself recognized that the states would violate them. Hence the stipulation that should a state exclude blacks from the suffrage, this denial would not be void; rather, an appropriate penalty would be attached—confining the representation of the state in Congress to the white basis of the population. Finally, Berger notes, even the enforcement of the Amendment was specifically entrusted to Congress, not to the Supreme Court.

Now, if Berger's reading of the intention of the framers of the Fourteenth Amendment is correct, and if judges are bound by that intention, then much if not all of our legal history under that Amendment will have to be jettisoned.

I shall argue, however, that Berger's single-factor analysis is both primitive and pernicious.

III

There is certainly room for doubt that Berger reads the intention of the framers correctly, or even that he knows who the framers were and how, after a century of time, their intention—if it was a single intention—is to be discovered.

Surely "the framers" cannot be reduced to the person of the draftsman of the Fourteenth Amendment, John A. Bingham, whom Berger in unwary moments describes as "a confused, imprecise, and vacillating witness," a man "given to windy oratory" and "frequent shifts of position." Yet Berger, ignoring the ancient maxim that the worst person to construe the meaning of a statute is generally the person who drafted it, because he tends to confuse what he intended to say with what he actually said—a maxim obviously to the point in Bingham's case—repeatedly cites and quotes Bingham to support his [Berger's] reading of that Amendment. Nor can "the framers" be the handful of congressional leaders whom Berger also invokes at length, including Thaddeus Stevens, leader of the Black Republicans, who said on the floor of the house to Bingham: "In all this contest about reconstruction I do not propose either to take his counsel, recognize his authority, or believe a word he says."

The framers of the Amendment include *all* the members of the legislative bodies and *all* the citizens of the states who voted for it. To discover what each of them intended that complex Amendment to mean is simply impossible. The Amendment was a bundle of compromises, with each of its crucial phrases the subject of hotly contested and prolonged debate. Who can say—especially in the age before public opinion polls and psychoanalysis—what motivated each legislator and each individual voter in the several states finally to support the Amendment as a whole, and what each intended the Amendment to mean, or thought it meant? Legislators and citizens may have disliked some parts of the Amendment, may have held different understandings of its many provisions, yet may have voted for it because, by and large, for one reason or another (given the fact that they had no power to select freely the provisions they approved and to reject those they did not), its advantages as they diversely understood and judged them seemed greater than its liabilities.

This is why a vote for a general statute or amendment cannot be construed as an approval of each item in it, or as entailing an identical understanding of the meaning or intention of each item. This is why parliamentary debates are of limited value in determining the interpretation of a law, and why courts do not in practice rely exclusively (or even heavily) on that legislative intent.

It is no great testimony to Berger's scholarship that, in arguing to the contrary, he quotes selectively from such distinguished Supreme Court justices as Holmes to establish that intention is both meaningful and binding; for Holmes also said (though Berger does not report this) that

> We must beware of the pitfalls of antiquarianism, and must remember that for our purposes our only interest in the past is for the light it throws upon the present. I look forward to a time when the part played by history in the explanation of dogma shall be very small, and instead of ingenious research we shall spend our energy on the study of the ends sought to be attained and the reasons for desiring them. . . . In the case of a statute . . . we do not inquire what the legislature meant; we ask only what the statute means.[3]

Nor does Berger report the fact that President Andrew Johnson—who might be expected to have known what his contemporaries in Congress were about— vetoed the Civil Rights Act of 1866 (which Berger himself argues was incorporated into the Fourteenth Amendment) because it attempted to fix "a perfect equality of the white and colored races ...in every State of the Union." In none of the enumerated rights, he said, "can any State ever exercise any power of discrimination between the different races." Many of the voters in the states also seem to have read it that way, as evidenced by Berger's interminable quotations from congressional spokesmen who sought to persuade those voters that the Amendment did not mean what they took it to mean. Why then did the 39th Congress not alter the language of the Amendment to make clear what was evidently unclear? Berger says it was not necessary, for everyone understood its meaning. Everyone—including President Johnson and many (Berger does not ask how many) of the voters?

For these and other reasons Chief Justice Warren was surely right to have held the historical evidence "inconclusive." But even if it were conclusive, it would not in itself decide the *meaning* of that Amendment.

IV

Berger thinks that the *meaning* of the fourteenth Amendment, as of any law, is determined by the intent of its framers, and that, consequently, any judicial departure from that meaning constitutes an unlawful exercise of legislative power. This notion is erroneous.

1. It confuses a constitution with a statute. A constitution consists of general provisions, designed to accommodate a multiplicity of specific statutes. It rests on "fundamental" principles concerned with enduring issues; statutes look more to immediate problems. Most important, a constitution evolves over time, altered (in keeping with the common-law tradition) less by formal amendment than by custom, what lawyers call "use and wont." Consequently rules of judicial interpretation governing a constitution are, and must be, markedly different from those controlling a statute. Berger, however, treats the Fourteenth Amendment, a part of our Constitution, as if it were a statute. This elementary confusion undermines his entire thesis.

2. This notion also mistakes the nature of the judicial process.

What Berger takes to be a piercing insight—that the Supreme Court often functions as a legislative body, not merely applying but making the law—is not a discovery but a commonplace. It was eleborated in massive detail, for example, by Louis B. Boudin in a widely discussed two-volume work bearing the same title, *Government by Judiciary,* back in 1932 (also in an article with that title in 1911), as well as by Morris R. Cohen in a celebrated essay, "The Process of Judicial Legislation" (1914), and by Gilbert E. Roe in an unduly neglected book, *Our Judicial Oligarchy* (1912). Berger cites none of these (or many other relevant) works, nor the quotation at the head of this review.[4]

Not only has judicial legislation been the prevailing practice since the founding of the Republic, its reaches are far greater, and the opposition to its restriction more intense, than Berger seems to reconize. Every critique of this practice, and every attempt to curb or otherwise control it, has foundered on an intractable reality: popular and congressional resistance to interference with what is taken to be the independence of the judiciary. As a result, the Supreme Court exercises a vast legislative power. It makes law through negative action: by vetoing or threatening to veto statutes enacted by national and state legislatures, the Court sets the contours of public policy, limiting what those legislatures may do by telling them what they may not do. The Court makes law through inaction: by refusing to hear certain cases on appeal it affirms the rulings of lower courts and enjoys the added convenience of not having to give reasons that might expose it to criticism. And most important, the Court makes law through positive action: by interpreting both the Constitution and statutes, it translates and applies the judges' understandings of those documents into law and social practice. Thus, as the "final arbiter" of what may or may not be done—a point to which I shall return—the Supreme Court has become a near-sovereign power.

The real issue, then, is not whether judges ought to legislate but the validity of the grounds on which they base their judgments. Those grounds entail precisely what Berger denies: the necessary (because unavoidable) interpretation of a law in accordance with social and ethical considerations—in terms, that is to say, of human consequences; they cannot be (and never have been) restricted to what Morris Cohen called "the phonograph theory of the judicial function": the legal fiction that in the adjudication of cases judges, like sales clerks in a music shop, find (or ought to find) and merely apply, but do not make (or ought not to make), the law. Justice Holmes, to invoke one of Berger's gods again, understood this full well, saying:

> The true science of the law does not consist mainly in a theological working out of dogma or a logical development as in mathematics, or only in a study of it as an anthropological document from the outside; an even more important part consists in the establishment of its postulates from within upon accurately measured social desires instead of tradition. . . . I think it most important to remember whenever a doubtful case arises, . . . that what really is before us is a conflict between two social desires, each of which seeks to extend its dominion over the case, and which cannot both have their way. The social question is which desire is stronger at the point of conflict. . . . When there is doubt, the simple tool of logic does not suffice, and even if it is disguised and unconscious, the judges are called on to exercise the sovereign prerogative of choice.

More pointedly, Holmes went on:

> I think that the judges themselves have failed adequately to recognize their duty of weighing considerations of social advantage. The duty is inevitable, and the result of the often proclaimed judicial aversion to deal with such considerations is simply to leave the very ground and foundation of judgments inarticulate, and often unconscious. . . .[5]

Berger thinks this is a monstrous notion. He wants our judges to be moral and political eunuchs, exempt from human passions, social interests, and economic bias, and deciding cases only in accord with the revealed intentions of the framers. But such creatures and imputed roles are figments of Berger's imagination; they do not and cannot exist in the real world. Moral and political considerations *always* play a compelling role in judicial deliberations and findings, as may be evidenced by a case in the headlines even as I write these lines.

The Nazi party sought to parade and display the swastika in Skokie, Illinois, a predominantly Jewish suburb of Chicago, whose residents include several thousand victims of Nazi concentration camps. Hastily drawn Skokie ordinances prohibited public demonstrations by "members of political parties wearing military style uniforms" and the distribution of any material that "promotes or incites hatred." Do such ordinances violate the constitutional protection of free speech and free assembly?

Neither we nor the judges know the answer to this question; rather, we do not know because the judges do not know. This is why the internally divided Illinois courts, abetted by split decisions (without opinions) of the United States Supreme Court, pursued a vacillating course: first upholding the ordinances, then allowing the march but banning the display of swastikas, finally permitting both the march and the Nazi insignia.

In all these rulings, neither the intention of the framers nor the language of the First Amendment was sufficient to determine the issue. The words of that Amendment provide for no exemptions whatever, not even libel or slander or "fighting words" or a "clear and present danger" of ensuing violence or unlawful conduct. Yet these and other exemptions have long been recognized. The judges disagreed as to whether such exemptions applied in this situation. But in ultimately ruling as they did, they decided that the "intense adverse emotional reactions" likely to be produced by the display of Nazi uniforms and swastikas, as psychiatrists argued,[6] is in effect less consequential than, say, shouting "fire" in a crowded theater. Whatever may be said of this judgment, the judges surely did not arrive at it by looking at the intention of the framers or the language of the First Amendment.

It is all too evident that if the Skokie case is ever fully argued on appeal, the Supreme Court's ruling will unavoidably turn on the justices' interpretation of the constitutive elements of free speech and of the proper balance between individual freedom and harm to others. The simple intention of the framers to protect critics from governmental suppression cannot dictate that determination. Nor does their language distinguish between symbolic and actual speech, or between speech to promote political discussion and speech to provoke violent action. Consequently, while the justices will of course look to our legal traditions, they cannot escape weighing the facts and estimating the outcomes in terms of moral and political values not spelled out in the First Amendment. Hence the cleavages that appeared in previous rulings will doubtless appear again.

What is true (and will be true) of the First Amendment in the Skokie case is true (and will remain true) of the Fourteenth Amendment in race cases, as the recent Bakke decision demonstrated only too well. It cannot be otherwise.

V

Constitutional law and statutory law, unlike natural law, are the products of human will. They bear a direct relationship to power and an ambiguous relationship to justice. To write of law and the judicial function without an adequate understanding of politics and power in a pluralist democracy, and of human conceptions of and yearnings for justice—as Berger does—is not only to move into a never-never-land but to invite disaster.

1. Where power is concentrated in a single place, one can only appeal for redress to the very power that has already inflicted the injury—hardly a promising prospect. Where power is divided, one obviously turns instead to an alternative power, seeking to correct a grievance not through petition or prayer but by playing one power against another; for in these struggles power, not principle, is decisive. Blacks, along with everyone else experienced in democratic politics, understand this quite well. They would be wildly irresponsible if they did not, in consequence, take advantage of democratic pluralism to maneuver as best they can to get what they want. For Berger to avow sympathy for their political aims but to deplore their recourse to judicial power as illegitimate is altogether unrealistic.

2. Berger roots much of his argument in what he takes to be historical facts, but he lacks a crucial historical insight: an insight into the perspective of a minority, especially black, perspective on American law and politics, and consequently on contemporary judicial practices and political possibilities.

In this view, many white Americans avowedly committed to equality have nontheless practiced (what is taken by its victims at least to be) a form of genocide with respect to the Indians and diverse forms of tyranny, not excluding wanton lynchings, with respect to the blacks. Such white Americans hate and fear the blacks and do not intend to admit them into politics, education, and society as free and equal persons. This is why, despite the Fourteenth Amendment, almost every judicial decision prior to 1954 on matters of race— e.g., *Plessy v. Ferguson* (1896), which held constitutional the "separate but equal" doctrine—has been but another obstruction to their legitimate aspirations, as have also political practices and arrangements that excluded blacks from the suffrage and hence from attaining their goals through channels readily accessible to others.

Their focus, therefore, is not on the right method but on right results. In a just society, perhaps for whites in a society where by and large they are treated justly, the right method is obviously crucial. But in an unjust society, or in a society where blacks are treated unjustly, the first item of business is to secure justice, to achieve the right results. Hence *Brown v. Board of Education* is not simply another legal case, to be debated by legal technicians and theorists. It is a major political and psychological event, a revolutionary breakthrough in the long struggle for human rights and equal justice.[7] Among other things, it created expectations that, when frustrated, drove the blacks into the streets and made possible the several subsequent Civil Rights Acts, including the Voting Rights Act of 1965, which enabled blacks effectively to participate in the suffrage and since then to gain an increasing share of political power. It has given blacks greater, if not yet fully equal, access to educational—and thus economic—opportunity. It has moved them from subjects to citizens.

In this perspective, to decry the Brown case and other decisions furthering civil rights—as Berger does—is to seek to turn back the clock. For how, without such judicial intervention, could the blacks have secured, or hope now to secure, their just claims? Without such intervention, they would still stand before Congress and state legislatures, and before public opinion, as servile petitioners, not equal citizens. Without further judicial intervention, even the rights they have seemingly secured will not be enforced. And if this constitutes judicial legislation, at least it is in a right cause; for it is, after all, the business of the courts to administer justice.

3. But Berger mistakes the meaning of justice. He confuses it with power and law. This is understandable, for over the entrance to the Supreme Court we read the motto: Equal Justice Under Law—*not* Law (Equal or Unequal) Under Justice. The law, made by those in power, determines what is just; justice, a product of knowledge and wisdom, does not determine what is law. To be sure, individuals and groups invoke the name of justice when they seek to change the law; but their success or failure in that effort will turn, as Thrasymachus and Hobbes understood, not on the justice of their cause but on the power they are able, or unable, to muster in its behalf.

Since, then, justice so conceived is not a matter of abstract right or utility but solely what the law declares it to be, Berger's notion of the proper judicial role—what is pietistically called the administration of justice—is to apply that law *as it is*. His is the voice of Javert: The law, the law, I live only by the law, and I will see to it that the law is obeyed. But the blacks, along with others primarily committed to justice, wish rather to hear the voice of Jean Valjean.

VI

To all these arguments Berger makes, in part, the same legalistic reply. Judges are bound not by justice but by the Constitution. Laws are to be made not by judges but by legislatures. But now he adds a crucial argument: that if judges are not so bound, if they are free to do whatever they will, our system will be converted from a government of laws into a government by a lawless judiciary.

Here, for the first time, I must register certain agreements with Berger. Judges should, in the American system, be bound by the Constitution; laws should be enacted by legislatures; we should not be ruled by an aristocracy of the robe. In emphasizing these elements of democratic theory Berger is on sound terrain.

But it remains true that to be bound by the Constitution judges must first know what the Constitution *means*, and this, I have argued, entails interpretation. Laws are of course made by legislatures, but in the nature of the case they cannot be made *only* by legislatures; for in applying the law (I have tried to show) judges must also make law. The real issue, then, if we are to avert rule by a judicial aristocracy, is to control that judicial rendering by subordinating it to the legislative will. At this point, however, Berger's case completely collapses; for, unlike Boudin and Cohen, he fails to understand that what is required to subordinate the judicial to the legislative will is the elimination not of judicial *legislation* but of judicial *review*, an entirely different principle. Indeed, by accepting and supporting judicial review—the power of the Court to declare unconstitutional an act of Congress or of the state legislatures—Berger abandons the most effective way to control judicial legislation and prevent judicial supremacy.

This is not the place to reopen the old and probably inconclusive debate as to whether or not the framers of the Constitution intended the Court to have this power—the literature is vast and still mounting—though I must enter my own belief, *contra* Berger, that it was not clearly given to the Court. What is necessary to note is that this power, which the Court exercises, makes possible the "absolute authority" of which Bishop Hoadly spoke and that enables the Court to become the "final arbiter" constitutive of near-sovereign power. It is this power, consequently, that is at odds with democratic theory; for without it, the Court's "improper" rulings can readily be corrected by congressional legislation.

1. A distinction must be drawn between judicial review in a federal system and in a system of coordinate branches of government. In a federal system the states cannot be allowed to override the Constitution; hence judicial review by the Supreme Court, or some equivalent body, is essential. But as one of three branches of the government, it is not easy to see why that power is required— apart from certain technical considerations, e.g., Marshall's refusal to accept the writ of mandamus in original proceedings so as to protect the Court's autonomy as a coordinate branch of the government.

It is true that judicial review is not beyond correction and control: through political pressure (say of a determined president like Jefferson or Grant or Franklin Roosevelt, or—as Mr. Dooley said—of the election returns) or constitutional amendment. But the first has proved to be little more than a temporary expedient; it has not altered the power of the Court, only (occasionally) its personnel and (for a time) its social and political direction. And the second, apart from its difficult procedures, has not touched the crucial fact that the Court still retains the power to interpret the amendment.

Other controlling devices are of course available: Congress can limit the Court's appellate jurisdiction or expand its size; the President can affect the character of the Court by his new appointments or impair its effectiveness by refusing to enforce its rulings; even public ire may move the Court; and impeachment, since Jefferson, always stands over the justices like a Damocletian sword.

But the more evident and realistic controls are internal to the judiciary itself, primarily the accountability of lower courts to the Supreme Court and the principle of judicial self-restraint.

2. These internal controls are at the center of the final, and perhaps most important—surely the most difficult—question: What if the justices do not properly exercise those internal controls? What if they go too far, as they have by injecting substantive meaning into the due process clause? How shall we know when they sufficiently restrain themselves? What are the standards appropriate to their work? What guidelines determine, or ought to determine, the limits of judicial interventionism?

Since the law, like politics, is not a mathematical science but an art—a product of compromises among conflicting power groups and interests, and hence less the incorporation of a coherent philosophy than a series of mutual adjustments that permit community survival—a clear answer to these questions cannot be vouchsafed. All that can be ventured is a set of considerations relevant to such an answer.

I put first the principle of equity: that courts must provide a remedy in proportion to the injury, so as to make that injured person whole. What Berger and critics of judicial interventionism too often forget is that the courts enter only by way of response to a plaintiff, who alleges he was unlawfully injured and asks restitution. The courts do not "invade" the legislative and administrative realms; they are dragged into them by the failures—of omission and commission—of deficient administrators and negligent legislators, as the treatment of black prisoners in Alabama and Arkansas jails, of mental patients in Willowbrook, and of black schoolchildren still under the operative (though outlawed) "separate but equal" doctrine make only too clear. In all these and similar cases, the Constitution may be colorblind but the remedy cannot be. The black plaintiff before the court has a right to redress, and judges cannot overlook his equity because the available remedies involve judicial legislation and administration, and recognition of his race.

Second, while the principle of equity requires that justice is paramount in the case of a particular individual or class, judges may undermine the *corpus juris* and impair their credibility if they extend that principle unduly, if they apply it to too many cases too much of the time. This maxim, a qualification of the previous point, is a matter of prudence, not of scientific exactitude. It reminds the judge that while he must at times wear the legislator's or administrator's hat, he should not do so regularly. He is primarily a judge, and as such must always look to the preservation and (as far as possible) coherence of the legal system.

An academic analogy may help to make this clear. If a university is a center of intellectual inquiry, and if diverse points of view should be represented to promote that inquiry, it follows that professors of different persuasions should be appointed. It does not follow that a Marxist, Thomist, Republican, Nihilist, Vegetarian, etc. must be placed in every social-science department, only that qualified persons holding such outlooks should, where relevant, be represented in some degree. How many such persons in how many such departments is a contestable question, and no definitive answer can be given. But every university administrator worth his salt is conscious of the validity of this requirement and will (or should) do what he can to meet it.

In these matters experience, not logic, is the ultimate guide. And for this experience court watchers should look not at extreme cases to emphasize what is wrong but at the more numerous moderate or intermediate cases—the continuum—that disclose the governing practice.

Finally, since the Supreme Court is a political and not merely a legal institution, a further test of proper judicial interventionism is the amount of opposition it arouses. Power in a democratic system is an element within a social process, and that process is sustained not only by coercion but by a large measure of consent. For the Court to take a position that alienates popular consent is to ensure the opposition of countervailing powers. A wise and prudent Court does not unnecessarily invite combat; much less does it engage in activities that threaten the community's or its own survival.

This is not to say that the Court should avoid conflict at all costs. There are advantages in conflict; indeed, our system is based on it, for where there is a Constitution there is already a built-in tension between temporary majorities and a Court charged with the maintenance of that Constitution. It is rather to say that judges (and lawyers) need to be political craftsmen and not simply legal technicians. They require training in and knowledge of the social sciences. Otherwise they might well stretch their powers to the breaking point.

VII

Many years ago an English judge, Edward A. Parry, opened his book *The Law and the Poor* (1914) with this sentence: "The rich have many law books written to protect their privileges, but the poor who are the greater nation, have the few."

The blacks all too obviously are the smaller rather than the greater part of the American nation, but they too have fewer books (and lawyers) to protect them. Given the existing state of injustice, Berger would have served a better purpose had he sought effective remedies to promote black rights, not crotchety doctrines to attack alleged judicial wrongs.

8

Justice for Sale:
The Justice of Property vs.
the Property of Justice

In the short time since its publication, Robert Nozick's book, *Anarchy, State, and Utopia*,[1] has received a quite extraordinary reception. Bernard Williams in the London *Times Literary Supplement* (January 17, 1975) described the author and his book as "original, remarkable, and strikingly intelligent," then subjected the work to devastating criticism. Peter Singer in the *New York Review of Books* (March 6, 1975), applauded its "rigorous argument and needle-sharp analysis," then gave a host of reasons belying this judgment. Sheldon Wolin in the *New York Times Book Review* (May 11, 1975) said that "the book is unquestionably a dazzling technical achievement," then treated it with biting contempt. In short, these and other serious critics dislike the book but yield it grudging respect.

Perhaps more extraordinary is the reported fact that President Ford's speechwriters are devouring the book for possible use. In one sense this is not surprising, for Nozick defends property rights and offers what appears to be a profound rationale for extreme individualism. But in another sense this is a mistake, for Nozick's ideas are not conservative but closer to anarchism than a contemporary capitalist (who is clearly also a statist) can abide.

That a technical philosophical work should become a primer for certain politicians is ultimately less consequential than its philosophical import. For a long time utilitarianism (along with perfectionism, whether in its Kantian or Platonic forms) reigned as our dominant philosophical doctrine. But the principle of utility, even as modified by John Stuart Mill, has come increasingly under attack. In the service of the greatest good for the greatest number, it seems to sacrifice individual rights, e.g., freedom, to economic and social welfare. Further, the greatest good is an imprecise standard, leaving room for prudential and therefore diverse judgments; it affronts those who crave certainty in moral and political affairs, especially those who seem to have found this precision and certainty in game theory, decision theory, and other modes of formal analysis. Moreover, the principle of utility does not seem to protect

Reprinted, by permission, from *Dissent* 23 (1976): 72–89.

minorities from the tyranny of a majority seeking (like the Nazis) its greatest pleasure. Hence many contemporary philosophers have either abandoned utilitarianism or sought to revise it. John Rawls's book, *A Theory of Justice*,[2] is perhaps the most ambitious and significant recent effort at this revision, setting forth minimum rules of justice to circumscribe an otherwise utilitarian doctrine. Nozick's book is a full-scale assault on both Rawls and utilitarianism, on both the welfare state and the principle of equality. As such, it challenges contemporary liberalism.

Since, however, I believe the book to be politically naive, philosophically deficient, and historically irrelevant, I find myself in a quandary. I can treat it briefly and perhaps satirically, in which case it might be more instructive to review Nozick's reviewers rather than his book. Or I can seek seriously to demonstrate why I think it is a bad book—which neither demolishes its antagonists nor proposes an adequate alternative—in which case I must deal with it in painstaking detail. In this latter case, however, I cannot—without writing at book length—consider *all* of Nozick's arguments, e.g., his extensive critique of Rawls. I will confine myself instead to the central principles of Nozick's enterprise.

I

The thesis of the book, at least initially, may be stated briefly.

Everything, including freedom and human rights, is for sale. It's only a matter of price.

What each individual has legitimately acquired, he may legitimately transfer. What he is and what he has is his alone to dispose of, provided only that he not interfere with the rights of others, who also may dispose of what they have or are. Each individual is his own sovereign. To oblige him to help others, e.g., through taxation, is nothing less than extortion; it is also "cruel paternalism" to those helped, i.e., maintained in what they have not. The state—if or to the extent that there must be a state— should be no more than a minimal state, limited to the protection of sovereign individuals from force, theft, and fraud, to the enforcement of contracts, and so on. Anything more—"But how *dare* any state or group of individuals do more. Or less."

Lest the reader think this is an inordinately extreme statement of Nozick's views, I add Nozick's blunt assertion that "a free system will allow [an individual] to sell himself into slavery"; indeed, "any individual may contract into any particular constraints over himself." And, what he offers as a simplified version of what he calls the entitlement theory of justice: "*From each as they choose, to each as they are chosen.*"

141   **Justice for Sale:**
The Justice of Property vs.
the Property of Justice

Some Preliminary Observations

First, Nozick's propositions, startling as they may appear, are by no means new. They derive from the 18th-century "invisible hand" theory of Adam Smith; from the 19th-century teachings of Josiah Warren, Stephen Pearl Andrews, Lysander Spooner, and Benjamin R. Tucker—though without the diverse commitments of these thinkers to spiritualism, phrenology, and other fads;[3] and from the present-day writings of Murray Rothbard and other so-called libertarians.

Second, Nozick's book is an exercise in formal, not empirical or causal theory. Those who think that history or sociology or political and economic events have something to do with moral and political philosophy will look in vain for concrete examples taken from those fields. Nozick is concerned only with principles that he believes apply to political and social life, but those principles—both descriptive and normative—flow only as logical deductions and inferences from given axioms. Whether his book demonstrates the strength or aridity of formal theory turns in part on whether or not one believes that a fictional explanation of how a thing—such as rights—may possibly have been produced furthers our understanding more than does a correct explanation of how it was actually produced (or more than does a reasoned account of how it ought to have been produced); and in larger part on the extent to which one agrees with Nozick that economic concepts and models, buttressed by mathematics and game theory, constitute the proper vehicle for the understanding of morals and politics. (A market, like a family, is not a state.)

Third, Nozick must show not only that his principles are correct but also that they are relevant to, that is, can actually be applied in, social and political life.

Moral teachings generally call upon individuals to perform acts contrary to, or to abstain from acts in furtherance of, their traditional ways, customary beliefs, conceived self-interests. This is generally sufficient to denude a teaching of its supporters, if not in espoused principle then certainly in practice. It does not, of course, invalidate that teaching as a standard by which human behavior should be governed and judged, provided that teaching is psychologically feasible, that is, that individuals can actually live according to the stipulations of the creed. Nothing in Nozick's book supports the expectation that this might happen.

Politically, Nozick's creed requires universal or at least general, not partial, consent if it is to be made operative. But in the face of widely opposing philosophies and traditions, and in the absence of coercion (which his libertarian doctrine eschews), that creed cannot hope to gain more than partial consent. To win what little it can through compromise is both insufficient and wrong, for this is to compromise inviolable rights. How, then, does Nozick propose to bring his theory to earth?

Finally, Nozick employs the neutral language of logical or philosophical analysis in the service of nonneutral ideas. This has the inestimable advantage of lulling the reader unfamiliar with the assumptions behind this language to accompany him through a seemingly unbiased argument before he arrives at those ideas. A less innocent terminology would alert an otherwise unwary reader to the fact that Nozick advances nothing less than a radically reactionary doctrine: radical, in that it fundamentally departs from accepted ideas and institutions, whether liberal or conservative; reactionary, in that it calls for a return to (the *concept* of) a world of atomistic individuals, living not in community (with all that this entails) but first in a state of nature and then in enclaves of self-selected protective associations, motivated only by self-interest, and led by an invisible hand to a larger (but narrowly limited) association that "may" be termed a state.

Now for some detail.

II

"Individuals," says Nozick, "have rights, and there are things no person or group may do to them (without violating their rights). . . . [T]he state may not use its coercive apparatus for the purpose of getting some citizens to aid others, or in order to prohibit activities to people for their *own* good or protection."

What is an individual, and how do we know that an individual has rights? What are these rights, and to what extent, if at all, may they be limited? What does it mean to be a citizen, or a member of "the people," as distinct from an individual? Does membership in a community entail no obligations for that community's preservation and welfare? Does an individual who is a member of a community, especially of a "good" or "just" community, retain all the rights he may be said to have had in a state of nature? And what *is* the state of nature?

If it did not actually exist (as it assuredly did not), if it is but a fiction, a hypothetical construct designed to enable us to arrive at a notion of rights through imagination (and reason), why rely on a state-of-nature theory—in particular, on Nozick's version—rather than on the historical realities pertaining to the actual formation and evolution of communities and states? Such questions need to be answered if we are to make sense of Nozick's argument.

Let us begin with the notion of isolated "individuals" in a state of nature. Suppose Adam[4] without Eve, that is, suppose a single organism capable of independent existence, a single person as distinguished from a group. In what sense can such a person be *human*, or exist? Surely only as a physical specimen, not as a moral being, not even one who can reproduce his own kind (and will

143   Justice for Sale:
The Justice of Property vs.
the Property of Justice

therefore very soon be extinct). If he is a rational animal, who is to know this when there is no other person with whom he can communicate? If he has rights (and perhaps obligations), against whom or with respect to what person does he have them when there is no other person to whom he can relate? It is impossible to speak of his individuality, for individuality entails the possession of qualities or characteristics that differentiate him from other human beings, and there are no others.

He becomes human only in relations with others, even if only with one other (Eve) and their progeny. He becomes human because he is then a *social* animal, a member of a community. As the community is enlarged, his humanity and individuality enlarge too. Only then can he begin to assert the notion of (and we can entertain the idea of his having) rights, for rights are claims made against *others*; they require modifications in the behavior of those others toward him. They are claims that those others may not do certain things to him, nor he (presumably) to them.

Insofar as an individual advances those claims, he denies that he, or any other individual, is his own sovereign. He affirms that there are limits on what any person, including himself, may do with respect to another. *Contra* Nozick, who argues that rights "are already possessed by each individual in a state of nature," there is no state of nature, i.e., a world of discrete individuals living independently of each other. Consequently there are no rights in such a state of nature, for there are no others against whom to assert those rights, nor any need for others or for the assertion of rights.

To the extent that an individual can claim rights, it is only because he is an individual within society and only because other individuals respect (or ought to respect) those claims, which makes them not individual but social rights— rights perhaps necessary to the development of individuality. If we use the term "individual rights," it is simply as shorthand for this conception. All rights are social rights.

It may be said that a state of nature does not mean the absence of society but only the absence of *civil* society, that is, of government, a state. But this is to mistake the nature of government and does nothing to salvage Nozick's notion of individual rights.

Government exists everywhere—in the family, the group, the larger association. Always there are rules that govern the relations of individuals to each other, even in the smallest unit, the family—rules, for example, concerning sex (such as the ban on incest), property (such as clothing or tools), and the socialization (education) of the young. And always there is an authoritative power to enforce those rules, whether a parent or priest or king or elected official. In this sense every society is a civil society, for every society is governed. And what rights one has as an individual one has only by virtue of the fact that they are rights recognized, i.e., *given* to individuals, by the society of which they are members. One may of course claim as rights things one does not yet possess but believes—as a matter of moral law or in accord with one's conception of one's nature as a human being—one should possess; but however conceived—whether as actual rights or moral claims—these remain rights within a social context; they are among the rules by which men and women are (or ought to be) governed.

Let us, however, waive the fictitious nature of the state of nature and of the supposed social compact by which individuals are held to be obliged to respect each other's rights or to obey some sort of sovereign (whether this be the doctrine of Hobbes or Locke or Rousseau). What sort of obligation is it that binds me to a promise made by some unknown ancestors? By what "right" do I lose *my* "right" to enter into promises of my own? Why indeed should I be bound to keep any promise, whether by others or by myself? Surely it cannot be because someone, somewhere, at some now-forgotten time decided this was the way individuals should live together in civil or political society; that property (as John Locke for example would have it) should be acquired in such a way and be transferred in such a manner, and that property so acquired and transferred is an individual right that cannot be transgressed. (Would one really feel bound by the agreement of some 17th- or 18th-century ancestors that two of their 20th-century progeny, one decidedly unsavory to the other, should now be married?) It can only be because I and others recognize that certain arrangements and practices, including promise-keeping (though not of course without regard to extenuating circumstances),[5] are necessary to the maintenance of a common life, of society; that they promote the interests of the society, and of the individuals who compose it; that we should therefore be bound to respect certain arrangements and practices, including rights, lest we suffer mischievous consequences. We do not then need a state-of-nature theory at all. Nor are we bound by rights and promises supposed to exist in that fictional state.

Nozick's entitlement theory, which relies heavily on a modified version of Locke's state-of-nature teaching, seeks to escape some of these obvious difficulties by substituting for the social compact doctrine the notion of self-generating protective associations. But this substitution deviates in no way from the fundamental principle of the social compact: that rights men possess in the state of nature are transferred to a collective agency only through an initial agreement (or purchase).

Thus the entitlement theory remains doubly flawed at the outset: it builds on a fictitious and unexamined individualist conception of the origins of rights; and it looks only to the origins of rights and not also to their purposes and consequences for their justification.

145   Justice for Sale:
The Justice of Property vs.
the Property of Justice

III

Individuals, I have argued, cannot be understood apart from community. To remove that social context and talk only of individuals and their unassailable rights is to operate in an unreal world.

No rights are, or can be held, inviolable. Consequently, rights—which entail duties and obligations on the part of others, e.g., to respect those rights and perhaps to do what may be necessary to render them actual—are held at the sufferance of the community, because the community believes those rights are essential and are necessarily subject to limitation according to circumstance and the community's conception of the common good and the good man.

It is meaningless to waive these considerations in order to be able to talk of rights in a state of nature. For what can it mean to speak (as Nozick does) of a right to property in the state of nature? Property is not a thing (say a timepiece or a plot of land) but *ownership*—already a social concept—of that thing. And ownership is not merely possession or use of that thing, for then anyone can take it and by using it make it his own, which reduces ownership to a matter of preponderant force. Ownership is a *legal*, or (if we must talk of a state of nature) socially sanctioned, right. As such, it requires moral (or social) justification, as Proudhon well understood when he argued that private property is theft.

By what "right," then, can an individual acquire property?

Suppose it were technologically possible to bottle up all the air. Would we recognize a single person's "right" to do so, either by initial acquisition (appropriation) or by purchase, and to sell it to others who otherwise could not live? Suppose one man claimed ownership of all the drinkable water, or all the land, so that no one else could drink or find a place on which to stand, save at the owner's sufferance. Would this be acceptable? Suppose instead of but a single person such ownership were divided among a few individuals. Would this be any more acceptable? Assuredly this (at least with respect to some water and a great deal of land) has been done; but by what *right*—even in a state of nature?

It will not do to say, as Nozick does at one point, that this is precluded in any practical sense because the scarcer a substance becomes that others want, "the higher the price of the rest will go, and the more difficult it will become for him to acquire it all." It is patently absurd to rest such a determination on economic considerations alone. More important, by introducing such terms as money and price, the issue is moved out of the state of nature and into civil society, into community. What Nozick requires is a theory that will justify a right to property within the state of nature.

Nor will it do for Nozick to rely on the Lockean proviso that there be "enough, and as good left in common for others," which he interprets to mean that the situation of others is not worsened, as it would be, for example, if someone was the first to come upon the only water in a desert and appropriated it all. Why shouldn't the situation be worsened for others if there are only "individual rights," and how can the situation of others be anything but worsened if a portion of the earth is taken from them?

In an all-too-neglected chapter in the first edition of his *Social Statics*, entitled "The Right to the Use of the Earth," Herbert Spencer—whom Nozick cites approvingly in another context but conveniently ignores here—argued that equity does not permit private property in land:

> For if *one* portion of the earth's surface may justly become the posses-
> sion of an individual, and may be held by him for his sole use and ben-
> efit, as a thing to which he has an exclusive right, then other portions of
> the earth's surface may be so held; and eventually the *whole* of the
> earth's surface may be so held; and our planet may thus lapse altogether
> into private hands. Observe now the dilemma to which this leads. Sup-
> posing the entire habitable globe to be so enclosed, it follows that if the
> landowners have a valid right to its surface, all who are not landowners,
> have no right at all to its surface. Hence, such can exist on the earth by
> sufferance only. They are all trespassers. Save by the permission of the
> lords of the soil, they can have no room for the soles of their feet. Nay,
> should the others think fit to deny them a resting-place, these landless
> men might equitably be expelled from the earth altogether. If, then, the
> assumption that land can be held as property, involves that the whole
> globe may become the private domain of a part of its inhabitants; and if,
> by consequence, the rest of its inhabitants can then exercise their facul-
> ties—can then exist even—only by consent of the landowners; it is man-
> ifest, that an exclusive possession of the soil necessitates an infringement
> of the law of equal freedom. For, men who cannot "live and move and
> have their being" without the leave of others, cannot be equally free
> with those others.[6]

Nor is this all. If (Spencer continues) we move from the possible to the actual, we find still less reason to uphold the rectitude of property in land. *No existing titles to property are legitimate.* Why? Because the sources from which such titles are derived are "violence, fraud, the prerogative of force, the claims of superior cunning." Since no valid claims can thus be constituted, the sale or bequest of such holdings is equally invalid. It is equally impossible, Spencer further maintains, "to discover any mode in which land *can* become private property," for what belongs to the human race cannot be claimed or appor-tioned by any one generation; else "men born after a certain date are doomed to slavery." The land—all the land—belongs only to society.

147   Justice for Sale:
The Justice of Property vs.
the Property of Justice

But what of Locke's contention that

> Though the Earth, and all inferior Creatures be common to all Men, yet every Man has a *Property* in his own *Person*. This no Body has any Right to but himselfe. The *Labour* of his Body, and the *Work* of his Hands, we may say, are properly his. Whatsoever then he removes out of the State that Nature hath provided, and left it in, he hath mixed his *Labour* with, and joyned to it something that is his own, and thereby makes it his *Property*. It being by him removed from the common state Nature placed it in, hath by this *labour* something annexed to it, that excludes the common right of other Men. For this *Labour* being the unquestionable Property of the Labourer, no Man but he can have a right to what that is once joyned to, at least where there is enough, and as good left in common for others.[7]

This argument, so impressive to Nozick, leaves Spencer utterly cold. In the first place, Spencer argues, if the earth is common to all men, the consent of all men must obviously be required before any article can rightfully be removed from the state that nature has provided. To say that a man has mixed his labor with the land is to ignore the question: By what right did he gather, or mix his labor with, that which belongs to mankind at large? In the second place, to claim that any article of property is valid only "where there is enough, and as good left in common for others," is to raise a host of queries. How do we know that "enough" is left in common for others? Who is to determine whether what is left is "as good" as what was taken? If there is not enough left in common for others, how should the right of appropriation be exercised? Why, in such cases, does the mixing of one's labor with the acquired property cease to exclude "the common right of other men"? Suppose "enough" is attainable, but not all is equally "good," by what rule must each man choose? In short, Spencer argues, it is impossible, under state-of-nature conditions, to establish the rightness of such appropriation.

"Justice in holdings," Nozick says, "is historical; it depends upon what actually has happened." I should like to see his (or any other) account of *that* history. It is certainly not given here. What we are offered instead is a wildly implausible rendering of acquisitions in an alleged state of nature.

Can we then look to a moral (if not a historical) basis for his conception of individual rights? Alas, no, for "this book," Nozick admits, "does not present a precise theory of the moral basis of individual rights." On what foundation, then, does his theory of property rights, and consequently his entitlement theory of justice, rest? It is indeed a sad theory of justice that cannot itself be shown, either on historical or moral grounds, to be just.

IV

It would serve no useful purpose to analyze in similar detail Nozick's state-of-nature theory with respect to other rights, e.g., liberty. Among other things, a right to property is a right *over* liberty as much as (and perhaps more than) a right in the service of liberty. In any case, as Spencer has shown, in the state of nature it is incompatible with the equal liberty of others. If liberty and property are to be defended as rights—and it is scarcely surprising that Nozick excludes *equality* as one of his individual rights—that defense must look to an alternative mode of justification, e.g., to a theory of natural right (Aristotle) or natural law (Aquinas) or utility (J.S. Mill), in any event to a theory rooted in man as a social animal.[8] It must also build, not on the empty notion of liberty as a totality, but on the more realistic understanding of liberty as a complex of particular liberties and concomitant restraints, in which some liberties are necessarily curtailed in the service of more esteemed liberties. This in turn requires a theory of the proper hierarchy of liberties and of the relation of those liberties to other values, always within the social context of varying circumstances. This sort of theoretical inquiry is notably lacking in Nozick's book.

What needs now to be remarked, instead, is that Nozick's state-of-nature theory, which is a device to provide plausible (indeed necessary) grounds for his theory of individual rights, misreads (and therefore misuses) the crucial purpose that such a theory was designed to serve: namely, to discover the true nature of human nature. One does not discover this by assertion, certainly not by asserting the validity of another's (e.g., Locke's) assertion.[9] Nor can he discover this in history, for in this conception the nature of man must be discerned in what man is (or is thought to be) prior to history, prior to convention or accident or human design. One can only discover this through reason, that is, by imagining what man would be like were he in something that might be called a state of nature and by reasoning about the qualities or characteristics of man in that prehistorical, precivil state. It is one of the more obvious deficiencies of Nozick's book that, though he avoids a historical investigation into man's nature (even while he claims, but nowhere demonstrates, that his account is historically correct), he does not in fact reason about man's nature at all. He merely asserts that man's nature is what he proclaims it to be.[10]

This is decidedly not what Hobbes, who employed a state-of-nature theory (in Part One of *Leviathan*), did, and for good reason. He wanted to know what man was like in order to answer the question: Why should such a man—independent and equal and unbound by political (but not by *natural*) laws—want to enter into civil society? Why should he surrender some of his liberty, much of his equality, and all of his independence, and willingly submit to a civil authority?

149   Justice for Sale:
The Justice of Property vs.
the Property of Justice

The answer, Hobbes said, is fear. Since no man is so much stronger than another, or a combination of others, as to be secure in his life, he seeks protection. To save his life, to escape an untimely death, he willingly gives up all his alleged rights—except, obviously, his right to self-preservation.

Unlike Hobbes, Nozick attempts no detailed and incisive analysis of human nature in the state of nature. He recognizes, to be sure, that fear is a major motive for men to join together into protective associations; but what he makes primary is not fear of death but love of property, and hence the Lockean protection of one's "rights," above all, the right to one's property; for what Nozick incredibly believes is that man is an economic, not a social or political animal. Hence, what unites men, what leads them to form a community (or to join a protective association), is not (in Nozick's view) their common interest, their equality, in avoiding death and seeking peace, but avarice, the rational pursuit of self-interest, the grim determination to retain what holdings they have.

I set aside Nozick's neglect of the still earlier contention by classical philosophers (e.g., Socrates) that every sane man seeks not profit but justice, what is right by nature—by the nature of man, not by the state of nature. I set aside, too, his failure to address himself to the ensuing conflict between Socrates and Hobbes as to what is truly natural, or truly right by nature, and how this is properly to be known. I cannot set aside, however, Nozick's easy assumption that it is enough to adopt and restate (albeit in somewhat modified form) Locke's view of man in the state of nature. Why not the image of man given us by Hobbes (or Rousseau), all the more so since without fear there would be no need for Nozick's protective associations? Why not, then, *all* of Hobbes? Why, instead, Locke? Surely a philosopher needs to set forth reasons that would confirm the validity of Locke's portrait. Without such reasons that notion of human nature is no more than a statement of arbitrary preference. Indeed, it gives rise to the suspicion that Nozick embraces it only (or largely) because it is a premise required by the conclusions he wishes to reach.

That Nozick does not give reasons, and that the suspicion I have articulated is warranted, is attested to by Nozick's curious statement explaining (justifying?) his choice of Locke's vision. Since descriptions of individuals in the state of nature are in any case problematic, it will not do (he argues) to select the most pessimistic, or *worst*, rendering of that state; nor the most optimistic, or *best*; but rather the most *moderate*, one in which "people generally satisfy moral constraints and generally act *as they ought*" (my italics). This now introduces an external (moral) standard by which to judge whether individuals behave moderately, *as they should*. In view of Nozick's later rejection of what he calls "end-result principles," that is, principles by which actions are judged in terms of given ends or consequences, it is difficult to see how Nozick can make any judgment concerning the rightness or wrongness of individual or group behavior in the state of nature, or how he can term any such state best or worst or moderate. The state of nature is what it is; individuals in that state are what they are; the state-of-nature theorist can only discover and describe these things. To select from among them only those practices (or that reading of those practices) that yield the principles he wishes to deduce from them, and then to employ those principles as moral criteria by which to judge those practices is an elementary circular fallacy.

V

If Nozick has neither proved nor offered a plausible case for his theory of individual (primarily property) rights and individual sovereignty, the huge and intricate edifice he then seeks to construct on this foundation can be no more than a house of cards. To show that this is so, let us look at the three major themes of the ensuing doctrine: the notion of protective agencies and their development (without violation of anyone's rights) into a dominant association that is *de facto* a state; the entitlement theory of justice that limits that state's activities to no more than the minimal or nightwatchman role ascribed to it by late 18th- and early 19th-century economic theory; and the utopianism (or inspiring ideal) claimed for this sort of social organization.

Nozick begins by asking, Why the state? For him this is *the* fundamental question of political philosophy. One might suppose then that he would consider some of the more obvious answers that have been put forward in the history of political philosophy—e.g., the notion (in Plato's *Republic*) that the state came into being in response to natural needs; or the idea (in a long tradition from Aristotle to MacIver) that this is not really a serious question at all, since government naturally and necessarily exists wherever there is a social entity—the family, the tribe, the city, etc.; or the Marxist contention (forcefully argued by Franz Oppenheimer) that "The State, completely in its genesis . . . is a social institution, forced by a victorious group of men on a defeated group, with the sole purpose of . . . economic exploitation" [and securing itself against revolt and war].[11] But Nozick does not mention, let alone discuss, these or other traditional views. He presents only Locke versus the anarchists, surely a most curious estimate of what is important in the tradition of political philosophy.

Against the anarchists, who argue that no state can be moral because every state violates individual rights, Nozick wants to show that the minimal state can be and in fact is moral precisely because it comes into being, and persists, without any such violation of rights. He seeks to show this by building on Locke's "inconveniences of the state of nature" and by introducing the notion of protective associations.

151   Justice for Sale:
The Justice of Property vs.
the Property of Justice

Locke's inconveniences derive from the fact that in the state of nature some persons violate the rights of others. In response to this, Locke holds that everyone, acting alone or in concert with others, has a right to defend himself and punish the transgressors; hence *"Civil Government* is the proper remedy."[12]

Nozick concurs in all but the remedy. He argues, instead, that civil government need not come into being as a conscious and deliberate response to those inconveniences, but that it can (and does) emerge as an unconscious and unplanned consequence of a series of intermediate arrangements within the state of nature. These intermediate arrangements are the voluntary devices and agreements persons might reach while acting within their rights. In a state of nature an individual may himself enforce his rights, and others may join with him in his defense. Groups of individuals may thus form "mutual-protection associations." To resolve difficulties that attend such simple associations— e.g., that "cantankerous or paranoid members" might seek to use the association to violate the rights of others, or members of the same association may be in dispute with each other—these protective associations "will use some [any? or only a "just"?] procedure to determine how to act." In any case, "some people will be *hired* to perform protective functions, and some entrepreneurs will go into the business of selling protective services. Different sorts of protective policies would be offered, at different prices, for those who may desire more extensive or elaborate protection."[13]

Such protective associations will doubtless come into conflict with each other, where they operate within the same geographical area and seek to enforce the claims of their respective clients. The stronger agency will obviously prevail; it will also attract the clients of the losing or subordinate agency. In this way the strongest agency becomes the dominant association. As such, it provides a common system that judges between the competing claims of all the persons in its geographical area "and *enforces* their rights." Nozick (after Adam Smith) calls this an invisible-hand explanation; for without agreement or design, every individual seeking only his own gain is "led by an invisible hand to promote an end which was no part of his intention."

Nozick believes that this dominant protective association is not only a state but that it is a morally legitimate state. He believes this because the dominant association may properly "judge any procedure of justice to be applied to its clients" and properly defend its clients against "a procedure that it finds to be unreliable or unfair." Since it may thus punish the punisher of its clients and not allow anyone else to defend against its own procedures, the dominant agency—even while not claiming a monopoly—clearly comes to occupy "a unique position by virtue of its power. It, and it alone, enforces prohibitions on others' procedures of justice, *as it sees fit.* . . . It alone is in a position to act solely *by its own lights"* (my italics). The dominant agency thus enjoys a *de facto* monopoly of the right to enforce rights.

The legitimacy of this monopoly derives from two alleged facts: the powers of the association "are merely the sum of the individual rights that its members or clients transfer to the association . . . the agency protects those nonclients in its territory whom it prohibits from using self-help enforcement procedures on its clients," which it is "morally required" to do by the principle of compensation. Thus the dominant association, which now enjoys a monopoly of force and extends its reach to all in its territorial domain, is a state that violates no one's rights.

Among the many things that might be said concerning this extraordinary argument, I limit myself to but a few points.

1. It is not at all clear why only one—rather than two or more likely three—dominant protective association will emerge from the process Nozick describes. I say more likely three because, as Orwell understood in *1984*, if there were only two, a conflict between them would reduce the loser to a subordinate role or eliminate it completely; while if there were three, the third would enter to do battle with the enfeebled victor, thereby leaving the vanquished time and opportunity in which to recover, so that it may take on the new victor in turn. In this way irrational men can continue the enjoyable process of mutual slaughter to the end of time. Neither stability nor peace but perpetual strife, as Hobbes might have taught Nozick, is the characteristic feature of the state of nature. By what reason—historical or logical—*dare* Nozick presume the inevitable outcome will be a single dominant agency?

2. If, however, a single association were to become the dominant agency, it would rule by imposed fiat, on the obvious principle—since Nozick holds this rule is legitimate—that might makes right. Now Nozick says that he does not wish to assume or claim that might makes right. But since he looks not to purposes or consequences but only to origins, he must accept this absurd argument. And he does. For, even as he deprecates the claim that might makes right he argues that it is might alone that enables the dominant protective association to enforce its prohibitions against an opposing but weaker agency. "[M]ight does make enforced prohibitions, even if no one thinks the mighty have a *special* entitlement to have realized in the world their own view of which prohibitions are correctly enforced." Precisely: the mighty do not have a special entitlement; they have only the ordinary entitlement attached to each individual, and by grant of individuals to a protective association, to realize that individual's (or association's) view. What is required for anyone to realize his view is clearly power; hence the reign of the most powerful. And this is "right," Nozick believes, because as against a small agency, the dominant

153   Justice for Sale:
The Justice of Property vs.
the Property of Justice

agency, "having a greater number of individual entitlements, . . . has a greater entitlement."

Not only does Nozick thus commit himself to the doctrine that might makes right. What is worse (for his theory), he also commits himself to the principle of equality. For only if entitlements are equal can a greater number of entitlements make for a greater entitlement. Without equality, a greater number merely makes for a greater (or larger) number; if the numbers are not equal, if one counts for more than one, a greater number may in fact add up to a lesser number. Since Nozick rejects the idea of equality,[14] on what grounds may the dominant agency claim it has a right to be dominant?

3. Let us look more closely, and realistically, at the nature of this dominant protective association. Will it in fact protect the rights of its clients? Does its power come to no more than the sum of the rights ceded to it by its clients? May we reasonably apply to the entrepreneurs and hired mercenaries of the protective agency what Nozick assumes of mankind: "that generally people will do what they are morally required to do"? And if the answers to such questions are in some measure unfavorable, what instruments or arrangements has Nozick built into these associations that will ensure their right (i.e., limited) functioning, their legitimate behavior? Who or what, in short, will control the controllers of power should they (when they) exceed or abuse the powers entrusted to them?

An entity is always more than the sum of its parts. Ten determined men acting jointly constitute a far more formidable force, certainly physically (since might is an issue here), than do ten determined men acting each for himself. And a protective association, hiring mercenaries to enforce the rights of its clients and headed by an entrepreneurial *condottiere*, constitutes a far greater power than do the members (or the sum of those members) of the association. It may or may not be true that the legitimate rights of the association are no more than the sum of the individual rights that have been assigned to it. It is certainly not true, as Nozick asserts, that "the legitimate powers of a protective association are merely the *sum* of the individual rights that its members or clients transfer to the association." Nozick all too easily substitutes powers for rights in this equation, and this is patently illegitimate. The rights may be the same, but the powers are overwhelmingly different.

Even the rights, however, may not be the same. If A has the right to do X, and B has the right to do Y, then an association in which A and B are members has the right to do both X and Y, which we may call Z. Neither A nor B individually has the right to do Z, but the association now has that right, because it includes both A and B. Since the association now has the right to do Z, it may clearly exercise this right on behalf of both A and B, thereby giving each of them a right that neither had before (giving Y to A, and X to B). But how can any person or collection of persons give an individual a right to which he was not himself entitled? Clearly, only because the association gives it to him. Then the association becomes a source or distributor of rights, or at least a mechanism through which an individual may acquire, if not a right, access to or protection of a right possessed by another.

Thus, both the powers and the rights of the association are indeed more than the sum of individual powers and rights.[15] And this has portentous implications.

For we now know, from historical experience and organizational theory, quite a bit about the behavior of associations. We now know that all associations, at least with the range of power with which we are concerned here, have more than the single purpose for which they were ostensibly created. They exist not only to carry out the functions assigned to them, but also to promote the interests of those who control and serve them—the leaders and the bureaucracy. Those interests are primarily the survival and expansion of the association. Indeed, this last is actually required by Nozick's theory, which expects and even demands that the initial small protective association seek to become the dominant association.

The purpose of the association will not only inevitably be corrupted by the nature of the bureaucracy. It will be subverted, even more, by the leaders of the association. For what will those leaders do when a situation arises in which, called upon to defend the rights of their clients, they risk self-annihilation or—more mildly—put their power and positions in jeopardy? Doubtless some will readily sacrifice all for a right cause, but history is replete with contrary instances.

Similarly, the leaders may fail to protect their clients' rights even in less irksome situations, where the inconveniences attached to such protection are more than they wish to bear. It is, after all, no easy matter to defend the legitimate claim of a less influential client against the competing claim of a more prestigious or powerful client. Since individuals buy their membership in the association, i.e., they pay fees or purchase (as it were) life-insurance or property-insurance policies, is it really to be expected that the claims of poorer clients will be respected as much as will the claims of wealthier clients, especially when they are competing? Or, since the dominant agency is charged with the protection of nonclients as well, is it to be believed that they will receive equal consideration and treatment with the fee-paying members of the association, and be given compensation, as is "morally required"? Merely to ask these questions is to indicate the inadequacy of Nozick's invisible-hand explanation; for to the extent that the invisible hand operates at all, it may well lead individuals to promote an evil end that was no part of their intention.

How, then, do the members of the association control the corrupters of power? What restraints or controls, if any, are imposed on them to assure the correct performance of their duties?

155   Justice for Sale:
The Justice of Property vs.
the Property of Justice

The reader will look in vain in Nozick's book for the answers to these questions. In a work of some 350 pages purported to be a contribution to political and moral philosophy, no more than two or three pages even touch these obvious questions of political power. And those pages focus not on the dominant protective association but on the modern state (what he calls "the nonneutral state"). Here is his one crucial passage:

> The illegitimate use of a state by economic interests for their own ends is based upon a preexisting illegitimate power of the state to enrich some persons at the expense of others. Eliminate *that* illegitimate power of giving differential economic benefits and you eliminate or drastically restrict the motive for wanting political influence. True, some persons still will thirst for political power, finding intrinsic satisfaction in dominating others. The minimal state best reduces the chances of such takeover or manipulation of the state by persons desiring power or economic benefits, especially if combined with a reasonably alert citizenry, since it is the minimally desirable target for such takeover or manipulation. Nothing much is to be gained by doing so, and the cost to the citizens if it occurs is minimized.[16]

To argue that the thirst for domination is essentially inconsequential in the minimal state, because the prize is minimal, is to ignore not only the immense power and economic benefits attached even to that minimal state (if there were such a state) in the modern world—if we think, say, only of national defense and the contracts and profits this brings—but also to scant the most rudimentary propositions set forth in textbooks and monographs on the psychology and sociology of power. Wherever, and in whatever form, power exists, men will strive to obtain it. However small the range of that power, men will exercise it and seek to enlarge it. The lust for power, for ever-increasing power, is insatiable. And power once acquired gives rise to innumerable temptations, so strong and pervasive as to have led a host of political philosophers—e.g., Montesquieu, Madison, Tocqueville, John Stuart Mill—to warn against its corrosive effects, and to seek for principles and arrangements that might curb and control the abuses and misuses of power. Nozick's failure to come to grips with these crucial problems is but another indication of the political irrelevance of his theory of justice.

4. Insofar as Nozick seeks to meet these sorts of political problems, he does so by an extended disquisition on procedural rights and what he calls "reliable" procedures. But these, whatever their intrinsic merit, are irrelevant to the issue; for it is not Nozick who decides and institutionalizes such procedures for the protective association; it is the association that judges which procedures are reliable or unreliable ("calling them as it sees them"), that applies the principle and has "the muscle to do so," that alone "is in a position to act solely by its own lights." Why, then, should the association adopt Nozick's conception of a

reliable procedure rather than one that better serves its needs, as it sees this? It is not only the judge in its own case. By Nozick's own argument, it is *legitimately* the judge in its own case. Hence private interests determine what Locke called "The Publick Good." Indeed, the Good is whatever the dominant private interest proclaims it to be. Justice, then, as Thrasymachus said, is nothing else than the interest (at least the conceived interest, the stated and enforced will) of the strongest. And Nozick's state, his morally legitimate state, appears to be no more than a variant of Marx's state: an instrument through which a ruling class secures its domination.

Nozick could, perhaps, salvage much of his argument by insisting either (i) that the dominant protective association must adopt his "reliable" procedures, or (ii) that any system of justice—however conceived and however harsh—is better than none; that is, that a state in which the principles of, and procedural rights associated with, justice are known and therefore predictable, is preferable to tyranny, where justice is arbitrary and unpredictable. But the logic of his argument prevents him from advancing either of these arguments, and he doesn't. For one thing, he would then have to deny the principle of entitlement, which holds that an individual may do with himself and his possessions as he will, provided only that he not violate the rights of others—and we now understand that it is he, through his protective association, who decides whether or not he has violated another person's rights, and what should be done about it. More important, were Nozick to advance either or both of these arguments, he would have to hold that it is proper to make judgments in terms of end-result principles; and these he explicitly rejects. I turn now to his reasons for doing so.

VI

The entitlement theory of justice is historical: "whether a distribution is just depends upon how it came about"; consequently, "*any* set of holdings that emerges from a legitimate process . . . is just" (my italics). In contrast, end-result principles "hold that the justice of a distribution is determined by how things are distributed (who has what) as judged by some *structural* principle(s) of just distribution."

Here—perhaps for the only time in the book—Nozick offers a strikingly realistic (at least hypothetically realistic) case to buttress the argument for his entitlement theory. He says:

> . . . suppose that Wilt Chamberlain is greatly in demand by basketball teams, being a great gate attraction. (Also suppose contracts run for only a year, with players being free agents.) He signs the following sort of contract with a team: In each home game, twenty-five cents from the

157   Justice for Sale:
The Justice of Property vs.
the Property of Justice

price of each ticket of admission goes to him. . . . The season starts, and people cheerfully attend his team's games; they buy their tickets, each time dropping a separate twenty-five cents of their admission price into a special box with Chamberlain's name on it. They are excited about seeing him play; it is worth the total admission price to them. Let us suppose that in one season one million persons attend his home games, and Wilt Chamberlain winds up with $250,000, a much larger sum than the average income and larger even than anyone else has. Is he entitled to this income? Is this new distribution . . . unjust? If so, why?[17]

If each person in this situation was entitled to control the resources he held, the fact that he freely chose to give 25 cents of his money to Chamberlain—rather than (say) spending it on candy bars—is just. That inequalities eventuate from such a gift to, or exchange with, Wilt Chamberlain is (Nozick argues) no legitimate ground for complaint; for where men are entitled to X (say the money they have earned), they may justly transfer that X, or a share of that X, to another. To deny that right of transfer (say under socialism) is "to forbid capitalist acts between consenting adults." Hence, any end result or patterned principle of redistributive justice entails interference with another person's liberty and thus violates his rights.

Consider taxation. This not merely deprives people of the right to choose what to do with what they have. Even more: "Taxation of earnings from labor is on a par with forced labor . . . [T]aking the earnings of n hours labor is like taking n hours from that person; it is like forcing the person to work n hours for another's purpose." This too is a clear violation of that person's rights; for no one (Nozick holds) may interfere with another person's right to choose from among the constrained set of options available to him. Each person has a right to decide what he would make of himself and what to do, and to reap the benefits accordingly. And what is true of taxation on earnings is true of taxation on interest, entrepreneurial profits, and so on. "Individuals are ends and not merely means; they may not be sacrificed or used for the achieving of other ends without their consent. Individuals are inviolable."

Hence, as both examples demonstrate, no state beyond the minimal state can be justified. No end-result principles are warranted.[18]

Intuitively, one feels there is much to be said for Nozick's view. One wishes to do what he will with what he has. To interfere with him, to tell him that he *must* give some of his earnings to others or to this or that cause, that he may not do with his earnings what he wishes to do (e.g., buy what others believe to be noxious things like liquor and drugs), seems to violate his autonomy.

But in the real and unequal world, many do not have sufficient earnings, or any earnings, to buy the things they need or would like—say a ticket to a basketball game, with or without the added tax for Wilt Chamberlain. A woman may marry a hard-working but low-income-earning man who dies and leaves her with several children. Are she and they "entitled" only to suffer misery? What if a man sells himself into slavery? Do his children go with him into bondage? It is surely a strange notion of justice that exempts the rich and the better-off from responsibility to the less-fortunate. Surely outcomes cannot really be irrelevant to a well-founded theory of justice.

1. Suppose one were to hold, as I do, that on Nozick's terms (though not necessarily on other terms) *no* property rights are legitimate. No one has properly appropriated land that he may call his own. Consequently no one may legitimately transfer such land, or a portion of that land, to another. And no one may legitimately use the proceeds from that property, or from products directly or indirectly resulting from that property, to buy anything.

Suppose one were also to hold, with a Biblical teaching, that to lend money at interest—any interest—to a fellow human being in need is usury and therefore immoral. Or argue, as a humanist, that to earn money from investment that involves exploitation of or harm to others, is also unjust.

To justify *some* lending of money at interest (e.g., that in capitalist systems the lending of money is a form of investment, or part of a credit system necessary to business enterprise), Nozick would have to distinguish types of persons, and types of situations, where such lending is legitimate from those persons and situations where it is not. He would also have to consider what is an appropriate (just) rate of interest. He does not do this, in part because the entitlement theory does not call for it but actually excludes it as a legitimate concern. Whatever a person legitimately has, he may do with it as he will. Outcomes are indeed irrelevant. So too with the problem of earnings from investment.

For Benjamin Tucker, and now for Nozick, to mind your own business is the primary moral law; to interfere with another's business is the primary crime. But if, as I suggest, *no one* (on Nozick's terms) has a legitimate claim to a business in property, then no one has a business of his own to mind, or a right initially to acquire or later to transfer that business through sale or bequest, or a right to "hold" the business and what he has "earned" from it. Then it decidedly becomes someone else's business to interfere. It becomes society's business to reclaim its property and use it for the social good.

2. Here Nozick's principle of rectification comes into play. If the principles of acquisition and of transfer have been violated—as I contend—then end-result or patterned principles of distributive justice properly enter. As Nozick puts it: "then a *rough* rule of thumb for rectifying injustices might seem to be the following: organize society so as to maximize the position of whatever

159   Justice for Sale:
The Justice of Property vs.
the Property of Justice

group ends up least well-off in the society." I take this properly to apply to *all* existing societies where private property in land is still an operating principle.

3. In this way, on Nozick's own terms, the notion of community is reintroduced. Rectification requires a society of persons held together by a sense of common identity and hence of some common interests. Racial, religious, and ethnic discrimination—which Nozick ignores—is not a matter of private but of public interest; its elimination is crucial if all individuals are to be equally members of the community. Hence it requires a common Authority to deal with it. War, whatever its origins, is not something to be left to a dominant association's notion of which prohibitions it may properly enforce, but becomes central to the community's survival. Since all are affected, all must share—in the determination, conduct, and resolution of the war. If some are uneducated, or inadequately educated (as in the poorer states), this deprives them of what is necessary for their development as individuals; and where a community is concerned with this value for all its members, this too becomes a matter of the public interest. If life itself is precious, so that communities provide police and fire protection, sewage disposal systems and garbage collectors, lifeguards at beaches and hospitals, and the like—without regard to wealth or station—then this too becomes a matter of community concern and action. And so with the things that are necessary to life—food, clothing, shelter, medical care, etc.

To be sure, there is need for liberty—for areas of privacy within which, or situations in which, individuals must be left alone in order to cultivate their unique qualities and implement their diverse desires. A careful analysis of the legitimate domains of the individual and the community is surely essential. But this analysis, not to speak of its applications in practical affairs, cannot be left solely to those who have "holdings," to the dominant private interest. The rich—who would then surely combine into a protective association and "buy" the most powerful "enforcers"—can hardly be entrusted with the welfare or rights of the poor; indeed, why should they in Nozick's theory? Who, then, will take care of the widows, the orphans, the infirm, the less powerful, the poor?

Nozick would have them look to themselves, or—since many are unworthy objects of sale, whether of their labor or their bodies (and souls)—to the charity of the affluent. Since he is not concerned with outcomes, the obvious consequences (as we have experienced them) cannot trouble him. But even if we think only of individuals, as Nozick does, and not of community, is it really a matter of indifference to the rich that they live surrounded by poverty and misery and urban and rural blight? Is this the kind of world that is pleasant or productive for them and their children? Is it even safe for them? To invoke Aristotle yet again, it was the awareness of this danger, this threat to the stability of the state, that led him to warn against a too-great division between the rich and the poor, lest rebellion ensue. Does Nozick really think a protective association can do everything with bayonets, even sit on them? Is not will, the will of all—rather than force, enforcing the will of a few—the true basis of a state?

From this standpoint, taxation is not extortion but a necessary device to insure the welfare of the community, including its dominant members—even, if need be, against their will. For it is not a choice between we and they; it is a matter of us all. This is why an economic conservative like Justice Holmes could cheerfully say: "With taxes I buy civilization." And from this standpoint the ludicrousness of the Wilt Chamberlain episode becomes patent. The question is not whether an individual—the ticket-buyer—may do what he will with what he has, or even whether a state committed to equality may use coercive measures to prevent any inequalities from reappearing. The question is, first, to assure that all have the means to provide themselves with the necessities of life, and then to allow the freedom to make choices among the leisure activities, the luxuries of life—though the question must surely remain open whether a just society should not limit the otherwise bizarre consequences to which such freedom might lead, e.g., Chamberlain or a movie star receiving an income even greater than that of the president of the United States! Here, as everywhere, crucial distinctions must be drawn.

4. This brings me, finally, to the issue of freedom and human rights, of justice for sale. Nozick makes much of rights, and properly so; but in his extreme individualist version those rights are operative in the real world only for those who can afford them, who are in an economic position where they need not sacrifice them. For the rest, those rights are up for grabs, for sale. And by any standard of justice other than Nozick's, this is sheer madness.

Rights, especially the rights to life and liberty, are too precious to be sold. Even Locke proclaimed against the right to sell oneself into slavery.[19] John Stuart Mill—surely no enemy to libertarian thought—is particularly appropriate here, for what Mill said against slavery applies to all contracts in perpetuity. An individual, Mill contended, is not the best judge of his own interest when he

attempts to decide irrevocably now, what will be best for his interest at some future and distant time. The presumption in favour of individual judgment is only legitimate, where the judgment is grounded on actual, and especially on present, personal experience; not where it is formed antecedently to experience, and not suffered to be reversed even after experience has condemned it. When persons have bound themselves by a contract, not simply to do some one thing, but to continue doing something for ever or for a prolonged period, without any power of revoking the engagement, the presumption which their perseverance in

161   **Justice for Sale:**
The Justice of Property vs.
the Property of Justice

that course of conduct would otherwise raise in favour of its being advantageous to them, does not exist; and any such presumption which can be grounded on their having voluntarily entered into the contract, perhaps at an early age, and without any real knowledge of what they undertook, is commonly next to null.[20]

This is why, for Mill and for Western societies generally, the law will not enforce such contracts.

It is true that in order to live, within a system of property rights, individuals must often sell their labor. Does this mean, should it mean, that even then the community has no stake in the conditions of that sale, that the community should not set minimum wages and maximum hours, and regulate what otherwise might be (as they have been) noxious and unsafe working conditions? Do property rights really have, should they have, priority over life itself, and the conditions that make life viable?

Nozick's theory of entitlement, looking only to the rights that emanate from holdings, and caring little or nothing about what happens to the rights of others as a consequence,[21] produces end results that are not outside of but within his own theory. A theory that deals only with means but not ends is not a theory. The two are inextricably intertwined in a moral judgment, for only a total situation is susceptible of a moral judgment. And a moral theory that leads to immoral results is not a theory of justice at all. (This is but another instance of Nozick's failure to come adequately to terms with utilitarian and other end-result theories.)

Justice is not, and cannot be, for sale. Freedom and human rights are not, and cannot be, for sale. They are both means and ends: they are means to, or requisites of, what it means to be human; they are also among the reasons why it is important to be human. This is why the test of a decent theory of justice, as of a society, is what it does to individuals, what it makes of individuals, and what it enables individuals to make of themselves.

That Nozick's theory of entitlement is, at best, good for some individuals—those with holdings—but not for all, is a sufficient mark of its moral deficiency.

VII

Only a few words need to be said concerning Nozick's idea that his vision of a good society, the minimal state, constitutes utopianism—a utopia that, belying its name (which literally means nowhere), is actually, in his view, realizable in this world.

By utopia Nozick means not the best of all conceivable worlds, but the best of all possible worlds. It is that in which "each person receives his marginal contribution."

Since you and I will obviously differ as to which is the best world, there can be no one best society for everyone. "Utopia will consist of utopias, of many different and divergent communities in which people lead different kinds of lives under different institutions. . . . The utopian society is the society of utopianism." Utopianism, then, as a framework for many utopias, will be acceptable to almost every utopian at some future time and is compatible with the realization of almost all particular utopian visions. "Though the framework is libertarian and laissez-faire, *individual communities within it need not be*, and perhaps no community within it will choose to be so. . . . The utopian process is substituted for the utopian end state of other static theories of utopias."

At first blush, Nozick's utopianism exudes a certain charm, for what can be more appealing than a utopia of many utopias, a utopianism that is not monolithic and stifling of diversity and individuality but allows for every kind of diversity and individuality? But as with most everything else in Nozick's book, appearance has little to do with reality.

Consider the notion that the most desirable of all possible worlds is that in which "each person receives his marginal contribution." Not his happiness, not love or good health or the development of personality, but "his marginal contribution." Can so paltry an end really constitute an ideal worth striving for?

If Nozick's argument is to be taken seriously, then not the minimal state, but a world that accommodates almost every form of state, including what Nozick would himself call an oppressive (because more-than-minimal) state, is utopian. If this is what Nozick has in mind when he speaks of the actualization of his ideal, it is a most peculiar utopian vision indeed; for it not only permits, it justifies evil systems and practices—and I use the world "evil" here to include anyone's definition of that term, including Nozick's. In the name of libertarianism, Nozick would permit anyone to do anything, as long as this is done voluntarily—as a matter of moral right! It is a strange notion of utopianism that permits a mixture of good and evil worlds, and in no stated proportions.

But in fact Nozick's true ideal, a combination of minimal states, cannot be realized; or if it can, it can only be realized by a process and a power that in itself would destroy that ideal. To achieve the kind of world Nozick wants, we would have to reverse history, and keep it reversed. This would entail precisely the massive state interference, with all its bureaucratic malevolences, he rails against; for how else could we rectify the injustices of existing states?

Thus Nozick's utopianism is not a utopia, any more than his idea of entitlement is a theory of justice. Together they constitute a vision of hell.

9   **The Higher Reaches
of the Lower Orders:**
A Critique of the Theories
of B. F. Skinner

There is only one serious question in political philosophy: What manner of
men do we take ourselves and others to be? All other issues—not least the next
fundamental question, By what right does any man or class command the
services of another?—derive from the answer we give to this central question.

I wish to consider here B. F. Skinner's answers to these questions.[1] They
constitute, if I understand them correctly, an argument in contempt of man,
turning on a currently fashionable, though age-old, thesis: that the bulk of
mankind is unable or unfit to be free; that men should accordingly be divided,
on the basis of some fixed criteria, into superior and inferior orders; and that
some version of the closed rather than the open society is consequently the
proper (and indeed unavoidable) medium for realizing this principle. I shall
argue against these notions, which I take to be morally deficient, politically
pernicious, and unworkable. They are not, however, without certain elements
of plausibility, a circumstance that lends poignancy to the human situation in
our time. All the more so since the political authoritarianism entailed by
Skinner's teaching comes bedecked in fashionable "scientific" credentials and
wins approval of some people who even think of themselves as humanists and
liberals.

I

In every society—save perhaps for the "primitive"—there are pyramids of
status and power, reflecting differences of wealth and birth, income and
occupation, race and religion and sex, capacity and willingness to employ force
and fraud, mental and moral attainments.

I mean here by a closed society one in which inherited or assigned standings
in the pyramids of status and power are approved and maintained. By an open
society I mean one in which those at the base or on the lower rungs of those
pyramids refuse to accept their assigned roles and struggle to rise toward the

Reprinted, by permission, from *Dissent* 20 (1973): 243–69.

top, *and* where the beliefs and social and political arrangements make it reasonably possible for nearly all of them to engage in that struggle, if they so wish.

Merely to state so bald a polarity should rightly arouse the suspicion that these are at best ideal types. No closed society—apart, perhaps, from the extreme caste systems of fiefdoms in an earlier India or the great dynasties of an earlier Asia—has been completely closed; almost always there have been some areas in which men were at least partially free to rise. So too with open societies. There is always a considerable gap between rhetoric and practice: even those states we label democratic are disfigured by arrangements that hinder or block legitimate access to higher place and power. In the real world *all* societies have probably been mixed rather than pure types. The intriguing questions then are, How closed or open can a closed or open society be if it is to maintain and perpetuate itself? and what kinds of human beings live in and are likely to be produced by relatively closed or open societies?

In raising this last question I am returning to John Stuart Mill's insistence that the true test of a good government is not its power or wealth but the qualities—the virtue and intelligence—of its citizens. For if the state exists for man rather than man for the state, the only justification of a state is not mere survival but progress—understanding by progress a change in the quality of men's lives that will enable them to move from the sorry creatures many are to what they might and ought to be.

But what ought a man to be? What is the essence of a man as distinct from his historical or momentary existence? To this question political philosophers have given a multiplicity of answers.

Man, they have said, is a featherless biped. If so, replied the skeptic, he is a plucked chicken. Man is a rational animal. If so, how do you account for the madness with which he misgoverns himself? Man is a fragmented being, with many roles and faces, an entire *dramatis personae* within a single individual, and one therefore who will never be fully known. He is a stranger even to himself. If so, how shall we treat him, how indeed shall we know who he is? So the debate has gone.

But throughout this long debate one belief at least has seldom been challenged: that man is a sentient and (at his best) reflective creature; consequently, though he may at times act chaotically, more commonly he acts in accord with his feelings—whether we call these passions, sentiments, impulses, or desires—and what he thinks right. Disagreements concerning the nature of man have thus turned not on whether he feels and thinks but on the *character* of his thoughts and emotions, and on the relation of those thoughts and emotions to his actions: on whether "right" desires and "right" thoughts are the province of all men or only a gifted few, whether man's reason is the servant or the

165   The Higher Reaches of the
Lower Orders: A Critique of
the Theories of B. F. Skinner

master of his passions (or whether reason is itself but one of the more com-pelling passions), and whether his behavior follows from those thoughts and emotions or is sometimes in conflict with them.

Now, however, we are told that these are mistaken grounds of disagreement. B. F. Skinner, author of one of our less genial and more authoritarian utopias,[2] and of other works denigrating man's freedom,[3] has in *Beyond Freedom and Dignity,* The Summa Scientifica of his life's work, spelled out what man really is.

Man, according to Skinner, is a behaving, not a feeling and thinking animal; as such, he must be conditioned to behave rightly, not be permitted to act wrongly; and we can so condition him only if we understand that the causes of his behavior lie beyond the individual himself, not in his attitudes or states of mind but in his cultural and social environment. As Skinner puts it:

> What is being abolished is autonomous man—the inner man, . . . the man defended by the literatures of freedom and dignity. His abolition has long been overdue. . . . A scientific analysis of behavior dispossesses autonomous man and turns the control he has been said to exert over to the environment. . . . What is needed is more control, not less. . . . The problem is to design a world which will be liked not by people as they now are but by those who live in it. . . . It is science or nothing. . . .[4]

From this perspective, the issue of closed versus open societies turns on different conceptions of what it means to be a man—not, be it emphasized, man as he is but as he might and ought to be. In Skinner's view, man is and ought to be—indeed, he *must* be, for there is no choice—a controlled being, a creature rather than a creator of his environment. In another view—and I shall here oppose to Skinner only that liberal tradition which may be said to run from John Stuart Mill through Russell, MacIver, and Morris R. Cohen to Camus and the democratic socialists of our own day—man is the one creature on earth who refuses, and ought to refuse, to be what he is. If he is to acquire the full stature of a human being, he must be a discontented and, more important, a self-protecting and self-dependent animal.

He must be a discontented man, according to this liberal tradition, because, as a perceiving animal, he is aware that he lives in a disharmonious and (in certain crucial respects) an unjust world. What is needed, then, are power and intelligence and above all the passion for justice that will enable the legiti-mately discontented man (and others like him who will always exist in our imperfect world) to alter the seemingly unalterable order of things.

This is why Mill and other liberals insist that to be a man one should exercise one's own judgment, make one's own choices. It is of course impossible to imagine a life deprived of all choices; for even the failure or refusal to choose, which is a surrender to persons or impersonal forces outside one's self, is itself an act of choice. But the crucial choice, which is the ability and right to make choices, is above all others the distinctive quality of what it means to be human. Why, it must be asked, does a man have a mind if not to exercise it? And what does it mean to exercise one's mind if not to reflect upon and choose among alternatives? And what is the point of such reflection and choice if, after that decision, he is told that it is of no account, he must abide by the decision of another? That, if left alone, he may in fact choose wrongly is a distinct possibility. But apart from the fact that fallibility also attends the choices of a superior (even if allegedly wiser) power, it is the meaning of freedom that a man take the risk of his own option. The right to be wrong, the right to be different, is (in this view) precisely what determines his manhood.

Now it is axiomatic that rights are not self-enforcing. Nor, on the historical record, are the rights of men in the lower orders likely to be held inviolate if entrusted to the higher orders. To be a self-dependent (autonomous) man requires not merely intelligence but also a power to resist the will of those whose judgment runs counter to his own. He must look not to the forbearance of others but to himself. He must be able to protect himself effectively. And this means not that he be given more power than they—for what then would protect the others from his possible encroachments on *their* right to be wrong or different?—but that he be given an equal power and opportunity to use it.

This conception of equality, so necessary to the idea of liberty and of a self-dependent and self-protecting man, merits special emphasis as a distinguishing feature between closed and open societies. In closed societies, no matter how enlightened and virtuous the ruling or despotic class, inequality and degradation remain the fate of the lower orders; for the one thing even the best of despots cannot do is to produce a self-sufficient and virtuous citizenry. In open societies, despite all deficiencies in institutions, the egalitarian principle remains central. If Camus and Silone are right in saying that man is a rebel who affirms his existence by fighting against his own condition, then without equality of power and opportunity, neither reason nor passion will enable him to transcend his miserable existence.

So, too, the conception of liberty alluded to here requires special emphasis. Every society, closed or open, professes a love of liberty. Every society, closed or open, means by liberty at least the absence of alien rule. But what is characteristic of closed societies is that they also mean by liberty the right of the government officially to suppress undersirable views, most commonly on matters of morality and political right. Closed societies generally mean by liberty what has come to be called "true" or "real" freedom. This is, the freedom to do and say only the "right" things—as stipulated by God or nature or tradition or, what is decisive in practice, by those earthly powers who claim to know, and

167   The Higher Reaches of the
Lower Orders: A Critique of
the Theories of B. F. Skinner

who therefore claim the exclusive power to apply, those alleged teachings. Or, if we move from normal to bizarre closed societies, that is, to those totalitarian societies based not on some alleged objective truth or binding principle but on the sheer exertion of power—as embodied, for example, in the Nazi and Fascist systems—"true" or "real" freedom becomes no more than compliance with the dictator's intuitive will.

"What is curious about this position," to cite but one of our previously mentioned liberal writers, "is the belief that if impartial investigation were permitted it would lead men to the wrong conclusion, and that ignorance is, therefore, the only safeguard against error."[5] But even if we do not, for the moment, press this objection, it remains altogether clear that the point of view embraced by proponents of the closed society cannot be acceptable to any person who conceives of man as a rational and autonomous creature and who consequently wishes our action to be guided by reason.

Open societies not only tolerate but encourage the free expression and examination of "objectionable" ideas. In the open society *all* questions are, or ought to be, open to discussion; all rulers subject to public criticism and expulsion from office; all opinions, including—indeed especially—those of the government, viewed with greater or lesser measures of doubt. What is entailed is man's freedom to articulate not only the "right" but the "wrong" ideas. Also entailed may be a predisposition, in the name of freedom, to leave men alone, to allow them to pursue their actual rather than allegedly real wills, at least in realms (such as religion) that do not require them to come into injurious conflict with one another.

So we return to the central questions: What, really, is this thing called man? What do closed and open societies make of man and do with man? No less important, what do they require man to do for himself? And what justifications attend these different understandings and practices?

II

Surely we must distrust all those who give simple answers to these questions, and Skinner gives simple answers. But what lends some verisimilitude to his answers is the undeniable fact that human or social conditioning has always been attempted and has often, in some measure, been successful.

Consider education and law. Education has always had as a primary purpose the influencing of men's minds. It seeks to control (modify) human behavior by instructing (instilling, training, indoctrinating, manipulating) children in proper codes of belief and modes of behavior. And surely it is one of the functions of law to control (modify) human behavior, in part through a system of punishments, in part through persuasion. Nor are education and law the only

instruments through which men have sought to control (modify) human behavior. Force has regularly been employed to compel men to behave in ways
they dislike. And more recently drugs, whether tranquilizers or stimulants,
have come into widespread use for the same purpose. The techniques depicted
by Koestler in *Darkness at Noon* and by Orwell in *1984*, and those utilized by
the Chinese Communists in the "brainwashing" of prisoners, are testimonials
to the power of this idea in the modern world.

All this is familiar enough. If a society is to function as some sort of cohesive
entity, it must favor some doctrines and practices over others. It must develop
or reflect a consensus on values and procedures that "define" it. Without such a
consensus, however limited, a society can form neither a nation nor a state but
must remain an amorphous conglomeration of beings. But in another sense,
this closing of the environment may entail what Mosca has called "a real
unbalancing of the spirit," and overly careful circumscribing of life. Then,
unless the child is one of those rare individuals whose intellect and circumstances enable him to think for himself, he will, if raised a religious or political
fanatic, become such a fanatic. To admit rays of light from other moral and
intellectual worlds is to encourage doubts and desertions. In this way not only
do the sane sometimes lead the mad but the mad often force the sane to keep
them company.[6]

Insofar, then, as Skinner puts his faith in some form of conditioning, and
stresses in this context the importance of environment, he offers not a new idea
but simply a new technique to improve or more effectively implement an old
idea.

It is Skinner's contention that it is misleading and unscientific to describe
men in terms of "personalities, states of mind, feelings, traits of character,
plan, purposes, intentions, or the other perquisites of autonomous man." Men
are nothing but behaving animals, and human behavior is the automatic
outcome of environmental forces. We are what our environment compels us to
be. Through proper environmental manipulation or engineering—what Skinner calls "a technology of behavior" or "operant conditioning"—it should then
be possible to structure the environment (design the right culture) so as to
produce (control) right behavior. This involves a carefully planned (programmed, scheduled) sequence of contingencies or reinforcements, positive
rather than negative (or aversive), because negative reinforcements not only
lead to undesirable consequences—e.g., they reinforce the nagging parent
rather than the submitting child— but are ultimately self-defeating. As Skinner
says:

> All control is exerted by the environment. . . . No one directly changes
> a mind. By manipulating environmental contingencies, one makes
> changes which are said to indicate a change of mind, but if there is any

169   The Higher Reaches of the
Lower Orders: A Critique of
the Theories of B. F. Skinner

effect, it is on behavior. . . . In the scientific view . . . a person's behavior is determined by a genetic endowment traceable to the evolutionary history of the species and by the environmental circumstances to
which as an individual he has been exposed.[7]

But while Skinner talks of genetics and physics, what he means by environment is not the biological or physical—which one might suppose are what his
theory requires—but the cultural or social. It is this cultural or social environment that "can be changed" (manipulated, repaired) to produce consequences
that will modify behavior.

Now one might think that by expressing a preference for one type of culture
or pattern of behavior rather than another, Skinner is introducing a moral
dimension into his analysis—as indeed he is. But he insists throughout that
these issues are discussed "from a scientific point of view." One might also
think that if the environment can be changed, it cannot also be true that *all*
control is exerted by the environment. The argument is thus flawed from the
very outset, and becomes all the more egregiously wrong as one traces out its
consequences.

If the environment is a culture, and a culture is defined as "a set of contingencies of reinforcement" or "a set of practices," what does it mean to say that the
environment "acts," that "it does not push or pull, it *selects*," that it "is
'responsible' for objectionable behavior" (e.g., juvenile delinquency), that it
can "induce" people to change their behavior? A culture is a concept, not a
person, and to reify a concept by giving it a will, with the power to judge and
direct, is to move not into the science of human behavior but into a realm of
verbal magic. It is also to deny what Skinner no less vehemently affirms: that
"the environment can be manipulated," that "we can arrange contingencies,"
that "man must repair [the damage he has done to his environment] or all is
lost," that while man is indeed controlled by his environment, "it is an environment largely of his own making," that "the individual controls himself by
manipulating the world in which he lives." If these latter statements are to be
taken at face value, then the environment, the culture, is not some abstract or
even concrete thing "out there," which moves as a monolithic entity upon the
individual or nation, molding it to the environment's will, whatever that might
be. It is rather persons who make and mold the culture, which in turn constitutes the conditions within which and through which individuals function.

Skinner cannot have it both ways. Either he is an environmental or mechanistic determinist (which he avowedly is), in which case man is the creature but
not the creator of his environment, or he holds (as he also does) that man can
arrange "environments in which specific consequences are contingent upon it
[*sic*]," in which case man is the creator and not the creature of his environment.
If, however, man is both creature and creator, if there is some sort of reciprocal

relationship or feedback—a doctrine that Skinner also affirms—then there is no determinism at all. It is hard to understand precisely which view Skinner holds, since he variously asserts all of them.

But this is not all. Skinner recognizes that environments differ considerably. "People," he says at one point, "are extraordinarily different in different places, and possibly just because of the places." And when he argues for planned diversification—of which more later—he concedes that the environment even within a nation (or culture?) is not monolithic. It follows, though Skinner does not draw this inference, that people are often different even in the same place, and may be the same even in different places. What then should the controllers do? Should they adjust (say) the rich child to the slum environment, or the slum child to the affluent environment, or maintain each child in his own or in still another environment? Does it even follow, given genetic and other differences, that the same environment will have the same effect on all persons within that environment? Clearly the controllers, if they could do through "operant conditioning" what Skinner believes it is possible for them to do, must make an ethical along with a scientific choice: they can take the world as it is and fit man into it; they can take man as he is and change the world to conform to man's nature and requirements; or they can change both man and the world so that both will be other (and presumably better) than they are. But if the controllers no less than the controlled are environmentally determined, how can they choose? And if they can choose, they are not only *not* the subject of deterministic forces, they are confronted by the need to provide justifications for their choices. All of which is to move them from "behaving" to autonomous men.

I would dwell a bit longer on this problem of the controllers. If the values implanted in the controllers' minds are determined by environmental forces—or if, to adhere to Skinner's terminology, the behavior of the controllers is determined by the culture—as are the values (or behavior) of the controlled, on what grounds can Skinner argue that the controllers should arrange the contingencies that will alter people's behavior rather than the reverse? Clearly, this cannot be defended by invoking the environmental forces themselves, for these are common to both controllers and controlled and should, precisely because they are the same, produce the same behavior (or values) in both. Indeed, given this common impact, where did the controllers come from in the first place? Since none of us, in the pre-Skinnerian world, is a controller, what in the environment selects a fortunate (and gifted?) few and transforms them from the controlled creatures they (along with the rest of us) are, into a new ruling class that will now control the environment that up to this moment has controlled us all? What, that is to say, destroys the controlling power of the environment? Further, if the behavior of the controllers is different—and it

171   The Higher Reaches of the
        Lower Orders: A Critique of
        the Theories of B. F. Skinner

must be different, otherwise there is not point to Skinner's argument that the controllers can (and must) change the world from its present unsatisfactory state to a better one—then either there are different environmental forces at work or the same environmental forces produce different forms of behavior. On Skinner's terms, the latter possibility is self-evidently absurd. But the former possibility, if true, only returns us to the controllers' problem of choice. Skinner excludes choice, holding that men do not in fact choose, that the environment chooses for them, in which case of course it is meaningless to ask whether they ought to choose, and by what criteria. Yet it is impossible to escape the fact that the controllers must choose. Skinner concedes this in a revealing passage:

> Man as we know him, for better or for worse, is what man has made of man. . . . When a person changes his physical or social environment "intentionally"—that is, in order to change human behavior, possibly including his own—he plays two roles: one as a controller, as the designer of a controlling culture, and another as the controlled, as the product of a culture. . . . The man that man has made is the product of the culture man has divised.[8]

To the extent, then, that the controllers can and do choose—and they *must* choose if man is to be made by man—then Skinner denies his own case on empirical grounds. If he says (as he also does) that the controllers *ought* to choose one set of contingencies rather than another, to select one pattern of desired behavior over another, he denies his case on normative grounds. In the latter situation, of course, he needs to provide appropriate criteria for his preferences, which leads us again into the ethical realm.

"Operant conditioning" is attended by at least two other difficulties. One is the role of accident and of the unanticipated consequences of intended actions. Chance has played an unascertainable role in human history, yet no one will deny its importance—in scientific discovery, military engagements, the resolution of economic and political conflicts, the everyday occurrences of human behavior. Even Skinner admits (though typically by overstatement) that "accidents have been responsible for almost everything men have achieved to date, and they will no doubt continue to contribute to human accomplishments." He goes on to add, however, that "there is no virtue in accident as such." This last statement is of course unexceptionable, but it does not remove the difficulty accident poses for Skinner's thesis. For if it is true that accident has played the major role that Skinner concedes to it, how can he argue that it is always the environment that determines human behavior? Surely accident cannot be explained by contingencies of reinforcement. And if accident is likely to play as important a role in man's future, how can he place so much confidence in the efficacy of his behavioral engineering? Surely even carefully programmed sequences of contingencies will be afflicted again and again by unforeseen and uncontrollable events.

If Skinner seeks to design a better culture, he must know at least two things: that the culture he prefers is indeed "better" and that the contingencies he would arrange are appropriate means to achieving that end. It is more than problematical whether, qua scientist, he knows, or can know, either of these things. If he knows the former at all, he can know it only as a moral philosopher, not as a scientist; and he cannot know it as a moral philosopher because, on his own terms, it is not merely the environment which does the selecting but it is behavior, not knowing, that defines the human animal. Man, after all—including, presumably, Skinner and his "controllers"—is not a thinking or feeling animal, only a behaving animal; he does not possess a plan or purposes or intentions, nor is he governed by a state of mind or the other perquisites of autonomous man. Hence he designs only what he is compelled by his environment to design; he can neither choose that design nor know that it is better than what presently exists. In the same way, the contingencies he would schedule cannot produce "a better world," for they will be frustrated by accident, by the unanticipated consequences of the controllers' actions. And these actions, in turn, cannot even be "intended," for the controllers can have no purposes or intentions, since they are merely behaving animals in an environmentally determined world. If, to rescue his case, Skinner would retreat from his mechanistic determinism to the voluntaristic choices of men "intentionally" seeking to remake themselves (or others), he not only repudiates his central doctrine but relies on the foolishness of choice he has consistently decried.

A second difficulty plagues the idea of "operant conditioning." It is, as I have tried to point out, truistic to say that societies attempt to condition (socialize) their children (and also, perhaps, their adults), and that in some measure they frequently succeed. But it is not always simply truistic. Consider the following possibilities:

1. In heterogeneous and pluralistic societies, socialization or conditioning takes different forms and produces a variety of results. Differences of behavior may (probably will) make for conflict, in which case the controllers, if they are to achieve Skinner's better world, must resolve those conflicts by rearranging contingencies so as to produce a harmonious order. But which differences shall be suppressed and which contingencies chosen? Unavoidably, we are back once again to the problem of choice and its relation to environmental determinism.

2. Where a society values (behaves so as to produce) critical and inquiring minds, that is to say, people who go about asking questions and seeking

173   The Higher Reaches of the
Lower Orders: A Critique of
the Theories of B. F. Skinner

answers, it may be possible to arrange a sequence of contingencies that will bring about (or perpetuate) the very autonomous men Skinner deplores and seeks to abolish. Indeed, the very fact that Skinner seeks to abolish or dispossess autonomous men presupposes that they already exist. If so, to abolish them entails a judgment that autonomous men are evil or harmful or wrong and *ought*, therefore, to be eliminated. But how, if men are merely (and deterministically) behaving animals, can they be termed evil or harmful or wrong? If they are so judged, we require ethical criteria by which to validate such a judgment and to vindicate their calculated transformation to "better" men. Moreover, what are "better" men? Again, this is not a scientific but a moral determination. Accordingly, let us now turn to Skinner's conception of ethics and a better (just?) society.

III

Skinner cannot really be said to have an ethical system, for in an environmentally determined world—that is, a world bereft of conscious choice—men (including of necessity Skinner himself) behave as they must, not as they think they ought to. And where men do what they must do, they have no responsibility for their behavior, so that neither praise nor censure attaches to their actions. Those actions cannot be termed good or bad; they are merely forms of behavior to be observed.

If, furthermore, all this were true, there would be no point in seeking to change the world (and human behavior) from what it is to something else. Yet Skinner does mean to change the world. He wants men to be "happy, informed, skillful, well behaved and productive." He wants them to be not heroic but "automatically good." He wants them to

> live together without quarreling, maintain themselves by producing the food, shelter, and clothing they need, enjoy themselves and contribute to the enjoyment of others in art, music, literature, and games, consume only a reasonable part of the resources of the world and add as little as possible to its pollution, bear no more children than can be raised decently, continue to explore the world around them and discover better ways of dealing with it, and come to know themselves accurately and, therefore, manage themselves effectively.[9]

Above all, he wants the culture to survive, for survival is not merely the principal value, it is "the only value according to which a culture is eventually to be judged."

This last assertion, of course, is selfevidently untrue. If the elements mentioned by Skinner in the quoted statement—peace, affluence, creativity, decency, self-knowledge, effective management—are what he esteems, then not survival per se but survival of a particular kind of culture is the crucial value. But what, apart from such impossible (for a determinist) expectations as self-knowledge, can be meant by the survival (or death) of a culture?

We have already been told that a culture is "the social environment," "a set of practices," "a set of contingencies of reinforcement." Can these perish or die as an individual may be said to die? Is this the sense in which Athenian culture (say) may be said to have died? If so, it can only be because culture is something that is bound in space and time, in which case no culture can be said to have survived and no culture can hope to survive. But if culture embraces entities (or practices) that permeate and transcend spatial and temporal boundaries, then Athenian culture did not die with Sparta's conquest of Athens or with the emergence of the Roman Empire. The identity "Athens" may not have survived, at least not in the form we associate with classical Athens, but its culture survived. In this sense cultures do not die but are adapted and adopted by later cultures. Skinner himself does not seek totally to destroy our old culture, only to alter some of its practices so as to correct what he takes to be shortcomings. He values much of what it already contains. "Our culture," he tells us, "has produced the science and technology it needs to save itself." Surely, then, in designing the new culture, the needed science and technology will remain; some contingencies, some part of the environment will survive.

In point of fact, the term "culture" is not a wholly convincing unit of analysis. One cannot study American culture at any point in its development without taking account of a wider set of (conditioning) influences originating outside of America. We may grant that American culture can be made intelligible by a consideration of historic forces operating on a restricted geographic scale. But science and technology and even the idea of a national state were not sired in America. Nor can America claim exclusive paternity of its language and literature, art and music, dress, games and manners. To view the landscape of culture through Skinnerian eyes is to move into a grossly distorted world; it is also to miss the ever-continuing cross-fertilization of both American and nonAmerican cultures.[10]

That Skinner attaches his ill-conceived notion of culture to the equally ambiguous (and long-discredited) theory of the survival of the fittest only compounds the implausibility of his doctrine. To say that what is fittest to survive, survives, is really to say no more than that we shall choose to call fittest that which survives.[11] For it does not know what is fit to survive until after it has survived; and it can only say it was fit to survive because it survived. All of which is not merely a circular argument but is to beg the question, What in fact is the fittest? The reputable trader may be put out of business by his unscrupu-

175   The Higher Reaches of the
Lower Orders: A Critique of
the Theories of B. F. Skinner

lous competitor, the thoughtful statesman be thrust aside by the demagogue. If these survivors are the fittest, it ill behooves Skinner to recommend their cause.

Survival of a culture, then, is not a viable but an empty and meaningless value, recommending itself only to those who feel more comfortable with concepts of stability and adjustment than with the more difficult notions of freedom, justice, and equality. Can anything more be said for Skinner's other ethical prescriptions?

Consider his idea—if a behaviorist (in Skinner's understanding of the term) can be said to have an *idea*—of "automatic goodness." Skinner wants men to be happy and well behaved. But what does it mean to be happy, and why should men behave well? How, in fact, do we distinguish behaving well from behaving badly? And is not the very drawing of a distinction between good and bad behavior (for in Skinner's lexicon to "behave well" is to "be good") an affirmation of morality rather than of science?

To a moral philosopher these might appear to be difficult (and clearly ethical) questions. But to Skinner they are scientific and readily answerable. He begins by posing the issue this way: "If a scientific analysis can tell us how to change behavior, can it tell us what changes to make?" This is not (he insists) a question of morality but

> a question about the behavior of those who do in fact propose and make changes. People act to improve the world and to progress toward a better way of life for good reasons, and among the reasons are certain consequences of their behavior, and among those consequences are the things people value and call good. . . . Those who observe cultures do not see ideas or values. They see how people live, how they raise their children, how they gather or cultivate food, what kinds of dwellings they live in, what they wear, what games they play, how they treat each other, how they govern themselves, and so on. These are the customs, the customary *behaviors,* of a people. To explain them we must turn to the contingencies which generate them. . . . The social contingencies, or the behaviors they generate, are the "ideas" of a culture: the reinforcers that appear in the contingencies are its "values."
>
> To make a value judgment by calling something good or bad is to classify it in terms of its reinforcing effects. . . . Good things are positive reinforcers. . . . The things we call bad . . . are all negative reinforcers. . . . Things are good (positively reinforcing) or bad (negatively reinforcing) presumably because of the contingencies of survival under which the species evolved.[12]

The problem, then, "is to induce people not to be good but to behave well." Indeed,

We can conceive of moral training which is so adequate to the demands of the culture that men will be good practically automatically, but to that extent they will be deprived of the right to moral heroism, since we seldom admire automatic goodness. Yet if we consider the end of morals rather than certain virtuous means, is not "automatic goodness" a desirable state of affairs?[13]

Skinner, then, seeks to make it easier for men to be good (behave well). He wants to reduce what is (for autonomous men) the agonizing tension between individual inclinations and social precepts by habituating (conditioning) them to the requirements of proper ("virtuous") behavior, as this proper behavior is defined in the society. Such conformity is not to be achieved through repression, e.g., fear of punishment, but through that "operant conditioning" that will make them "automatically" desire, and consequently act in accordance with, what is socially approved. This, of course, requires a thorough understanding of human nature (behavior), a knowledge so complete that (as the skeptical Hobbes said) it would enable us to eliminate avarice and ambition and "enjoy . . . immortal peace." Skinner admits that we do not yet have such complete knowledge, that his behaviorist psychology "is not yet ready to solve all our problems"; but, he goes on to say, "it is a science in progress, and its ultimate adequacy cannot now be judged."

One might suppose that if Skinner's present knowledge is short of what is required for the implementation of his teaching, he would be loath to press his argument as vigorously as he does. But let this go for the moment. What is crucial here is his notion that if men can be conditioned to behave as society (or his controllers—and it is not clear that these are always the same, for the controllers, it must be remembered, are charged with *changing* the culture) requires them to behave, they will be automatically good; that this is the proper conception of what it means to be a man; and that such men behaving in those required ways will be happy.

Doubtless some things can be said in support of these views: that we will, in all likelihood, continue to increase our knowledge of human nature (behavior); that in consequence of this better understanding and of the further progress that will be made in behavioral engineering we will be able more effectively to condition (control) children, and thus men; that such conditioning will, to the degree that it is successful, eliminate the need for painful thought and thereby ease anxiety; that if proper behavior becomes effortless it becomes more certain, and society as a whole will benefit (in the sense that it will get what it demands); and that if "goodness" becomes automatic and therefore less difficult, human energies can be channeled more efficiently into other needed tasks.[14]

177   The Higher Reaches of the
       Lower Orders: A Critique of
       the Theories of B. F. Skinner

But all too much can be said against these views, not least that the hope it holds out is of a drab and morally deficient world. For suppose Skinner is correct, that he can do all he claims, that he can make men behave well (be "good" or "virtuous") through habit, without effort and thought. What, then, is he making of men? What is he doing with and to men? Is he not converting them into automated beings or humanized robots? Is he not reducing them to untroubled innocents dwelling in a state of perpetual childhood? If a better world means better men, what shall we say of a doctrine that quite literally imprisons man, substituting for one kind of containment a more radical and dangerous restriction of the mind? It may of course be argued, in strict adherence to Skinner's behaviorist psychology, that man has no mind, in which case we are dealing not with imprisonment but only with nonviolent (and presumably benevolent) control of man's behavior. Still, it is difficult to see why such control (conditioning) is not in fact the replacement of one form of power by another. It operates as a sort of prenatal excision or molding, which is not significantly different in principle from control exercised after the act. It may, indeed, because such prenatal control is more subtle and more difficult to detect or correct, constitute a far more threatening affront to man's critical faculties than if we were dealing with open and visible dangers. No less than violence, it is a form of coercion in that it compels man to act, or refrain from acting, in accordance with another's will. And where man has no choice but to do as he is told, where indeed he is compelled to do this even without being told, he is surely no more than a puppet on a prearranged stage.

From this perspective, as George Kateb has argued, Skinner is a kind of playwright creating a world of strictly patterned activity. Men move about in expected (stipulated) ways. They substitute no words (for language, which is "verbal behavior,"[15] is subject to the same Skinnerian rules) or gestures of their own, perform no unexpected acts, alter no scenes, introduce no improvisations. What they say and do is always controlled. They are predictable men.[16]

Now it is true that men whose actions are completely unpredictable are regarded as beyond the moral range, perhaps as lunatics. But there is a vast difference between normal (somewhat educated, somewhat socialized, perhaps somewhat conditioned) men and men totally conditioned to do what their controllers require. Such men lack all sense of, and must be relieved from, what we understand by moral responsibility; only their controllers are responsible for what they do. Such men, who are not men at all, are clearly incapable of performing Mill's self-protecting and self-dependent roles. Nor, since they are "automatically good" (behave well), can they be discontented men, or exercise—or worry about exercising—freedom of choice. That discontent, that freedom of choice, is reserved to the controllers, the new men of the higher orders, about whom, in spite of the awesome duties he assigns to them, Skinner says very little.

Here, perhaps—and we are still speaking, it must be recalled, of the moral realm—we confront the most damaging element in this indictment of Skinner's teaching. For by excluding choice from what he clearly considers the lower orders of men, he deprives them of the one quality that would still enable them to retain their humanity. To live is to think, for what but reason distinguishes man from the other animals? What but his critical and creative faculties separates the cultivated from the primitive man? And what does it mean to reason if man must then set his reason aside and forgo the right to choose? It is, I suppose, plausible to say that in primitive societies customary responses are generally sufficient to meet the problems of the day. But in complex societies, what are accounted moral problems are not choices between good and evil—such a choice is so simple (i.e., morally undemanding) as hardly to be accounted a choice at all—but choices between alternatives that are both good, or seemingly good, or sufficiently ambiguous as to require the determination of the good, or mixtures of good and bad so that in choosing to do good we may find, to our discomfiture, that it is also necessary to pay the price of doing some harm. How, in this setting, is it possible automatically, without painful reflection, without, at times, inordinate suffering, to do good (behave well)? And if to these considerations we add the further fact that no moral act makes sense that does not take into account the probable consequences of one's actions, we can see that moral choice is the most taxing, and elevating, demand put upon the individual. It is precisely this quality that—to revert to the liberal conception of the autonomous man—constitutes the hallmark of what it means to be a man. Nowhere was Mill more eloquent than in pressing this point:

> He who lets the world, or his own portion of it, choose his plan of life for him, has no need of any other faculty than the ape-like one of imitation. He who chooses his plan for himself, employs all his faculties. He must use observation to see, reasoning and judgment to foresee, activity to gather materials for decision, discrimination to decide, and when he has decided, firmness and selfcontrol to hold to his deliberate decision. And these qualities he requires and exercises exactly in proportion as the part of his conduct which he determines according to his own judgment and feelings is a large one. It is possible that he might be guided in some good path, and kept out of harm's way, without any of these things. But what will be his comparative worth as a human being? It really is of importance, not ony what men do, but also what manner of men they are that do it.[17]

Yet precisely these are the qualities Skinner would exclude in the name of automatic goodness.

179   The Higher Reaches of the
Lower Orders: A Critique of
the Theories of B. F. Skinner

Can there, however, be such a thing as automatic goodness or conditioned virtue? To do good (behave well) without knowing what, or why, or with what consequences, and in the face of what alternatives, one is doing it, is simply to do—not to do good, or, for that matter, evil. A man who acts automatically, that is, "unconsciously," without awareness of principles and reasons, causes and consequences, is at best going through certain motions. No rational conduct is involved here, no moral choices are made, nothing good—or bad—is done, for such a man knows nothing of good or bad; indeed, he knows nothing at all. He simply does.

He does what society (or the controllers) requires him to do. Conformity, not individuality (or creativity), is what Skinner esteems. It is true, says Skinner, that "life, liberty, and the pursuit of happiness are basic rights." But he quickly adds two things: first, these are the rights of the individual and "have only a minor bearing on the survival of a culture"; and second, apart from the fact that survival of the culture is the paramount, indeed the only value, what counts is not *being* free but *feeling* free.

Now to *be* free is to be able to act undeterred by external restraints. To *feel* free may entail no more than one's recognition of this objective condition. It has also, however, been taken to mean one's voluntary and happy compliance with the dictates of authority—either because one welcomes the imposition of those external restraints or does not recognize them to be constraints at all. Conditioning, it is clear, operates at this last level. By focusing on the internal and anterior causes of human behavior, it seeks not to impose external restraints on "improper" desires but to alter man's nature (behavior) so that he will desire only what is "proper," i.e., what he *ought* to desire. Skinner confuses here the philosophical problem of determinism versus free will with the quite separate social problem of freedom and restraint. Hence, despite his repeated animadversions against such "mentalistic expressions" as the word "feeling," he can innocently—without embarrassment and indeed with approval—say that a young Chinese follower of Mao may feel freer and happier than most young Americans in doing what he is required to do, if he does them because of positive rather than negative reinforcements.[18] Such is the wisdom of our prophet.

It is also true, says Skinner, that man's "individuality is unquestioned. . . . No intentional culture can destroy that uniqueness." But he qualifies this too by adding that "the individual nevertheless remains merely a stage in a process," and that it is "the culture which induces him" to act as he does. These remarks may help us to understand the cavalier way in which Skinner deals with the problem of the dissenter in contemporary America. He says:

A serious problem . . . arises when young people refuse to serve in the armed forces and desert or defect to other countries, but we shall not make an appreciable change by "inspiring greater loyalty or patriotism."

What must be changed are the contingencies which induce young people to behave in given ways toward their governments.[19]

Why is *this* the correct behavior to be induced? Why not, instead, change the contingencies that will induce the government to behave in different ways—toward their young people or toward the role of the armed forces? Surely this is an ethical question of the greatest moment, but it is noteworthy that Skinner does not address himself to the issues involved, least of all to the question of what justice requires. Justice, to Skinner, is an empty word. But if behavior is to be changed, how can this determination be made without both a power of choice and a sense of justice?

It may be objected at this point that I have been unfair to Skinner's portrayal of a viable (better? just?) society, in that Skinner explicitly argues against uniformity or regimentation, which "might indeed work against further evolution," and for "*planned* diversification, in which the importance of variety is recognized." But this does not really militate against the image of conformity I have imputed to him. For one thing, if in a given situation uniformity rather than diversity can be shown to promote the survival of a culture, and if that survival is the overriding (or only) value, then not change but uniformity is clearly to be preferred. But the more important key to Skinner's teaching here is his underscored term "*planned* diversification." His notion of variety is not that of the open society, in which men are free to become (even if within limits) what their desires, opportunities and circumstances allow them to become, but rather of the closed society, in which variety is carefully (and officially) circumscribed. He draws a revealing analogy when he says: "The breeding of plants and animals . . . also requires planned diversity." The variety that Skinner conceives is one in which the kinds and degrees of diversity, and the manner in which they may exist, are the result not of accident or free choice by the lower orders but of deliberate design, by the contingencies of reinforcement set into operation by the controllers.

Since the issue of fairness has been raised, it may be well at this point to insert Skinner's observation that "nothing in the behavioral process guarantees fair treatment, since the amount of behavior generated by a reinforcer depends upon the contingencies in which it appears."

In the face of all this, in what sense can men be deemed to be happy in Skinner's world? "The problem," I have already quoted him as having said, "is to design a world which will be liked not by people as they now are but by those who live in it." But how, in Skinner's scheme of things, can people "like" anything? To like something is to have a feeling, or to manifest a state of mind, or to employ what Skinner calls a "mentalistic expression"; and these, he has repeatedly said, do not exist. "What is ultimately good or bad," he insists, "are things, not feelings." Yet he falls back again and again on this proscribed word.

181   The Higher Reaches of the
Lower Orders: A Critique of
the Theories of B. F. Skinner

Somewhat curiously, he maintains that "a world that would be liked by contemporary people would perpetuate the status quo," as if contemporary people were a monolithic entity, all feeling content with things as they are and none of them seeking major, or even minor, changes. He believes that contemporary people like the status quo because they "have been taught to like it. A better world will be liked by those who live in it because it has been designed with an eye to what is, or can be, most reinforcing." This is in keeping with his view that "feelings about any institution depend upon the reinforcers the institution uses." If this is so, what people will like turns not on *their* preferences but on the preferences of the controller, who, Skinner affirms, will (to some extent) "necessarily design a world *he* likes." It is this world, this environment, that will shape (condition) people. They will "like" it because they will be taught (conditioned) to like it. Yet it is surely an elementary psychological truth that such a process of regression is likely to produce just the opposite result. As our rebellious youths have amply made clear, men do not and cannot really love those whose authority restricts their autonomy. If, despite this, they are happy, that happiness—if happiness it be—can only be the contentedness of men who are boring and do not even know they are bored.

IV

It is a commonplace that in politics and religion irrational beliefs and conduct are no bar to success. It is even arguable, perverse though this might seem (though not, of course, to a Dostoevsky or an Orwell), that all too many people look to a power in the universe greater than themselves; they seem to crave mystery and authority; they seek someone to whom they can entrust their conscience, someone who will remove the awful burdens of freedom, someone who will give them bread, security, and perhaps amusement, someone who will make them happy. It may well be, therefore, that Skinner's utopian vision will not founder—at least in its initial appeal—because of scientific and moral deficiencies. The fundamental question, or so he would have us believe, is not whether that vision is right or wrong (in any case meaningless terms) but, "Would it really work?" In Walden Two, he has argued, it did; and if there, why not everywhere?

Now we did not need a Marx to tell us that men have always been affected (somewhat conditioned) by impersonal forces outside themselves. Nor do we require unusual insight to understand that where there are monopolistic (or near-monopolistic) controls of the media of communication, not to speak of the deliberate use of terror, surveillance, and the concentration camp, the alternatives to which men are exposed are drastically limited; and that, if their horizons are narrowed, their thoughts and behavior are more easily channeled in desired directions. As techniques of conditioning are perfected we may expect greater and more effective socialization to take place.

Indeed, it was precisely because he recognized these things that Mill pleaded for a more autonomous man. Along with Tocqueville, he feared the increasing pressures of conformity. He understood that many (perhaps most) men were not free, did not wish to be free, and might not—in the absence of true understanding—become free. He sought, therefore, to set forth principles and institutions by which men might achieve what he believed only a very few superior intellects had thus far been able to achieve—the status of autonomous, self-reflective and self-dependent men. Such a status is not vouchsafed by history; it must be fought for and, with great difficulty, attained.

But this status, says Skinner, has not, cannot, and should not be attained. On the contrary, behavioral engineering ("operant conditioning") must prevail. There are, however, considerations that militate against his expectation.

Take, first, the problem of complexity and scale. It is one thing to control the behavior of rats in a maze or pigeons in a cage or infants in a carefully constructed box. It is more difficult (though according to Skinner quite possible) to control individuals and small groups of men. But it is surely an entirely different matter to control (as Skinner understands "control") hundreds of millions of people in a nation, or billions of people in the world. In the face of the variability and intractability of human nature, of qualitative as well as quantitative differences among men, to assume, as Skinner does, that "the behavioral processes in the world at large are the same as those in a utopian community, and practices have the same effects for the same reasons," is to gloss over the many (and I believe insuperable) difficulties that attend the vast distance between intention and achievement. For one thing it does not follow that controls that work over many (even most) people will work over every individual; there will always be the odd person or (more likely) numbers of persons who will stray from the fold. For another, even if we think only of the generality of men, the number and quality of the controllers required to perform the close supervision of the upbringing of children, not to speak of the ongoing behavior of adults, would be simply fantastic. If Skinner really means to apply his many and diverse contingencies—in a degree of control (though not of savagery) that exceeds the practices of even the totalitarian states—to all sorts of people in varying stages of mental and moral development, in diverse social environments and levels of economic and political evolution, he requires an unimaginable number of qualified personnel in constant attendance upon them. It is instructive to note how Skinner, almost as an incidental thought, deals with this problem. He says: "Ethical control may survive in small groups, but the control of the population as a whole [which whole—the nation? the world?] must be delegated to specialists—to police, priests, owners, teachers,

183   The Higher Reaches of the
Lower Orders: A Critique of
the Theories of B. F. Skinner

therapists, and so on, with their specialized reinforcers and their codified contingencies." How, and by what criteria, do owners (of what?) and police (as we know them in what country? as they might become?) emerge as equivalent to such therapists as the almighty Frazier, founder and czar of Walden Two? Clearly, Skinner's methods, if they apply at all, are applicable only to some (perhaps many, but certainly not all) individuals and small communities.

(I must note, if parenthetically, Skinner's curious failure to confront the problem of class and class consciousness with respect to his controllers. He talks throughout as if his controllers will behave [create contingencies] in a remarkably consistent and proper way so as to bring about his desired results. This presupposes not simply a community of rulers but of their interests, purposes, shared values. But Skinner offers no evidence that his rulers will constitute such a class. It is, after all, one thing to have a single person [and mind?], the scientist-king Frazier, direct a society. It is quite another to form [by labeling] police, priests, owners, teachers, therapists, and the like, into a ruling class and expect these disparate persons to behave in a unified way. Since they have no "purposes" or "interests" but only behave as the environment compels them to behave, what in that environment will make them do the same things at the same times? Why should we expect them to act *as a class* when they lack the very consciousness that is crucial to their existence as a class?)

Modern societies are complexities of large-scale organizations, involving vast and complicated systems. The rules and codes employed in those systems are numerous and by no means unambiguous. Their internal arrangements are imperfect. The messages sent (the contingencies put into operation)—and errors or accidents may of course enter even at the point of origin—are neither consistent nor constant, and so too with the course they follow. If the message employs language (verbal behavior?), this is notoriously vague and its reception, by that strange and complex animal called man, often involves a transformation of the sender's intent into a variety of misinterpretations. The whole process makes certainty of transmission a very risky business.[20] Skinner seems utterly unaware of this problem.

He seems oblivious, too, to the vast problems entailed by the modification of a complex environment. Problems are not merely many and complex in our chaotic (at least disharmonious) universe; they are interrelated, so that to deal (say) with the problems of the blacks in contemporary America, we must come simultaneously to terms with poverty, education, employment, housing, medical care, family structure, and the like—as well as with (though Skinner will reject the phrase) the psychology of prejudice. What is the demonstrated competence of Skinner's therapists—or teachers, owners, police, and priests (and are there really to be priests in Skinner's utopian world?)—to resolve these problems? They cannot adequately solve any one of them without simultaneouly solving all the others, and if, as Skinner proposes, they deal with them in piecemeal fashion instead, he must confront the further fact that a change in any one of these matters is itself likely to produce a change in another, and that this latter change (more accurately, series of changes) may be one of the unintended consequences of the controllers' actions. Thus to speak, as Skinner does, of modifying behavior and changing the environment is to ignore the complex realities hidden behind these simplistic terms.

Take, now, Skinner's idea of *planned* diversification. It has already been noted that the kinds and measure of diversity to be found in Skinner's new society will be determined by the controllers. The question now to be raised is, How shall we know in advance whether the prescribed diversities will blend together into a coherent unity or be disruptive of that unity? And further: what shall we do if the controllers make a mistake, or misuse their power? One all too obvious answer is that *we*—if members of the lower orders—will not and cannot know these things. For not only can we not "know" (we can only behave); we will have been conditioned to behave as the controllers want us to behave, which is to say, we will do as we are told. But surely, unless the controllers are gods (and even Socrates did not contend that his philosopher-kings were gods), they are likely to make *some* mistakes, they are likely to misuse some of their powers some of the time and thereby endanger the working of the system. Is there, within Skinner's arrangements, a self-correcting mechanism or principle that will deal adequately with this problem?
Here is what Skinner says:

> The misuse of a technology of behavior is a serious matter, but we can guard against it best by looking not at putative controllers but at the contingencies under which they control. It is not the benevolence of a controller but the contingencies under which he controls benevolently which must be examined. All control is reciprocal, and an interchange between control and countercontrol is essential to the evolution of a culture.

And again:

> Self-government often seems to solve the problem by identifying the controller with the controlled. The principle of making the controller a member of the group he controls should apply to the designer of a culture. . . . *He* will select goods or values which are important to *him* and arrange the kind of contingencies to which *he* can adapt.[21]

I have underscored certain words in the foregoing quotation to make it clear that what Skinner is talking about is not selfgovernment (or countercontrol) at

185   The Higher Reaches of the
Lower Orders: A Critique of
the Theories of B. F. Skinner

all. Like the Persian potentate (as recounted in the *History* of Herodotus) who addresses a group of fellow conspirators, he in effect says: "Let *us* choose out from the citizens a certain number of the worthiest, and put the government into their hands." Or, in keeping with a celebrated line in the *Iliad,* he argues: "Good sir, sit still and hearken to the words of others that are thy betters." The controller is a member of the group he governs only in the way in which an absolute monarch or tyrant may be said to be a member of the group he governs. He is *in* but not *of* the group. He is certainly not chosen *by* the group. Above all, if he too is a conditioned man, if he too is subject to contingencies of reinforcement designed to control his behavior, he is conditioned not by other persons—as he conditions others—and is subject only to contingencies of his own making—whereas others are subject to the contingencies that he has made.

In what sense, then, can it be said that there is a reciprocal relationship between the controller and the controlled? Only in the sense that there may be said to be a reciprocal relationship between the jailer and his prisoner. An influence there may well be: the behavior of the prisoner may elicit pity or compassion and kind treatment, or contempt or hatred and harsh treatment, from his superior, but this does not make them equals or promote effective control of the jailer by the prisoner; for it is still the superior who determines, and alone has the power to determine, the treatment that shall be accorded the fellow-member of his "group." After all, did not Skinner say that it is the controller who will select goods or values important to him, not to them, and that he will arrange the kind of contingencies to which he, not they, can adapt?

In effect, there is no way within Skinner's system to correct the misuse of power by the controller. Skinner has divided his world into higher and lower orders, and between the two there is an unbridgeable gap. The members of the lower orders are conditioned, not conditioning, men; creatures of automatic goodness, they behave properly not because they have an awareness of problems and make intelligent choices, but because they have no awareness and make no choices but do as they are required (have been conditioned) to do. How, then, can such men, who are not men but mindless beings, question the policies of the controllers? How can such robotlike creatures correct unwise or unworkable policies? If it be said that the controllers too are conditioned men, the response must surely be that they are conditioned, if conditioned at all, in a quite different way—not by other men, other controllers, but by contingencies that they have themselves made, in other words, by themselves. And while history may be said to teach many and diverse (perhaps inconsistent) things, there is one thing it teaches that transcends all reasonable doubt: namely, that the possession of power is dangerous (even if also useful) and that to guard against its wrongful uses is the first obligation of a responsible society.

To all this we must add: the great technical difficulties in planning a harmonious and efficient social order; the extraordinary qualities required in the men responsible for such planning (and it ought not to be forgotten that Skinner's planning—both in range and intimate details—goes far beyond all hitherto known schemes for human control); and the fact that such planning must take place in ongoing, not *de novo* societies, populated by previously (and, from Skinner's standpoint, erroneously) conditioned men, passionately committed to the traditional and the familiar. We can see that the feasibility of his proposals rests on a morass of perplexities.

Take, finally, Skinner's notion of a stable (though evolving) society. He does not mean by stability a static order, for central to his teaching is a program of deliberate change. But the changes he proposes have a particular purpose, to transform the existing order and bring into being a new culture. This new culture, once achieved, will approximate if not embody utopia. Hence, though it will continue to evolve, its evolution cannot be expected to admit major alterations. Tranquility, or the removal of tension, and peace, or the removal (or near removal) of conflict, become the hallmark of Skinner's stable—and if not static, certainly not dynamic—society.

Would such a society really work? Is it even attainable? I do not believe so, and for two reasons primarily. One is psychological, turning on the tensions and discontents that always attend differences and inequalities. The other is structural, turning on the resentments and ambitions that always attach to hierarchy. Together these make for perpetual conflict and occasional rebellion, and require, therefore, a method of resolution appropriate to a turbulent rather than a tranquil society. Let us consider these points in turn.

One striking omission in Skinner's book is his failure to treat the problem of equality. He talks, to be sure, of differences, which he prefers to uniformity. But he does not confront the problems that emerge when men impute attributes of superiority or inferiority to these differences. There is, of course, no necessary reason for such imputations, any more than there would be if we were talking of the differences between an apple and an orange. But for thousands of years men have somehow believed that differences—whether of race, sex, religion, nationality, intelligence, talent, creativity, or any number of consequential and inconsequential things—do and should entail such judgments. Indeed, the striving for preeminence is so pervasive as to warrant the suspicion that inequality in *some* form is an abiding characteristic of the human condition.

I am arguing, that is to say, that by nature *and by inclination* men are *and want to be* different, that they associate differences with imputations of super-

187   The Higher Reaches of the
        Lower Orders: A Critique of
        the Theories of B. F. Skinner

iority and inferiority, and that if they can no longer hope to better themselves they seek to improve the status of their children.

From time to time, moreover, some men and groups see themselves as outside of (alienated from, often because they believe they are regarded as inferior to) the larger group of which they are allegedly a part. Thus, when a black man today says, "I have nothing in common with whites," we may deplore his statement as a betrayal of his humanity, but we cannot fail to recognize the reality (and intensity) of his belief (feeling). And when any man, black or white, resents the superior position held by another man, generally because he believes that the other man is no more and perhaps less deserving than he, we can regret or sympathize with his judgment, but we cannot, if we seek a stable society, ignore it. Skinner may tell us that beliefs and feelings and attitudes do not exist, that only relevant behavior counts. But the fact is that the behavior of such men draws upon such feelings and beliefs and can be understood only in terms of such attitudes. For Skinner to hold, therefore, that his controllers can both assign men to fixed tasks and also (through "operant conditioning") keep them there in some sort of cooperative action, is to flout all we know of human behavior.

As long, then, as differences and inequalities of some sort exist—and they will always exist—not tranquility but tensions and discontents will constitute essential characteristics of the social order.

These reflections are reinforced when we consider the further problem of hierarchy. In modern industrial society, specialization of function and the division of labor are not matters of choice but technical necessities. Workers cannot be freely interchangeable. Differences of function entail inequalities of skill and (generally) productivity, and consequently inequalities of reward. Now if the ideal of equality of opportunity had been, or could be, fully realized—if all men had been, or could be, given the same opportunities to reach higher positions—men at various levels in the pyramid of hierarchical power and reward might feel no sense of injustice. But the reality, of course, is that this ideal has never been realized, and if we are to take seriously the Socratic teaching that equality of opportunity requires, among other things, that all children be taken from their parents immediately after birth and raised in common—and I see no other way to achieve complete equality of opportunity—it is unlikely that the ideal can ever be fulfilled. Even if, with Edward Bellamy, we look also to equality of income or reward, the problem of differentiated power and the touchy question of incentives (which has bedeviled even the "socialist" countries of our time) remain.

It follows, then, in the face of the heterogeneity in power, fame, reward, and the like, produced by hierarchical structures, that men at the lower levels will (as they do) resent their positions and strive in various ways to rise above them. They object, too, to the arbitrary rules (or what they take to be arbitrary rules) and the irresponsibility (lack of democratic accountability) of men at the higher levels of those pyramids. Whatever the merits of their complaints, certain facts are clear: that hierarchy makes for a variety of differences, that these differences entail a variety of inequalities, and these inequalities produce not merely a variety of tensions but also a striving for betterment that cannot (Skinner notwithstanding) be programmed out of existence.

What is true of hierarchies in the industrial sphere is true of hierarchies in other areas of society, e.g., the political, the religious, the educational. The difficulties—the resentments, tensions, conflicts, strivings—are thus all-pervasive. How implausible, then, is the extraordinary remark by Skinner's alter ago, the psychologist Frazier in *Walden Two*: "We simply arrange a world in which serious conflicts occur as seldom as possible or, with a little luck, not at all." Conflicts will be absent only in a world where men have ceased to be human, where they have been converted into robots and are consequently "automatically good"; or in an entirely just world populated by entirely just men, which is to say, Heaven. But as Lucifer demonstrated, not even the most perfect ruler can order the continuance of perfection.

Skinner's recipe—conditioned virtue—is both ineffectual and destructive. Ineffectual, because it cannot eliminate the conflicts that endanger the stability of a state. Destructive because, in seeking only to eliminate those conflicts, it provides no mechanism by which to contain them when they erupt. Thus Skinner's theory not merely invites the rebellions of the lower orders; it ensures that those rebellions, when they occur, will be unmanageable.

V

Two considerations more than any others seem to underlie the idea of a closed society: that the truth is known and that it can and should govern human societies. Both are demonstrably false.

The truth is not known, at least not the whole truth. Always we know only a fraction of what there is to be known; always the things we do not know vastly exceed the things we know; hence we cannot be sure that we know even what we think we know. We act, of course, on the basis of what we think we know, and we must do so. But action dictated by faith or circumstance or limited (because partial) understanding is a far cry from absolute knowledge.

Since *the* truth is not known, it follows (as Mill argued) that men must be free to inquire into the validity of conflicting claims to truth. The alternative is the imposition of an alleged truth on the ground that power is rightfully employed in a true cause. But whether that cause is a true cause is precisely what is at

189   The Higher Reaches of the
Lower Orders: A Critique of
the Theories of B. F. Skinner

issue. Hence domination not merely evades the issue of truth, it corrupts the process by which it might be ascertained.

What is distressing about Skinner, who is presumably committed to scientific method, is that he not only claims to know the truth, or enough of it to warrant the conviction that in time he will embrace it all, but wants the power to preclude the possibility of anyone ever again challenging that truth, or the men who implement it.

From this point of view, it is less important to argue that Skinner is wrong in his conception of what human nature (or behavior) is, than it is to argue that uncertainty is the first condition of rational thought, and that whatever one's conviction about his own or another person's ideas, it is never legitimate to hold that those ideas are beyond criticism. For the moment Skinner is content to meet this requirement, as is evidenced by his participation in public discussions of his work. But the logic of his position is such that should he obtain the power to put his ideas into practice, those ideas and that power could not be reversed. If he can do what he claims to be able to do, and if he has the power to do it, then men conditioned by his methods will no longer be capable—as they are now—to make the free choice to reject his system. This irreversibility converts Skinner and his controllers into authoritarian, oligarchical men.

This authoritarianism, inherent in Skinner's thought, should come as no surprise to a reader of *Walden Two*. There Skinner has Frazier say:

> The government of Walden Two has the virtues of democracy, but none of the defects. . . . We have no election campaigns to falsify issues or obscure them with emotional appeals, but a careful study of the satisfaction of the membership is made. Every member has a direct channel through which he may protest to the Managers or even the Planners. And these protests are taken as seriously as the pilot of an airplane takes a sputtering engine. We don't need laws and a police force to compel a pilot to pay attention to a defective engine. Nor do we need laws to compel our Dairy Manager to pay attention to an epidemic among his cows.
>
> Let's not stop with democracy. It isn't, and can't be, the best form of government, because it's based on a scientifically invalid conception of man. It fails to take account of the fact that in the long run *man is determined by the state*.[22]

And if one should wonder what is entailed by channels of protest and studies of satisfaction of the membership, Frazier explains that Walden Two has effectively controlled the *inclination* to behave; that through a wise choice of techniques what has been increased is the *feeling* of freedom; and that in any case a social structure has been built "which will satisfy the needs of everyone and in which everyone will want to observe the supporting code."

Skinner underscores these points in *Beyond Freedom and Dignity* when, to avert possible misunderstanding, he says: "People who get along together well under the mild contingencies of approval and disapproval are controlled as effectively as (and in many ways more effectively than) the citizens of a police state."

Thus Skinner moves, not simply "beyond" (by which he means "short of") freedom and dignity, but "beyond" ("short of") science and rationality. He moves "beyond" science in that he removes his system and the men who operate it from the self-corrective controls of experience. One of the great merits of democracy is that it can provide an effective mechanism through which those who live under a system are able to inform the rulers of their experiences under that system. But this information is worthless if it has been prearranged. Nor is it consequential if is enters only as a petition or prayer, dependent for its reception on the arbitrary will of the ruler. But in Skinner's system, apart from an individual's presumed capacity to reveal his suffering as a cow reveals its affliction or an engine its defect, there is no way for a citizen to express his discomfort or to compel a change in its cause.

Skinner moves "beyond" rationality in that he does not understand the limits of reason in politics. It is a truism that in politics *the* truth, in whatever measure known, does not wholly govern men. There is a certain recalcitrance in human nature, a grim resistance to the surrender of one's habits and prejudices, a love for what is, a commitment to people and places and possessions. What *can* be done is vastly different from what a scientist-king believes *ought* to be done. This is why Aristotle carefully distinguished theoretical wisdom (knowledge of the truly good) from practical wisdom (knowledge of what is possible in a given situation). Totalitarian rulers, not knowing or indifferent to this distinction, resorted to terror in the abortive attempt to achieve their unattainable ends. Similarly, Skinner, who would use the carrot rather than the whip, requires manipulation (a form of coercion in that it violates man's autonomy) to pursue his stated objectives, and would put that manipulation outside the reaches of popular control. All of which becomes particularly irrational when we understand that many problems are not capable of permanent solution at all.

I mean here no more than that, where diversity and thus conflict are permanent features of the human condition, it is necessary to provide not "a" solution but a method that will admit of continuing (and at best partial) resolutions. This is why Mill and other writers in the liberal tradition have stressed the crucial importance of democracy and the open society, from which there emerges a certain conception of dignity, embodied in the rights of man.

Among these rights three are of such importance that they merit special emphasis: the right to be wrong; the right to be Left; and the right to be left alone.

191   The Higher Reaches of the
       Lower Orders: A Critique of
       the Theories of B. F. Skinner

It is often said that while every man has a right to speak as he may please, it should please him to speak only what is right and good; for no man should wish to utter false or wicked things. He has a right to be right, but not to be wrong. This is pernicious doctrine. He who claims to know what is right and true and good really asserts no more than that he thinks he knows. Even if he does know, he knows not by authority—for as Hobbes remarked, when a man says that God spoke to him in a dream he is really saying he dreamed God spoke to him—but by observation and reasoning. As these were open to him, so they must be open to other men.

It is also often said that men should not disturb accepted traditions and practices, especially since (as would be the case if Skinner's policies prevailed) they are the "right" practices. What is most objectionable here is the notion that conformity and tranquillity are the noblest of virtues. One need not insist that all traditions and practices are wrong in order to insist on the right to question them. The right to be Left is the right to point out derangements and propose remedies. The right to be Left denies that tranquillity is the highest achievement of the human race.

Finally, the right to be left alone. It is often said that what liberalism lacks is a sense of and respect for community, that it sets men apart in isolation from each other and thereby deprives them of their brotherhood. This is surely a tawdry caricature, both of Mill and other liberals (Russell, MacIver, Dewey, Cohen, etc.). Man does not and cannot exist apart from community. Community forms him, gives him his substance and identity. What liberals contend is that community is a necessary and ennobling reality, but not the only or complete reality. Individuality is a reality, and a value, too. Men must be given room for their own differentiation. To realize oneself as a unique person, a man must in some measure be left alone.

Nor does this mean that he will be the straw man Skinner attacks—a fully autonomous creature. There is no such thing as a completely free and autonomous man. What autonomy means in the real world is not freedom from all restraints, not the denial of socialization (some "conditioning"), but the insistence that where an individual's practices do not militate against the interests of others, his mode of life has a privileged claim to respect. Where his actions do not directly violate the welfare and interests of others, he should be left undisturbed.

We live, in some respects, in a deranged world. Through accident and design, men have been divided into higher and lower orders. But it is not written in the stars that those at the bottom are forever destined to reside there, or were properly put there initially. The right system, the only just system, must have as its prerequisite a mechanism that will enable the lower orders not merely to reach out for their legitimate higher claims but actually to attain them. Equality in all things is an impossible goal. But equality in crucial things is a reasonable goal. What those crucial things are is properly a matter of dispute. Hence men must be free to discuss and resolve that dispute. In this at least they must be equal. Such freedom and such equality are the core of what we mean by dignity. The "right" human objective, then, is not to move beyond freedom and dignity but to secure them.

VI

Despite all that has been said here, some sensitive and idealistic persons have found in Skinner's theory a plausible answer to their concerns. Why is this so?

1. Clearly, they do not see in that theory and its explanatory account anything markedly different from what they conceive American practices already to be. In their view, America is not a liberal or democratic state but a society ruled by hidden elites. These elites condition us now—through controlled "information" from the government and mass media, through authoritative indoctrination from the churches and schools, through programmed advertising from the controllers of Madison Avenue. This conditioning works. It has produced a conformist culture made up of one-dimensional men.

The choice before us, therefore, is not between programming and the absence of programming but between two kinds of programming—that of Skinner and that of hidden elites. It is not a choice between two ideal types—authoritarian rule and democracy; but between two realities—the benevolent authoritarianism of Skinner's scientist-kings and the inchoate (and wicked) authoritarianism of the political-military-industrial complex. Indeed, they do not even take Skinner's controllers to be scientist-kings or authoritarians at all; rather, the controllers (as Skinner has repeatedly emphasized) are themselves controlled men, they are like us, of us. Hence their programming is more likely to be "right."

2. They are attracted as much by Skinner's methods as by his promised results. Some see him as he sees himself, as a humanist, "one of those who, because of the environment to which he has been exposed, is concerned for the future of mankind."[23] Others (rejecting his world outlook) are attracted by his techniques, which they see as improved shortcuts of technological manipulation that may be used to achieve their own ideological ends.

It is a grim fact, they note, that good ends are not always attainable by good means. If economic development is to take place in the "backward" nations, for example, despotic rather than democratic rule may be required. If children are to be taught mathematics, language, and "right" principles, authoritarian rather than democratic methods may be the more effective. And if good men

193   The Higher Reaches of the
     Lower Orders: A Critique of
     the Theories of B. F. Skinner

are to realize their right causes in a world where persuasion, addressed to previously conditioned (and therefore unreceptive) men, can never be effective, Skinnerian techniques may be the only device to break the bonds of conformity.

3. They are bemused, then, by the quest for certainty. Like Hobbes, they want peace and tranquillity and a commodious life, and they believe that Skinner will help to provide these. Here many correctly sense what Skinner himself does not see: that Skinner is essentially a mystic, not a scientist or behaviorist at all. What drives Skinner, and what attracts them to Skinner, is his faith—not in reason, or science, or scientists, or even that limited breed of scientists known as behaviorist psychologists, but in a sort of Invisible Hand that will transcend environmental determinism to control the environment that controls us, and in that way lead us to utopia. And Skinner's utopia, like all utopias, cannot be said to be harmful or wrong, for how can one criticize what does not exist and never has? There are no imperfections, no meannesses, no inequities, in Skinner's world. We cannot disprove empirically what is not yet real. His hypothetical utopia, like all mystical systems, is invulnerable to criticism.[24]

This fascination with utopia must not be minimized. For well over two millennia men have been gripped by the Socratic portrayal of an ideal Republic ruled by philosopher-kings. Bacon's *New Atlantis* anticipated much present-day disillusionment with philosophy by putting scientists at the helm instead. What Skinner does is to plumb the hearts of those who want freedom but do not want to make choices, who want to *feel* free but not to *be* free, by giving them what they want (or will want after proper conditioning) while absolving them of all burdens—the fears, uncertainties, and responsibilities—of decision-making. He offers them a royal road to salvation—led and controlled by behaviorist scientist-kings.

Similarly, we must not mistake the profound appeal of the doctrine of environmental determinism. Listen again to Skinner:

> Do I mean to say that Plato never discovered the mind? Or that
> Aquinas, Descartes, Locke, and Kant were preoccupied with incidental,
> often irrelevant by-products of human behavior? Or that the mental laws
> of physiological psychologists like Wundt, or the stream of consciousness
> of William James, or the mental apparatus of Sigmund Freud have no
> useful place in the understanding of human behavior? Yes, I do. And I
> put the matter strongly because, if we are to solve the problems that
> face us in the world today, this concern for mental life must no longer
> divert our attention from the environmental conditions of which human
> behavior is a function.[25]

Here, at one stroke, Skinner imputes responsibility for our many problems not merely to all the thinkers who have preceded him but to the fact that they exercised "thought" at all. Skinner thus presents himself as a humble, not an arrogant man. It is not *his* "mind" that is superior to theirs. It is rather the environment that is above us all. The "evil," the weakness, the fallibility in man—these are not the products of man's will, or of his "nature," but of an uncontrolled environment that makes us what we are. Control the environment and you control the conditions of life; control the conditions of life and you control man.

4. It follows, paradoxically, that Skinner appeals precisely to those who would argue men should not be governed by forces outside their own control. That, he contends, is how they are governed now—with catastrophic results. Consequently, with the help of science, men who wish to be ("feel") free must seize control of those external forces (the environment) which determine their behavior in order that they may themselves determine that behavior "correctly." Not to control the environment is in fact to surrender to the forces that now control them.

Doubtless there are further reasons for Skinner's widespread appeal, but these may be sufficient to suggest why that appeal is widespread, and why the grounds that sustain it appear so plausible.

It is pointless to repeat here the considerations I have already advanced to show that *all* of these interpretations of Skinner are either erroneous, in that they mistake Skinner's teachings, or warrant condemnation, in that they lead to harmful results. A few additional remarks, however, may be in order.

1. Skinner's system *is* markedly different from current American practices in at least two major respects: it substitutes for the present conditioning from a variety of uncoordinated sources a carefully coordinated and univocal pattern of conditioning; and it substitutes for the present reality of imperfect democracy an ideal or perfect, because total, system of authoritarian rule.

It may or may not be true that America is governed rather than merely (or widely) permeated by "hidden elites." But to the extent that it is true those elites are not merely many, they are often discordant and opposed. They are also specific rather than general, in the sense that while an elite may dominate a realm of activity at a particular time, it does not dominate all sectors of the society always. It is contested by other elites, and it depends for its success on its ability to win the support of the masses. And where elites compete for mass support, that support is forthcoming only where the masses can exact a price in return. To this extent at least, the masses do choose. A particular elite does not always ascend to power, as business elites have learned to their discomfiture in the age of the welfare state, and as labor elites learned in the age of capitalism

195   The Higher Reaches of the
Lower Orders: A Critique of
the Theories of B. F. Skinner

and are still learning in the age of the mixed economy. In Skinner's system, however, the masses never choose; a particular elite always governs.

The very fact that Skinner is free to prescribe wholesale remedies for change; even more, the fact that he believes those remedies not only should but can be implemented—these testify to the relative openness of existing arrangements, both in ideas and political practices. It is all too clear that under his system there can be no opposing ideas, indeed no "ideas" at all, and no political instruments for change counter to the will of his new ruling class.

2. Skinner is not a humanist, for he dehumanizes man. No less important, in scorning process for results, he deprecates humanistic values in the procedures he advocates.

I know it is fashionable, today as always, for men convinced of the rightness of their cause to become impatient with and ultimately to reject the tedious delays and inevitable compromises that emerge from the formal rules of consultation, bargaining, and popular acquiescence. They want not "right" procedures but "right" results; hence they are prepared to jettison those procedures when they do not get what they want.

This is the principle of oligarchy, a principle that respects "superior" minds and is contemptuous of the "inferior." But it is not a principle consistent with humanism. In the humanist conception, all men require opportunities for education and growth, all men count. To neglect their judgments, to impose the judgment of an allegedly superior will, is to diminish their humanity. And if it is the business of a people to correct the errors of government, procedures that enable them to criticize, to participate, and effectively to remove rulers are vital.

The bad-means/good-ends relationship accepted by Skinner's devotees is equally dangerous. This is of course the ancient problem of "dirty hands," the notion that good men may have to do unjust things in order to achieve just goals. But this is a false and pernicious statement of the problem. If a particular means is *necessary* to the achievement of a "good" end, such means—even though it may entail painful acts, such as the surgical removal of a leg to save a man's life, or the resort to war to save a people from Nazi barbarism—cannot be condemned. Means and ends are never to be judged in disjunction. They must always be taken together and assessed in terms of the total situation.

From this perspective, despotism for the advancement of "backward" peoples and authoritarian techniques for the improvement of children have little or no relevance for what Mill called mature and enlightened peoples. It is even questionable whether despotism will "advance" a "backward" people rather than more effectively bind it in subjection, or whether authoritarian controls will "educate" children rather than turn them into mechanical beings. Certainly, the ineffectiveness of Chinese "brainwashing" lends little support to the notion that modern techniques of conditioning can effectively reeducate men.[26] It requires more than a little faith to believe that Skinner's conditioning of rats, pigeons, infants, and retardates proves his ability to condition mature adults.

3. Skinner is indeed a mystic, and his utopia is much to be feared. Utopia, to be sure, has always appealed to men conscious of the injustices of an existing order and attracted to an ideal commonwealth where disharmony and inequity no longer prevail. But this is not the lot of men. Utopias of whatever kind are always rooted in a rigid authoritarian mold. This is because the new system, being perfect (or nearly perfect), cannot admit of change lest it lose its perfection. Utopias are thus static societies, and men within them, frozen into higher and lower orders, are soon frustrated and bored. The impulse to change cannot be eliminated, for while men have limited needs they have unlimited wants; but if suppressed, that impulse will assume unorthodox and revolutionary forms. Hence the inevitable dilemma of utopia: to assure the maintenance of its perfect arrangements, it must preclude orderly processes of change; by precluding those processes, it only facilitates the emergence of other, disorderly, and (probably) violent social movements. The reality of utopia becomes the death of utopia.

Like Plato, whom he oddly dismisses, Skinner believes that knowledge—*his* knowledge—is virtue; that *his* understanding of human behavior will lead always to the "right" controls, the "right" results. He should hearken instead to the words of sanity uttered by a madman:

> Knowledge and pain go together. The more we know, the greater our despair. The more we advance, the more we clash with the immensity of evil. . . . Not all your scientists put together could guarantee the serenity of a single human being.[27]

Skinner looks to external (environmental) forces as determining the nature (behavior) of men. But the curious fact (I must repeat) is that if his notion of environmental determinism is correct, Skinner *cannot* bring about the changes he prescribes. If we are what we are because of deterministic forces outside out control, we *cannot* become other than what we are or are destined to become. To be other than we are, to become other than what we are already destined to become, we would have to control the environment that controls us. But if *it* controls us, we cannot control *it*. Hence Skinner's proposal is self-defeating.

To put this another way: If Skinner's goal is survival of the culture, and if survival requires that his controllers gain power, then his doctrine of environmental determinism precludes their getting that power and hence of providing for that survival. To get that power they would have to break the chains of environmental determinism. The logic of Skinner's theory makes it impossible for them to do this, though Skinner curiously believes that they can and should

197 **The Higher Reaches of the
Lower Orders: A Critique of
the Theories of B. F. Skinner**

do this. If they can do it, despite his theory, then his theory is wrong: the environment does not deterministically control men. And if they can do it, we are back of course to the ethical question: survival for what? Why is X culture—*our* culture—worthy of survival? Why is it more worthy of survival than Y or Z (*their*) cultures? Indeed, given a deterministic doctrine, in what sense can it be said that we choose survival at all? It is really no answer to say, as Skinner said in a television broadcast (October 17, 1971): "We do not choose survival as a value. It chooses us." For if it chooses us, we need neither Skinner nor his concerns; all will be done despite him or ourselves.

4. To avoid being governed by forces outside their own control, Skinner would have men seize control of their environment. But which men? If Skinner's controllers, the new men of the higher orders, in what sense can men of the lowers orders be said to control? Clearly, whether the environment controls men, or Skinner's controllers control the environment that controls men, the bulk of mankind remains subjects, not citizens. A citizen is one who rules and is ruled; a subject is only ruled. In Skinner's world there are rulers and subjects. There is, in this relationship, no significant difference between the current world as Skinner depicts it and the world he would create. The future world is not better or worse than the present world; it is fundamentally the same. But to the extent that the actual world is different from the world he depicts, what he envisions is decidedly worse; for to turn citizens into subjects is effectively to bind them to governments and forces he would set permanently outside their own control.

VII

A final world: No credit or blame should attach to Skinner for the achievements or failures of *Beyond Freedom and Dignity*, or of his life's work. Clearly, these are the products of external circumstance, the environment, over which as a determinist he can have had little or no control. For the same reason, no credit or blame should attach to this writer for what is said here, or to the reader for his reactions. As Skinner would be the first to insist, both writer and reader are also behaving only as they must. If, then, none of us is an autonomous man, if none of us is responsible for what we do and say, what is the point of writing, reading, reflecting upon, or talking about this book?

10　　　How New Are the
　　　　　　New Conservatives?

What are the new conservatives telling us that the old conservatives have not told us before? Are they articulating new principles or merely applying old principles to new problems—or to old problems in new settings? Have they resolved the tensions within, and contradictions between, the diverse schools of conservative thought so as to present a new synthesis, a unified and coherent body of ideas that may properly be called the new conservatism? And have they, along the way, adequately met the many criticisms that have been brought against traditional conservative doctrines?

To answer these and related questions, I propose to state briefly the major tenets and leading criticisms of the old conservatism and to consider some of the recent contributions of the so-called new conservatives.

I

Some Preliminary Observations

It may be objected, first, that I have posed the wrong questions. What counts, it may be argued, is not the truth or validity of an idea but its utility and influence. Why is conservatism significant today? What circumstances explain its resurgence as an important political force? And why do so many people, including any number of sensitive and reasonable men and women, now embrace it?

Political and psychological inquiries of this kind are important, of course. But the philosophical question, the truth or validity of an idea, is also part of its utility, and *belief* in the truth or validity of an idea is part of its influence. Men continue to debate the truth or falsity of conflicting doctrines, presumably because to establish the one or the other would make a difference. Hence, while many people doubtless embrace ideas for psychological and strategic reasons—because they satisfy a deep craving for security or rationalize preferred positions, powers, and privileges—serious thinkers still seek to rest their

views on morally defensible grounds. The conservatives we will consider
here—men like Friedrich A. Hayek, Michael Oakeshott, and Leo Strauss—are
serious thinkers. Their arguments must be met if they are not to carry the day.

Second, it may be objected that conservatism is not to be defined by any one
set of principles or even by, simply, opposition to drastic change. An intelligent
mind draws distinctions; hence one who, like Daniel Bell, asserts that he is
radical in economics, liberal in politics, and conservative in culture is displaying
not multiple schizophrenia but sensitive discernment. It may be unfair, then, to
apply the label "conservative" to a particular individual or group or to insist
that such a person or entity be conservative in all aspects of his or its being.

Much of this is incontestable. Conservatism is in part a disposition or mood,
not simply an "essentialist" body of principles. But conservatism cannot be
said to be defined by no principles or policies at all; for what then could
conservatism mean? To say that X is or is not a conservative is to presuppose
certain principles in terms of which such an assertion may properly be made.
That particular individuals and groups are conservative in some things but not
in others only argues that there *are* standards or criteria that legitimately enable
them to be termed conservative but that the label must be applied carefully.

It may be objected, third, that the disjunction made by conservatives like
William Buckley and his mentor Willmoore Kendall—that conservatism must
be understood in *contradistinction* to liberalism—is overly simplistic, perhaps
not even sensible. Conservative criticisms of liberalism *and* vice versa, it may
accordingly be said, are but family squabbles, not to be taken seriously; against
both doctrines, only a radical politics is meaningful.

In one sense, this contention is evidently true. The decisive issue for our time
is not Mill vs. Burke but Mill vs. Marx; hence liberals and conservatives stand
together, at least here and now, in defense of democracy against dictatorship.
But liberals and conservatives are by no means agreed on what democracy
means or entails; and while all liberals are logically committed to democracy,
some conservatives accept it only as a matter of historical necessity or ex-
pediency. Moreover, in the divergent responses they make to radical critiques,
the issues between liberals and conservatives take on a crucial dimension
indeed.

Finally, it may be objected that the question posed in my title has already
been answered. As a major left-wing critic and editor recently said to me, the
new conservatives have told us three important things: that the welfare state
doesn't work; that liberals are bewildered by, and have no explanation for, the
breakdown in traditional styles of culture; and that the old problems of order
and peace and purposefulness have, in the immediate historical situation, a
new and commanding urgency.

But if the problems have long been recognized, then the new conservatives are not in fact offering a new analysis of our political situation. If liberals cannot adequately account for our cultural disorders—a dubious allegation—this but shifts the burden of that explanation to the conservatives. Have they pinpointed what, precisely, has broken down? Is all breakdown equally to be condemned? How do conservatives propose to repair the damage?

Further, what is meant by the statement that the welfare state doesn't work? If conservatives mean that the welfare state has not produced utopia, they are correct; but who has ever contended otherwise? If they mean that welfare-state countries are worse off than they were before, this is surely a contestable, and I think an unwarranted, assertion; but even if true, or partly true, it but raises the question, why?

If the welfare state has failed or is seriously deficient, is this because it has been insufficiently a welfare state? Or excessively so? What, precisely, is "excessive"? *Any* form of governmental regulation or assistance, such as our miserly Social Security system? And if the well-being of the citizenry is one of the acknowledged objects of government, how can any government be other than a welfare state? Conservatives do not denigrate all governmental activities. They do not argue, like the anarchists, for no state at all. They distinguish, as most people usually do, between good and bad governmental activities. They want, not a no-welfare state, but a particular kind of welfare state. Because it cannot take account of these important perplexities, the journalists' rendition of the new conservatism is not sufficiently illuminating. We still need to know the conservative principles and policies that a particular state—given its resources, level of social and economic development, traditions and institutions, constellations of powers and interests, and the like—ought to pursue if it is to advance the general welfare. What, with respect to this problem, are the new conservatives telling us that the old conservatives have not told us before?

II

In turning to the tenets of the old conservatism, I distinguish three major schools of thought. There are of course many shadings, refinements, departures, and overlappings in the writings of theorists within and across these schools. Nevertheless, these "ideal types" sufficiently account for the main streams of the old—and perhaps also of the new—conservatism.

The Politics of Virtue, or the Counterrevolution of the Saints

I include here a group of thinkers who advocate what may be called the politics of right conduct. These conservatives are not automatic defenders of the status quo. On the contrary, they are primarily concerned with the world as it ought to be. Their principles constitute both ideal goals toward which existing societies should move and criteria by which such societies may properly be judged. Hence they are often critics, even radical critics, of the world as it is, especially of what they take to be liberal societies. They are, to be sure, radical in a quite reactionary way, for they propound essentially aristocratic principles. But if to be radical is to go to the roots, to seek not cosmetic reforms but fundamental changes in contemporary practices and arrangements, they are certainly radical.

There is considerable disagreement among these conservatives as to the proper metaphysical or epistemological grounds on which to rest their principles.

According to Leo Strauss, correct moral and political principles can be, and have been, discovered through human reason alone. Reason enables man to apprehend what is "right by nature" and also to apply those right principles prudentially according to their circumstances, either directly through the rule of wise men, Plato's philosoper-kings, or indirectly through philosophers advising kings, or through statesmen where there are no kings.

Opposed to this notion of natural right is the doctrine of natural law, expounded by Christian theologians and lay political philosophers, e.g., Jacques Maritain and Bertrand de Jouvenel. Right principles are indeed to be discovered (not invented), but not through reason alone; they are manifested to us primarily through revelation. Their legitimacy is to be found either in Scripture itself or in God's words as interpreted by the Christian Fathers, notably Aquinas. Instructive too, as in Jouvenel's case, are the practices and arrangements of the Christian Church in the Middle Ages.

Whatever their *differentia specifica*, these groups unite on the politics of virtue. Walter Lippmann, for example, had little difficulty in arguing that natural-right and natural-law theorists belong together in a single camp, which he labeled "The Public Philosophy." Their principles, he said, are needed; we must "repair the capacity to believe" in them.

For this school, the fundamental political question is: What type of men, and what principles, should govern the community? This is fundamental because its right settlement ensures the excellence rather than the depravity of political legislation. Now, to settle anything rightly, one must first know what is right, and such knowledge is independent of one's opinion or claim that one is right. Invariably, conflicts among individuals and groups involve assertions by each claimant that he (or it) is right, that his cause is just, that what he wants is good for himself and for the community. To negotiate and compromise these conflicting claims so as to give each side a measure of what it wants is to accede to the legitimacy of such claims. But what if the claimants are wrong? What if they merely *think* they know but do not *really* know what is right or just or good?

Then to give them what they want rather than what they deserve is to do what is wrong, to treat both them and the community unjustly.

Knowledge of right principles, in this view, is not given to all men, only to a few, the best—persons of "quality, excellence, or virtue," as Strauss put it; "the people of light and leading," in Lippmann's construction. These superior few know what is good, what is the right or noble thing to do, and they do what is right or noble simply because this is the thing to do. Always they put the common interest above private interests. That is why they are the best. Consequently, the right political order is that which discovers, trains, and elevates the best into positions of power, each according to his or her merit or excellence.

Moreover, ordinary men—ordinary because they do not know what is right—cannot by their own reason behave virtuously themselves. They must, therefore, be guided by right rulers. They must do, not what they *think* is best, but what is *really* best; that is, what those who know what is good tell them to do. In this way they will act rightly, and by acting rightly they will attain True Freedom; for then they will actually do only what they would themselves have chosen to do had they but had the rational knowledge to know the good and the will to choose it when known.

This is why, in the politics of virtue, the good cannot be derived from the subjective desires of men. Such desires yield diverse and incompatible things, even harmful things. But what is really good, and what therefore men ought to desire, is what satisfies their needs. Accordingly, Strauss argues, "absolute tolerance is altogether impossible; . . . there are unchangeable standards in the nature of man and the nature of things." These standards, or "fixed norms," are absolute because they are "right by nature"; they are not "negotiable." They constitute the public morality of a closed society appropriate to, because natural to, man.

In these terms democracy and modern liberalism are clearly deficient. By relying on numbers instead of quality, on the false principle of equality rather than the true principle of inequality, democracy enables the unwise (or less wise), simply because they are more numerous, to govern the wise. By accepting Mill's principles of tolerance and an open society, liberalism (they argue) celebrates pluralist and relativist confusions over right moral convictions. Conservatives committed to the politics of virtue cannot, in principle, also be committed to democracy; they can accept it only as a momentary expedient. Liberalism they dismiss as a contemptible mistake.

The Politics of Restraint,
or Tradition and the Limits of Social Policy

Unlike the politics of virtue, which seeks (like Marx) not simply to interpret but also to change the world, the politics of restraint attempts primarily to preserve it. This is not because the world and everything in it are deemed good but because, as Michael Oakeshott put it, "The world is the best of all possible worlds, and *everything* in it is a necessary evil."

Why then ought we to preserve, not change, the world? The answer is fourfold.

First, human reason—or what Oakeshott calls Rationalism—neither knows nor can know what constitutes a better world. As Hobbes said, there is no such thing as the real good or ultimate end, no *summum bonum* or *finis ultimus*. Even Strauss conceded that his distinctions between justice and injustice, and the like, cannot be "demonstrated" and that "they are exposed to grave theoretical doubts." Why then should such claims to knowledge of right principles be obeyed? Because they claim to know what is good, rationalists, whether they are liberals, radicals, or conservatives, all suffer from the same fatal disease. They are all mistaken. There are only objects of desire, only what men *take* to be good.

Rationalism also erroneously assumes that we not only know what is good but also how to attain it, how to move the world to what it ought to be. But men are driven less by abstract principles than by prejudice, habit, and conceived self-interest; they are bound by customary arrangements and conform to traditional manners of behavior. Politics is not, for them, a war between principles, not the pursuit of a dream or ideology, but a conversation, in which the language they employ is that of acknowledgement and accommodation, not of combative assertion and denial. These intractable realities set limits to social policy. They make politics the art of the possible, not of perfection.

Of course there are evils in the world: poverty, crime, war; the list is interminable. But who really believes that all evils can be eliminated? That we can, for example, legislate prostitution or murder out of existence? This is not to say that nothing can or should be done. But what can be done is only what is *intimated* by existing elements within the tradition itself. A tradition is not static but dynamic, ever changing, containing and revealing intimations that may fruitfully be pursued. To essay more than this, to attempt vast and fundamental change, is futile. Worse, it may produce unanticipated and perhaps more disagreeable consequences. Moreover, any "solution" of a problem but exposes or leads to new problems. Hence, every pursuit of an intimation must be attended with a wary eye, with skepticism and reserve.

This leads to Oakeshott's greatest divergence from the politics of virtue, as also (or so it initially seems) from all rationalist thought. If there is no fixed design in, or intrinsic purpose to, human history, then our first obligation is simply to survive, "to keep afloat on an even keel." The proper business of the state is not to satisfy substantive wants or to impose a public morality in the alleged cause of True Freedom or the Public Good. It should only establish conditions to be observed by those seeking the satisfaction of their wants, rules of procedure that allow self-determined, autonomous beings to engage freely in self-chosen transactions with others. But in this cause the politics of restraint requires a politics of restoration, namely to change the (socialist or welfare-state) world that is to the (unhampered market-economy) world that once was and ought again, as the "right" tradition, to be. On the other hand, if this world is the best possible world, and everything in it is necessary, then to preserve it is to resist attempts to change it. Oakeshott "resolves" this anomaly apparently by abandoning the antirationalist politics of restraint for a rationalist restruc-turing based on economic individualism and limited government. Whatever the internal tensions of Oakeshott's thought, the primary import of his teaching has been a heightened sense of the limits of social policy.

Despite the sharp cleavage between the politics of virtue and the politics of restraint, a number of conservatives embrace both. This is self-contradictory on its face. The appeal to natural right or natural law is an appeal to principle, to allegedly objective criteria and standards independent of national practice. The appeal to tradition is an appeal to subjective experience, to what communities have done and believed. One who accepts the politics of virtue can respect tradition only to the extent that it incorporates right principles. He may also respect it (in the sense that he must take account of it) to the extent that municipal customs and arrangements impose practical impediments to the ready application of those right principles. He must, however, always sub-ordinate tradition to virtue; in praising or condemning tradition and in his treatment of it, he must be guided by virtue. That some conservatives celebrate both schools of thought is an interesting oddity.

The Politics of Economic Individualism, or the Libertarian Resurrection of the Invisible Hand

I turn now to a group of theorists so far removed from both the politics of virtue and the politics of restraint as to appear, in some respects, more liberal than conservative. In fact, some among them, e.g., Friedrich A. Hayek, Ludwig von Mises, and Milton Friedman, like their patron saint, Herbert Spencer, insist that they alone are the "true" liberals.

These thinkers oppose the politics of tradition because, as Hayek observes, it distrusts both abstract theories and general principles and consequently neither understands what social arrangements and "spontaneous forces" are necessary for freedom nor possesses a base from which to formulate principles of policy. New ideas more than anything else cause change, Hayek further argues; but a conservatism that looks to tradition fears new ideas: in part because, being hostile not merely to too rapid change but to change as such, it defends "popular prejudices, entrenched positions, and firmly established privileges";

in part because, having no distinctive principles of its own to oppose to them, it lacks the weapons needed in the struggle of ideas. In part it fails to perceive that the advance of knowledge makes possible the gradual solution of such problems and difficulties as we can hope to solve. Most decisively, this conservatism "by its very nature"—i.e., its obscurantism—"cannot offer an alternative to the [socialist] direction in which we are moving." It may slow down "undesirable developments," but it cannot eliminate them.

In contrast, Hayek and his fellow libertarians believe that they possess the right principles and can offer a better road for mankind. Unlike those who champion the politics of restraint, they mean, then, to restructure the world. But they are also unlike those who champion the politics of virtue; for the world they would bring into being—more accurately, restore—is the world of Adam Smith or that of the Old Whigs, a pluralist world in which differing standards of right jostle each other and public order consists only of what is necessary to insure the freedom to compete.

These libertarians depart from the politics of virtue in certain important respects. For one thing, they deny that moral and religious beliefs or matters of conduct are proper objects of coercion; the state should not interfere with individual liberty in the private as distinct from the public domain and should foster the development of multiple goals rather than promote a single morality. Moreover, because they hold that intolerance of moral values different from one's own makes it impossible to maintain a peaceful society with a minimum of force, they support widespread toleration. While these libertarians are not egalitarians, they are not in principle antidemocratic. Unlike the politics of virtue, rooted in concepts of order and hierarchy and the rule of superior persons, libertarian politics looks to democracy as an advantageous method for achieving peaceful change and political education. In any case, "the chief evil" is not majority rule but unlimited and omnipotent government, which is what elite rule ensures. The centrality of this "chief evil" to his thought explains not only what separates Hayek from Strauss (and Oakeshott) but why he breaks decisively with John Stuart Mill and opposes democratic socialism. He and Mill hold different notions of liberty.

This requires a brief explanation.

In an earlier period, individual liberty was conceived as freedom from law. The issue, as Spencer put it, was man versus the state, and every law was seen as a restraint on freedom. But we have since learned that property, too, is a form of power and that freedom is consequently threatened not only by the state but also by private or nongovernmental powers, e.g., corporations. State intervention is then invoked to protect individual liberty from the coercive acts of private powers; the state enters to restrain restraints. This is not to say that governmental intervention does not interfere with individual freedom; it is rather to say that economic anarchy or corporate despotism may also interfere with individual freedom.

To rectify the coercive practices that strong private power imposes, Mill's intellectual heirs turn to a positive version of the state. Whatever the problems, and they are indeed many and complex, the positive state at least employs an egalitarian form of power—one man, one vote—to counteract those radical disparities, especially economic differences, that interfere with genuine individual freedom of choice. Hence, when twentieth-century liberals defend the state, they do so precisely on liberal grounds: in the name of individual liberty. Their ends remain the same as those of their nineteenth-century forebears; but the old means—the negative state—are no longer adequate.

Much of this was anticipated and treated in Mill's *Principles of Political Economy* and *Chapters on Socialism*, which is why Marx excluded him from "the herd of vulgar economic apologists" and why conservatives correctly see him as their major antagonist. Hayek, because he remains committed to the view that individualism is incompatible with political intervention in economic affairs, diverges sharply from Mill, whom he otherwise reveres. Hayek and the libertarians continue to support competitive private enterprise within a relatively unhampered market society (with Hayek accepting more extensive state provision of social services than Ludwig von Mises or Lionel Robbins). They want limited government because they wish to limit that coercion that makes a person "a base tool in the achievement of the ends of another." A meritocracy, because it forces some to act in accordance with ideas of moral merit conceived by others, is "the exact opposite of a free society."

As an alternative to modern liberalism, the libertarians urge that individuals be rewarded on the basis of their economic value to society. This involves incentive rewards and, generally, the inegalitarianism of a competitive economic order fully responsive to needs and wants. Thus, with various degrees of vociferousness, adherents of this camp oppose the welfare state, especially its redistributivist policies. They resist all notions of state planning, urging, instead, the merits of individual initiative and private charity. They are quick to identify whatever unforeseen problems arise from massive public programs; deficiencies in government policies demonstrate the correctness of their anti-state position; and official interference in the heretofore private affairs of citizens always captures their attention.

These libertarian critics of our society bear an important message—one that liberals admittedly cannot afford to ignore; and indeed, their concern for liberty, for a society with a multiplicity of ends, habitually arouses liberal sympathies. Yet there is a gulf between these conservatives and the liberals they castigate, and the differences that separate them have telling political consequences.

An economy responsive only to freely formed needs and free choices to provide for them loses some of its appeal if it is grounded not on individual effort and decision but on force or fraud or inherited entitlement. Goods and services are not often acquired or produced under conditions of unfettered competition, and monopolistic control or other practices effectively deprive some of any real choice about the plan of life they wish to pursue. "Property," said Herbert Spencer, echoing Proudhon as he contemplated the reality of landholding, "is theft." Libertarians tend to ignore the origins of property or the actual modes of its acquisition, while liberals have accepted Spencer's notion and, through their doctrine of equality of opportunity, have attempted to provide whatever compensatory mechanisms prove necessary to rectify the injustices of market societies. Liberals, in short, are not economic determinists. Political democracy plays as crucial a role in constructing a free society as do economic arrangements. Thus any tendency of markets to emasculate individual choice turns modern liberals to state regulation (while it turns devotees of Ayn Rand to a celebration of strength and selfishness and the will to power as qualities more praiseworthy than individuality, which free choice, in liberal thought, is intended to promote).

To avoid extreme formulations (such as those of Rand) and to oppose the kinds of coercion created by a market system, a recognition of man's situation as a dweller among others, a social creature dependent to some extent on a communal understanding of how human relations are to proceed, must modify pure individualism. Once again, contemporary liberals turn to a positive version of the state and countenance wide rule-making activity, while libertarians remain convinced that simple "law and order" provide ample protection to all.

To put it in other terms, liberalism sits astride the age-old tension between liberty and equality and develops ad hoc ways of maintaining a balance amenable to currently perceived canons of justice. The libertarians abandon equality in the name of liberty without resolving the dilemma that this abandonment poses for the very libertarian principles of justice they espouse. In their thought, individualism comes to replace individuality, and freedom, as a result, develops hierarchical gradations. Consequently, in spite of Hayek's remarkable essay, "Why I Am Not a Conservative," and his pointed criticism of certain conservative doctrines, his thought fits comfortably, even if not snugly, among conservative ideas. He is correctly viewed as an opponent of the liberal persuasion.

In their distrust of elites and their opposition to government interference in matters of morality, libertarians differ sharply with those who subscribe to the politics of virtue. They have closer affinities with the politics of restraint (e.g., in their shared opposition to rationalism). Caution is warranted, however, for libertarians have a more positive view of man's development and a more activist conception of human problem-solving than the politics of tradition usually finds congenial. Further, in their rampant individualism they lack respect for those social forces and common arrangements that traditionalists celebrate as necessary to voluntary human interaction or as elements of being too important to self-understanding to be lightly obliterated. ("Every change," says Michael Oakeshott, is "a threat to identity" and "an emblem of extinction.") Curiously, in spite of these striking incompatabilities, some conservatives seem equally fascinated by the doctrines of all three schools of thought.

The New Conservatives, or the Ascendancy of Declining Expectations

We come, finally, to those called the "new conservatives." As *Esquire's* feature story about them observed, they include inner circles of friends and outer circles of sympathizers, their links forged by mutual interest in public policies, journals, or organizations. Some were illogically thrown together by their reaction to the barbarism of the New Left, and they retain a common heritage of bitterness over battles with the Movement. Others are coupled only by their common antipathy to liberalism, and still others appear to be liberals who simply have written superbly well on some old conservative themes.

The catch-all quality in this upsurge of conservative thought is rendered intelligible as soon as one searches for a coherent underlying philosophy unifying this set of writings and discovers that the search is vain, not only for an integrative philosophy but for any philosophy at all.

To some extent, these newly popular writers have borrowed from the three strands of conservative thought outlined above. Irving Kristol's concern for civilizing standards of public morality resembles, at least superficially, Leo Strauss's teachings about the politics of virtue. Edward Banfield's hopelessly unheavenly city seems to expand on themes from Oakeshott's politics of restraint. Milton Friedman's emphasis on freedom apparently follows closely Hayek's libertarianism. But what is most striking about the new conservatives is not that their doctrines are merely staples from old schools of thought but that they have nothing to add to the positions of their mentors.

As a group, the new conservatives have no philosophical interests. They lack a theory of history, they do not consciously espouse an ethics, their writings contain no conception of the nature of knowledge or, for that matter, any metaphysical base whatsoever. These absences help explain such seeming incoherences as, for example, the alliance between disciples of Strauss and followers of Oakeshott. Thus Gertrude Himmelfarb castigates liberals for their insufficient trust in human reason and their consequent praise of uncertainty, which, allegedly, leads to an erosion of public morals. But Aaron Wildavsky bemoans liberalism's overextended trust in human reason and its consequent overconfidence in social engineering. These contradictory outlooks conjoin without common ground, with only a common enemy, because a philosophic groundwork is not an abiding concern of these authors.

Indeed, the greatest consistency to be found in the new camp is perhaps a readiness to gloss over philosophic issues. Robert Nozick begins his most famous book with a simple assertion: "People have rights." But, if you then expect to discover how people got them, you will be disappointed. That interesting question is simply bypassed, and the tracks are covered by some vague references to John Locke and some offhand remarks about the serviceability of that philosopher's ideas.

Or take the case of Nathan Glazer, who has written extensively about the judiciary and its allegedly improper activities as it runs schools to promote integration, or administers mental hospitals to insure fair treatment, or supervises jails to protect criminals from abuse. At no point in his discussions does he stop to consider the nature of law. What is the relation of law to society? In what ways, if any, do law and justice correspond? What ought to be the relationship between justice and a legal system? Glazer is not interested in these questions, and his work is uninformed by any point of view about them. Like a good journalist, he tells lively stories, but the meaning of his tales, the structure of reality they incorporate, never occupies his attention.

Glazer's colleague James Q. Wilson maintains the same sort of nonphilosophic stance. Typically, he once began a lecture to a college audience with the assertion that our government needs to prevent heroin addiction and then went on to explain the difficulties of doing so and why his criminology based on punishment is superior to others based on rehabilitation. The philosophical issue was thus passed over in the first sentence, and, for the remainder, crime and punishment were discussed without any attempt to argue from a foundation that might explain what makes something a crime. Not even the very specific legacy of John Stuart Mill on the very issue of drugs in society could entice him into an exploration of the public/private dichotomy and its significance. In its place, we find only the same vague antirationalism that runs through so many articles in *The Public Interest*.

Irving Kristol, the catalyst, the organizer, the procurer of money and media exposure, and thus the single most important name associated with the new conservatives, writes about republican virtue and the need to refurbish the character of the American people. However, not only does he fail to distinguish between the classical Stoic conception of virtue (in which self-sacrifice and community service fulfill man's nature) and the more institution-oriented civic-humanist notion of the virtuous republic (in which balanced groups and the clash of ambitions promote the good of society), but he adds an elitist orientation of a sort quite different from that found in either previous version. Kristol wants to rely on leadership and wisdom even to the exclusion of consent. Thus the masses must be protected, against their will, from the corrupting effects of pornography by those wise enough to comprehend the requirements of virtue (see, for example, Walter Berns on the First Amendment's free speech as "wise free speech"). In the economic realm, however, no regulation is needed. The fear of bankruptcy and the need to accumulate capital promote bourgeois virtues sufficient to deter evil. Such obviously shallow use of the politics of virtue can sustain neither a serious critique of politics nor a serious defense of capitalism.

No one has filled out the picture of the virtuous commercial society that most new conservatives probably wish to celebrate. Perhaps, for slightly different reasons, all three schools of conservatives would be happy to see the general run of folk too engaged in acquisitive activities to find time for any egoistic design of grandiose plans to better the human condition, too preoccupied for any passionate pursuit of noble dreams about doing away with poverty and oppression, too busy for any narcissistic focus on work or relationships that yield personal gratification. Commerce, in the modern scientific world, uses self-serving passions to provide for a respectable way of life. It may be a second-best regime, but the only viable alternative is totalitarianism (science in the service of centralized tyrannies). From this point of view, liberalism's rational planning and wholesale tolerance encourage the wrong values, those that lead to the worst outcome, and they interfere with the right values, those that distract people from risky adventures.

Liberalism unleashes too much confusion. It is disorderly and unsettling. Here, perhaps, is the crux of the matter. The new conservatives are part of the newest worldwide quest for greater certainty. They yearn for a structured society that will impart meaning to life, a manner of living that clearly labels the good and the bad, observes lucid standards of merit, and announces unambiguously what counts as success or failure. In such an ordered society the camaraderie of the alienated will be replaced by a sense of belonging.

From this common existential base, various themes from the three different schools of conservatism converge on the common enemy, liberalism. Harmony, the Straussian conservatives insist, must precede community. Perpetual reform, the liberals answer, is compatible with the successful and moral organization of a political unit, for the only unity worth having is the agreement to utilize diversity and conflict in the cause of human betterment. The common good, liberals argue, is an open-ended concept best arrived at through democratic processes. Justice, the new conservatives counter, consists of a truth, an absolute standard of right (and, they often add, an absolute truth sufficiently knowable only by an elite whose dominance is a necessary or important part of its fulfillment). Liberal egalitarianism, especially its belief in those compensatory mechanisms necessary to equalize conditions and make equality of opportunity meaningful for both rich and poor, is perceived by the new conservatives as a threat. It is a threat to their truth (merit must be rewarded), a threat to individual freedom (the mob will elect demogogues), a threat to their correct standards of behavior (mass debasement of culture is intolerable), and a threat to the essential goals of collective action (men will seek security, not development).

People, the liberals claim, can never know their own limits until they push against them, for, just as you break the four-minute mile by straining against the possible, in politics you must experiment and reach for the stars in order to discover what can actually be done. In sharp disagreement, the Oakeshott school of thought pessimistically declares that politics is the art of the possible and that, therefore, a "counterrevolution of declining expectations," as Lewis Coser has dubbed it, is the only appropriate response to the overextended hopes of the welfare state. Further, reliance on prejudices, interests, and habits is always more prudent than innovation and the encouragement of untried remedies, which breed new problems rather than effective solutions.

Human rights, especially the right to be free from government interference, the libertarian conservatives add, provides the only safe bulwark against injustice. However sympathetic a chord that particular barb strikes, liberals, acutely sensitive to the social origins of rights, to the duality of freedom and community, and to the inextricably intertwined needs of individuals and groups, must politely demur. They have no faith in the resurrection of the invisible hand that will arrange individual actions so that they produce justice. Leviathan is no doubt a scary creature. But possibilities for democratic control of the beast make liberals into socialists of varying degrees.

Resuscitation of efforts to forge an allegedly essential public morality in the twentieth century is a not uninteresting development. It is an effort to sustain the enlightenment that could protect us from the current revival of religious fundamentalism, which threatens to compete with nihilism for the honor of undoing Western civilization. But formulation of such an ideology is also dangerous, for it forges a link between intellectuals and industry that portends a power bloc of considerable magnitude. At the very moment when intellectuals have been catapulted to center stage as knowledgeable actors, possessors of analytic and communication skills indispensable to the modern economic order, they turn to an ideology that sustains current hierarchies of power. Instead of letting philosophy play its traditional role, of maintaining a stance from which society can be criticized, some political commentators have become interested in reinforcing existing standards. Those willing to ally themselves with business and put their talents at the service of corporate power will be, and in fact are being, encouraged by highly lucrative offers (to write ads for Mobil Oil or to do research at the American Enterprise Institute). Corporate patronage then thrusts these writers into prominence. As capitalism buys itself sophisticated ideological justification, large numbers of intellectuals will be tempted to jump aboard the gravy train. The significance of the new conservatives may lie, therefore, not in the profundity of their ideas but in the large sums of money they can generate to propagate an ideology serviceable to American businesses. Considerable talent will suddenly find topics with conservative import attractive, and the media will increasingly carry conservative messages. The conservatives may well succeed in leaving an imprint on the 1980s for reasons having little to do with the merits of their ideas.

Perhaps the resurgence of interest in a civil religion, to which all conservatives can agree in principle if not in content, will prod liberals to develop more fully the revolutionary proposition inherent in their own philosophy: that there is no need for a public orthodoxy, that society can and ought to function without one. There is much new material in philosophy to reinforce the liberal concept of politics as an open-ended enterprise, and it needs amplification. In spirit and content, liberalism has within itself the material necessary to counteract the retreat to certainty. A conviction that people, unlike crabs, ought not to crawl backward, is irrepressible. The conservative appeal may not be long lived. But, in a fast-changing liberal world, in which nothing is sacrosanct and everyone is invited to question every authority, all three camps of conservatives will experience a revival because they are presented with an opportunity to defend transcendent, absolute truth and contrast it with the surrounding turbulence. Liberalism is the common enemy because it threatens their notion of ordered civilization. It is too radical for safety. But that, of course, is also liberalism's glory.

Afterword

A Credo for Liberals

1. Esteem liberty above all other values, even over equality and justice.

As long as inequalities exist—and in some form and measure they always will—liberty is necessary if men are to discuss and correct those inequalities they deem unjust. Liberty is also to be given priority over abstract claims to justice, for, since men disagree not only about what justice means but about what it entails, liberty is essential if men are peacefully and reasonably to examine and resolve those disagreements. Beyond this, liberty is essential to the discovery of truth, if only because freedom of inquiry and expression are indispensable to the correction of error. And it is, of course, necessary for solitude, without which no person can detach himself from the crowd and discover his individuality. Liberty is so good, so important, that its battle cry, "Leave me alone," may well be the most frequent phrase uttered by individuals from childhood to the grave.

2. Respect people, not property; but do not ignore the positive role of property in promoting human well-being.

Insofar as property is useful for liberty—as a countervailing power against government, as a means of self-dependence and self-development, and as an instrument that promotes variety of experimentation—defend people's claim to private property. Insofar as property is a form of sovereignty, enabling those who own it to stand in a superior relation to others and to exercise power over them, as well as to employ it for private purposes contrary to the public good, limit and control that property. The test is one of social utility, not of natural right; for rights adhere only to human beings, and only that is right which safeguards and ennobles mankind. "Leave me alone" is not equivalent to "Leave business alone."

213

3. *Distrust power, even that of majorities.*

Power may indeed enable good men to do good things, but power, as also the lack of power, always tends to corrupt. In the case of the possessor of power, it fills his mind with an undue sense of his own importance; it surrounds his person with fawning courtiers who tell him what he wants to hear, not what he needs to be told; and . . .
In the case of those who lack power, . . .

4. *Distrust authority.*

When one is a child, he accepts authority, because authority is all that he knows. When one is an ignorant adult, he accepts authority, at least in those realms (such as science and religion) where he recognizes his ignorance. But precisely because of that ignorance he knows that he cannot know whether the authority he accepts is right. And when he moves into areas, not simply of his competence but of his familiarity, he knows enough to know that there is no certainty in this world. Whatever we know, we know but partially.

5. *Be tolerant.*

It is always more comfortable to be certain, but this is why it is important to be tolerant.
Certainty is given only to gods . . .
Evils of suppression . . .

6. *Adhere to democracy.*

It is true that the right process may on occasion yield a wrong result, but, unless we are prepared to argue that free discussion and the careful examination of empirical evidence are calculated to mislead men, it is more likely to yield a right result. The wrong process in any case will yield a right result only accidentally and hence infrequently. What is crucial, however, is that what makes democracy the right process is that it includes provision for the correction of error.

7. *Revere truth and rationality.*

Myths may be useful, but it is the business of a rational man to understand both the myths and the reasons for their utility, not to be beguiled by them.

8. *Accept the inevitability of change.*

Nothing lasts forever, neither persons nor nations nor institutions, and tranquillity is an illusion. Fear revolution, for the success of a revolution is but the victory of revolutionaries and the corruption of both their principles and their honor. Look instead to reform, for, though slow, it is lasting; it will produce a minimum of harm; and it will make possible successive reforms that bring the ever-changing reality closer to the ideal.

9. *Do not disparage compromise.*

10. *Above all, retain the critical spirit.*

Oppose violence. (Distinguish force [by gov't] from violence [against government or persons or property].)

Notes

Chapter Two

1. For this exposition, see David Spitz, *The Liberal Idea of Freedom* (Tucson: University of Arizona Press, 1964). The seminal figure in this tradition is, of course, John Stuart Mill. In recent times its leading spokesmen surely include Morris R. Cohen, John Dewey, R. M. MacIver, and Bertrand Russell. Their writings, however they may differ in other respects, portray the meaning and implications of liberalism with clarity, cogency, and remarkable completeness.

Chapter Three

1. John Plamenatz, *The English Utilitarians* (Oxford, 1949), p. 122.
2. Bertrand Russell, *Portraits from Memory* (London, 1956), pp. 114–15.
3. George H. Sabine, *A History of Political Theory*, rev. ed. (1950), pp. 714, 706–7. That Mill and his *On Liberty* were treated no more indulgently by his contemporaries than by critics in our own day is amply documented by J. C. Rees in his excellent little volume *Mill and His Early Critics* (Leicester, Eng., 1956) and by James Fitzjames Stephen in his sweeping attack, *Liberty, Equality, Fraternity* (1873). For a present-day indictment which reflects much of the adverse literature on Mill and his essay ever since its publication, see Theodore B. Fleming, Jr., "John Stuart Mill's Essay On Liberty: A Critical Analysis" (Ph.D. dissertation, Yale University, 1957).
4. John Morley, *Recollections*, 2 vols. (New York, 1917), 2:363, 1:53.
5. For example, Albert W. Levi, "The Value of Freedom: Mill's Liberty (1859–1959)," *Ethics* 70 (October 1959): 37–46.
6. Elie Halévy, *The Growth of Philosophic Radicalism* (1949), p. 285.
7. Sabine, *History of Political Theory*, p. 709.
8. Benedetto Croce, "The Roots of Liberty," in *Freedom: Its Meaning*, ed. Ruth N. Anshen (1940), p. 34.
9. All three of these points were advanced by Professor Currin V. Shields in a paper read at the annual meeting of the American Political Science Association, Washington, D.C., September 11, 1959, as also in his introduction to the Library of Liberal Arts edition of Mill's *On Liberty* (New York, 1956), pp. xx–xxi.
10. For an account of this incident, which goes unmentioned in Mill's *Autobiography*, see Bertrand and Patricia Russell, *The Amberley Papers* (New York, 1937), 2:247–49.

11. Plamenatz, *The English Utilitarians*, p. 123.

12. Fleming, "John Stuart Mill's Essay *On Liberty*," p. 70 and passim.

13. See, for example, Gertrude Himmelfarb, *Lord Acton: A Study in Conscience and Politics* (Chicago, 1952), p. 75.

14. Fleming, p. 68.

15. Mill, *Dissertations and Discussions* (Boston and New York, 1864–75), 1:191.

16. See the citations in Rees, *Mill and His Early Critics,* pp. 9–14, 56.

17. See, for example, the comments of Jared Sparks in H. B. Adams, *Jared Sparks and Alexis de Tocqueville* (Baltimore, 1898), pp. 43–44.

18. So, for example, Louis Hartz, *The Liberal Tradition in America* (New York, 1958), esp. pp. 128–34.

19. I have argued this point in greater detail in my *Democracy and the Challenge of Power* (New York, 1958), chap. 5.

20. It is to be noted, for example, that Mill carefully distinguishes "questions of social morality," where he thinks the public, or the overruling majority, is likely to be right more often than not—because there it is asked to judge of its own interests—from "questions of self-regarding conduct," where he thinks the public, considering only its own preference, is likely to be wrong (*On Liberty,* chap. 4).

21. Mill, *Autobiography* (New York, 1924), pp. 162–64.

22. The phrase is professor Shields'; see note 9, above.

23. The passage concerning education on which this misconception of Mill is based is to be found in *On Liberty*, chap. 5, p. 161. It is easy to show, however, that throughout his life Mill was a consistent defender and advocate of the principle that the state has an obligation not merely to require but also *to provide in some measure* for the education of its children. This demonstration I must leave for a later occasion. Here it may be enough to call attention to but two of many facts that do not square with the impression of his critics: one, that Herbert Spencer, who was no stranger to Mill, castigated Mill precisely for his defense of, rather than opposition to, government intervention in education (see Spencer's *Social Statics* [New York, 1873], pp. 367 ff.); the other, that Mill explicitly committed himself to this position in earlier works—for example, his *Principles of Political Economy*—where he said: "Education . . . is one of those things which it is admissible in principle that a government should provide for the people. The case is one in which the reasons of the noninterference principle do not necessarily or universally extend" (*Principles of Political Economy, 7th ed., ed. Ashley, [Clifton, N.J., 1909], Book 5, chap. 11, pp. 953–54).

24. Published in two installments in the first volume of the *Oxford and Cambridge Review* (June and Michaelmas Term, 1907), with authorship imputed to Mill. The first (and larger) portion was republished as a separate volume by Columbia University Press in 1941, with an introduction by Dorothy Fosdick and with authorship again imputed to Mill.

25. For an ingenious (but, to this writer, unconvincing) argument to the contrary, see James P. Scanlan, "J. S. Mill and the Definition of Freedom," *Ethics* 68 (1958): 194–206, esp. 201–6.

26. Rees, *Mill and His Early Critics,* pp. 38–54, 61–63.

27. Bernard Bosanquet, *The Philosophical Theory of the State,* 4th ed. (London, 1923), esp. chap. 3, sec. 3.

28. For an analysis of certain deficiencies in Mill's style that make for troublesome construction, see, for example, Alexander Bain, *John Stuart Mill* (London, 1882), pp. 174–83.

29. The essays by Mill that have given greatest credence to this twofold yet seemingly disparate commitment are those on Bentham and Coleridge, reprinted in his *Disserta-tions and Discussion*, 1:355–417 and 2:5–78. For the substitution of Aristotle for Coleridge, see Levi, "The Value of Freedom: Mill's *Liberty* (1859–1959)," p. 43.

30. Some critics have gone so far as to make a *reductio ad absurdum* out of this concession by Mill. Thus Christian Bay, *The Structure of Freedom* (Stanford, 1958), p. 127, argues that, once a breach is made with regard to freedom of expression in general, the principle victim is bound to be freedom of expression on political issues. In the same vein, some of the "new conservatives" would even have us believe that in this respect Mill was, of all things, a totalitarian *malgré lui*!

31. *Utilitarianism*, Everyman ed. (London and New York, 1910), chap. 2, p. 22; and see, further, chap. 5, p. 59.

32. If any doubt remains on this score, one need only advert to Mill's rejection of the notion of essences (e.g., as in his *System of Logic*, Book 1, chap. 6, sec. 3) as proof that he did not subscribe to any species of natural right doctrine.

33. Sabine, *A History of Political Theory*, p. 711.

34. H. J. Laski, *Authority in the Modern State* (New Haven, 1919), p. 55.

35. In fact, Mill himself was fully aware of many of these difficulties. In his *System of Logic*, Book 6, chap. 9, secs. 2–3, he noted the impossibility of isolating any single phenomenon and denied that human actions, for example, are unrelated to or un-affected by other phenomena. In his correspondence, moreover, he repeatedly stressed the importance of unforeseen or, as he termed them, "unobvious" consequences and called attention to the difficulty of attempting to draw a line in practical affairs on the basis of a general principle. See *The Letters of John Stuart Mill*, ed. Elliot (London, 1910), 2:9, 95, 185.

36. In an article which appeared too late for consideration here, Professor Rees contends that Mill's critics are wrong in their indictment of Mill on this point because they fail to note the significance of the terms Mill employs in drawing his distinction between self-regarding and other-regarding acts. There is an important difference, Rees holds, between saying that an action merely affects or concerns another person and saying that it affects his *interests*. See "A Re-Reading of Mill on Liberty," *Political Studies* 8 (1960): 113–29. Unfortunately, this point deserves lengthier consideration than it is possible to give in this article.

37. Earnest Barker, *Political Thought in England, 1848 to 1914*, 2d ed. (London, 1928), pp. 7, 10; and cf. the bizarre statement by Crane Brinton, *Ideas and Men* (New York, 1950), pp. 432–33, who, by tearing Mill's words out of all meaningful context, would have us believe that "parts of Mill's writings sound today like the writing of a conservative defender of old-fashioned individualism against the New Deal." Brinton's statement is all the more incomprehensible in view of what Mill says in his *Socialism* (Chicago, 1879) and, even more pointedly, in his *Principles of Political Economy*, Book 2, chap. 1, sec. 3, where he goes so far as to assert that, if he had to choose, he would prefer communism with all its evils to the society of his day.

38. Georg Brandes, *Creative Spirits of the Nineteenth Century* (London, 1924), p. 200.

39. R. A. Nisbet, *The Quest for Community* (New York, 1953), p. 228.

40. So, for example, L. W. Lancaster, in his *Masters of Political Thought, III: Hegel to Dewey* (Boston, 1959), p. 132, alleges that Mill talks "as if the individual and society were two distinct things. . . . [But] surely, society and the state cannot exist apart from the individual persons composing them . . . ; it does not seem possible to put the

'individual' and 'society' into different categories, regarding the former as the only reality and the latter as purely imaginary."

41. Fleming calls attention to the fact that the original editions of Mill's essay, both in England and in the United States, speak of "man" but that the later People's edition, which is also the text of the Everyman's edition, renders this as "a man." Since I have not seen the drafts of Mill's original manuscript, I do not know whether the insertion of the article "a," which gives the text a different connotation, was intended by Mill or was merely the result of a printer's error, as seems more likely in view of Mill's stated refusal ever to revise this work. It would be pointless, therefore, to discuss the bearing of this on the problem stated in the text.

42. It does not argue against Mill's values here to say, as does Isaiah Berlin, for example (*Two Concepts of Liberty* [Oxford, 1958], pp. 40 ff.), that most men are content merely to be recognized as individuals by others without aspiring to anything more. Mill could have rightly insisted that one is a precondition of the other.

43. Sabine, *A History of Political Theory,* pp. 707–8.

44. Michael St. John Packe, *The Life of John Stuart Mill* (New York, 1954), p. 490.

45. Mill, "Periodical Literature–Edinburgh Review," *Westminster Review* 1 (1824): 509.

46. Bosanquet, *The Philosophical Theory of the State,* pp. 64–65.

47. D. G. Ritchie, *The Principles of State Interference* (London, 1891), p. 86.

48. Lancaster, *Masters of Political Thought,* p. 134.

49. Bosanquet, *Philosophical Theory of the State,* p. 65.

50. H. J. Laski, *Liberty in the Modern State,* rev. ed. (New York, 1949), p. 15. But compare Mill's statement in 1871 that "the land question and the relation between labour and capital are the points on which the whole of politics will shortly turn" (*Letters,* 2:311).

51 For example, *Principles of Political Economy,* Book 4, chap. 7, and Book 5.

52. See his essay on civilization in *Dissertations and Discussions,* vol. 1. esp. pp. 189–218; the quotations are on pp. 189, 214, 215.

53. Bertrand Russell, *Portraits from Memory,* p. 127.

54. As alleged, for example, by H. M. Roelofs, *The Tension of Citizenship* (New York, 1957), p. 182.

55. John Morley, *Recollections,* 1:61.

56. Cf. Fustel de Coulanges, *The Ancient City,* trans. Small, 4th ed. (Boston, 1882), Book 3, chap. 17; but see, *contra,* A. H. M. Jones, *Athenian Democracy* (Oxford, 1957), chap. 3, esp. pp. 43–45, and E. A. Havelock, *The Liberal Temper in Greek Politics* (New Haven, 1957), especially the Introduction and chap. 13.

57. In what must surely be one of the more remarkable utterances in political literature, Crane Brinton *does* deny this, saying of *On Liberty* that "it is not a prescient book. . . . Neither Mill's hopes nor his forebodings are quite pertinent today" (*English Political Thought in the Nineteenth Century* [London, 1933], p. 98).

58. Compare with David Riesman, *The Lonely Crowd* (New Haven, 1950), esp. pp. 166, 266, 300–302, 304.

59. R. M. MacIver, *The Modern State* (London, 1926), p. 456.

60. John Morley, *Critical Miscellanies* (London, 1904–8), 3:47.

61. See Mill's early speech on the Church (1829), reprinted in the World's Classics edition of his *Autobiography,* ed. Laski (London, 1924), p. 322; see also his *Spirit of the Age,* ed. Hayek (Chicago, 1942), p. 14.

62. Thus Gerhart Niemeyer, "A Reappraisal of the Doctrine of Free Speech," *Thought* 25 (1950): 251–74, esp. 257, 271–72. See, in the same vein, Walter Berns, *Freedom, Virtue, and the First Amendment* (Baton Rouge, La., 1957); but see, *contra,* my paper "Freedom, Virtue, and the New Scholasticism," *Commentary* 28 (1959): 313–21.

63. Niemeyer, "A Reappraisal of the Doctrine of Free Speech," p. 273.

64. G. J. Holyoake, *Bygones Worth Remembering* (London, 1905), 1:279.

65. Quoted in Rees, *Mill and His Early Critics,* p. 33.

66. Niemeyer, "A Reappraisal," p. 273.

Chapter Four

1. Robert Paul Wolff, Barrington Moore, Jr., and Herbert Marcuse, *A Critique of Pure Tolerance* (Boston: Beacon Press, 1965).

Chapter Six

1. Sometimes, oddly enough, as in France and England, strong and ambitious kings granted some political power to the common people in order to limit the power of the aristocracy. Such kings, Tocqueville sardonically observed, "assisted democracy by their talents, others by their vices."

2. Giovanni Sartori, *Democratic Theory* (New York: Praeger, 1965), paperback ed., p. 327.

3. Cf. John Rees, *Equality* (London: Macmillan, 1972), paperback ed., chap. 1.

4. Thomas Hobbes, *Leviathan* (1651 ed.), Part I, chap. 13.

5. Jean-Jacques Rousseau, *The Social Contract,* trans. Cole, Everyman's ed. (1913), Book II, chap. 11, p. 45.

6. Aristotle, *Politics,* trans. Barker (New York: Oxford University Press, 1946), Book V, chap. 2, p. 207.

7. For Mill's doctrine, see his essays *On Liberty* (1859), *Utilitarianism* (1861), and *Representative Government* (1861).

8. Albert Hofstadter, "The Career Open to Personality: The Meaning of Equality of Opportunity for an Ethics for Our Time," in *Aspects of Human Equality*, ed. Lyman Bryson et al. (New York: Harper, 1956), pp. 123, 136.

9. Dorothy D. Lee, "Equality of Opportunity as a Cultural Value," ibid., pp. 259, 261, 268.

10. This may explain why certain "socialist" and allegedly egalitarian countries, such as Czechoslovakia, seek to rationalize *their* differences and systems of hierarchy as constitutive of "socialist stratification," as distinct from capitalist, bureaucratic, technocratic, and other "debased" forms of stratification. See Ernest Gellner, "The Pluralist Antilevelers of Prague," *Dissent,* Summer 1972, pp. 471–82. It may also explain the curious argument of Professor John H. Schaar, who, after denouncing hierarchy and the equal-opportunity principle, concludes by affirming that "of course there must be hierarchy" and that "the equal-opportunity principle is certainly not without value." See his "Equality of Opportunity, and Beyond," in *Equality,* ed. J. R. Pennock and J. W. Chapman (New York: Atherton, 1967), chap. 13.

11. I forgo for reasons of space a range of further problems that should at least be indicated here: whether equality entails a right to equal property or an equal right to property; whether equality before the law requires a public defender no less adequately staffed and funded than a public prosecutor; whether, as the transformation of Eliza Doolittle from a flower girl into a duchess suggests, it is in fact true that persons who are treated alike tend to become alike; and whether equality within a single realm of social life (say the political), or within an aspect of that realm (say the suffrage), can meaningfully coexist with inequalities in other realms (the family, the school, the church, the army, the corporation).

12. Isaiah Berlin, "Equality as an Ideal," in *Justice and Social Policy*, ed. F. A. Olafson (Englewood Cliffs, N. J.: Prentice-Hall, 1961), p. 150.

13. I am especially indebted here to Rees, *Equality*, pp. 134-38.

14. Cf. John Rawls, *A Theory of Justice* Cambridge: Harvard University Press, 1971), and Brian Barry, *Political Argument* (London: Routledge & Kegan Paul, 1965), esp. chaps. 6 and 7.

15. Cf. John P. Plamenatz, "Equality of Opportunity," in Bryson, ed., *Aspects of Human Equality*, chap. 4.

16. Daniel Bell, "On Meritocracy and Equality," *Public Interest*, Fall 1972, pp. 29–68; Irving Kristol, "About Equality," *Commentary*, November 1972, pp. 41–47.

Chapter Seven

1. For some of the problems, see Nathan Glazer, "Should Judges Administer Social Services?" *Public Interest*, Winter 1978, pp. 64–80; see also Berger, pp. 428–31.

2. Raoul Berger, *Government by Judiciary: The Transformation of the Fourteenth Amendment* (Cambridge, Mass.: Harvard University Press, 1977).

3. Oliver Wendell Holmes, *Collected Legal Papers* (New York: Harcourt, Brace, 1920), pp. 194–95, 207.

4. Obviously, a writer need cite only references he deems requisite or useful. But in so painstaking a scholarly work—I count no less than 1,647 footnotes including 131 books and 108 articles—I find inexplicable the omission of these and other leading items, such as Rodney Mott's *Due Process of Laws*, E. S. Corwin's *Twilight of the Supreme Court* and *Court over Constitution*, A. C. McLaughlin's *Constitutional History of the United States*, and W. W. Crosskey's *Politics and the Constitution in the History of the United States*, not to speak of the writings of a host of legal philosophers, e.g., Felix S. Cohen, Ronald Dworkin, Jerome Frank, H. L. A. Hart, and Julius Stone. I cite these—and could add others—only because, like Boudin and Morris Cohen, they deal directly and insightfully with Berger's themes and contain many of the points and leading arguments he advances as well as counterconsiderations he ignores.

5. Holmes, *Collected Legal Papers*, pp. 225–26, 239, 184.

6. Cf. Dr. William G. Niederland, letter to the *New York Times*, February 7, 1978.

7. A number of earlier cases, beginning a decade before, did much to prepare the way. Thus, in *Smith* v. *Allwright* (1944) the Supreme Court outlawed the Texas white primary (and, more significantly, paved the way for the *Brown* case by also rejecting the doctrine of *stare decisis* in the realm of constitutional law); in *Morgan* v. *Virginia* (1946) the Court declared invalid state laws requiring segregation in interstate buses; in 1948 a series of cases did away with racial restrictive covenants; and in 1950 the *Sweatt* and *McLaurin* cases practically outlawed segregation in public higher education. For these

and related documents, as well as the general history, see any of the standard antholo-
gies: *Civil Rights and the American Negro: A Documentary History,* ed. Albert P.
Blaustein and Robert L. Zangrando (New York: Washington Square Press, 1968);
Documents of American History, ed. Henry Steele Commager, 6th ed. (New York:
Appleton-Century-Crofts, 1958); and *The Negro in 20th Century America,* ed. John
Hope Franklin and Isidore Starr (New York: Vintage, 1967).

The sociopolitical significance of these cases further demonstrates Berger's unrealistic notion of the judiciary as simply a technical legal body.

Chapter Eight

1. New York: Basic Books, 1974.
2. Cambridge: Harvard University Press, 1971.
3. The bizarre doctrines of these early American thinkers—a curious mélange of
Owen, Fourier, Proudhon, and Max Stirner, along with such indigenous curiosities as
Warren's time store—defy easy classification. Some commentators have thought they
add up to "left-wing individualism," others, to "right-wing anarchism." Dean McEl-
downey, from whose doctoral dissertation on these writers I have profited greatly,
employs the term "bourgeois radicalism." Nozick seems to prefer "individualist anarchism." But, whatever the label, they remain *divertissements.*
4. Not Robinson Crusoe, for Crusoe was already a *social* animal before he was
stranded on an island.
5. Such as the refusal to keep a promise extracted through coercive means or to pay a
debt at a stipulated time when the one to whom the debt is legitimately owed is at that
moment drunk.
6. Herbert Spencer, *Social Statics* (1850) (New York: D. Appleton, 1873), chap. 9,
p. 132.
7. John Locke, *Second Treatise of Government,* in *Two Treatises of Government*
(1690), ed. Peter Laslett (Cambridge, Eng.: At the University Press, 1960) chap. V, sec.
27, pp. 305–6.
8. Nozick (*Anarchy, State, and Utopia,* p. 177) notes certain "familiar social considerations favoring private property" but doubts (even as he argues for the proposition)
that they support the Lockean enough-and-as-good-left-over proviso. He denies that
they enter into a utilitarian justification of property but offers no reasons for asserting
that this is so.
9. For Locke, as Nozick recognizes (p. 9), "does not provide anything remotely
resembling a satisfactory explanation of the status and basis of the law of nature in his
Second Treatise."
10. It is obviously no accident that, despite the recent revival of interest in social
contract theory, Rawls does not root his theory in an alleged state of nature. His
"original position" and "the veil of ignorance" associated with it are significantly
different. This is also why, to anticipate what follows, my concern is not so much to show
that Hobbes rather than Locke (or Rousseau) reads the state of nature correctly, but
rather to argue that the entire appeal to state-of-nature theory is misguided and that,
consequently, Nozick's theory of rights, which derives from his reading of that state of
nature, is without theoretical (or factual) justification.
11. Franz Oppenheimer, *The State,* trans. J. M. Gitterman (1908), 2d American ed.
(New York: Vanguard Press, 1926), p. 15.

12. Locke, *Second Treatise,* chap. II, secs. 6–7, 13, pp. 288–90, 293–94.

13. Again, I am at a loss to understand how within a state of nature, which is a state without a common Authority, there can be such things as prices—which presuppose not only a common system of currency and a common standard of exchange but such arrangements as hiring and selling—which presuppose an established market and an Authority to enforce contracts. I find Nozick's argument (p. 18), taken from Ludwig von Mises, absurd.

14. Some readers may take Nozick's arguments against equality and against state efforts to promote equality (chap. 8) as a major challenge to liberal and socialist theory. I do not share this view. But to explain why this is so would require an intensive analysis of the different meanings of, and arguments for and against, equality, which I cannot undertake here. I have dealt with some of the relevant issues in my article, "A Grammar of Equality," *Dissent,* Winter 1974, pp. 63–78.

15. This is among the reasons Aristotle gives in defense of the idea that the people should be sovereign. One person may lack sufficient wisdom to rule, but a multiplicity of such persons constitutes an entity that becomes something different—one to which each brings his share of goodness and moral prudence. "Some appreciate one part, some another, and all together appreciate all." This is why it makes a difference to understand man as a social animal rather than an isolated individual. See Aristotle, *Politics,* trans. Ernest Barker (Oxford: Clarendon Press, 1946), Book III, chap. XI, p. 123.

16. Nozick, p. 272.

17. Nozick, p. 161.

18. Further to support his argument, Nozick considers—and finds deficient—some opposing end-result theories, primarily John Rawls's theory of justice and, less extensively, Bernard Williams's case for equality. Considerations of space preclude a critical evaluation of that debate here, all the more since Nozick omits other important alternative views—e.g., the classical ideas of Plato and Aristotle—and gives insufficient attention to still others—e.g., views on utilitarianism, both by Bentham and John Stuart Mill. Nor is it necessary to do so in order to assess his own argument.

19. Locke, *Second Treatise,* chap. IV, secs. 22–24, pp. 301–3.

20. John Stuart Mill, *Principles of Political Economy* (1848), 7th ed. (1871), in *Collected Works,* ed. J. M. Robson (Toronto: University of Toronto Press, 1965), vol. III, Book V, chap. XI, sec. 10, pp. 953–54.

21. Nozick's proviso—that any exercise of rights must not violate the rights of others—would of course enter here; but we have already seen what that means.

Chapter Nine

This is a revised version of a paper prepared for the conference on the Open Society, Bellagio, Italy, June 28–July 4, 1972. I am indebted to the Rockefeller Foundation, to Professor Dante Germino, organizer of the Conference, and to my colleagues at the Villa Serbelloni.

1. In his book *Beyond Freedom and Dignity* (New York, Knopf, 1971).

2. *Walden Two* (New York: Macmillan, 1948; paperback ed., 1962).

3. E.g., *Science and Human Behavior* (New York: Macmillan, 1953) and "Freedom and the Control of Men," *American Scholar,* Winter 1955–56, pp. 47–65.

4. *Beyond Freedom and Dignity,* pp. 200, 205, 177, 164, 160.

5. Bertrand Russell, *Why I Am Not a Christian* (New York: Simon & Schuster, 1957), pp. 182–83.

6. Gaetano Mosca, *The Ruling Class,* trans. Kahn, ed. Livingston (New York: McGraw-Hill, 1939), pp. 184–87.

7. *Beyond Freedom and Dignity*, pp. 82, 92, 101.

8. Ibid., pp. 206–8.

9. "Freedom and the Control of Men," p. 47; see also *Beyond Freedom and Dignity,* p. 214.

10. Cf. Morris Watnick, "Toynbee's Nine Books of History against the Pagans," *Antioch Review* 7 (1947): 587–602.

11. Skinner has repeated this tautology in a recent article, where he says: "A practice that makes a culture more likely to survive survives with the culture" ("Humanism and Behaviorism," *Humanist,* July–August 1972, p. 20).

12. *Beyond Freedom and Dignity*, pp. 103–5, 127–28.

13. "Freedom and the Control of Men," pp. 60–61.

14. See George Kateb, *Utopia and Its Enemies* (New York: Free Press of Glencoe, 1963), chap. 6—though it should be noted that Kateb's careful and searching analysis, which appeared prior to the publication of Skinner's *Beyond Freedom and Dignity,* contains the most trenchant criticism of Skinner's views known to me. Kateb has commented on Skinner's last book in the *Atlantic,* October 1971, 122–25.

15. B. F. Skinner, *Verbal Behavior* (New York: Appleton-Century-Crofts,. 1957); see also the now classic review by Noam Chomsky in *Language* 35 (1959): 26–58.

16. See also Andrew Hacker, "The Specter of Predictable Man," *Antioch Review* 14 (1954): 195–207, and "Dostoevsky's Disciples: Man and Sheep in Political Theory," *Journal of Politics* 17 (1955): 590–613.

17. John Stuart Mill, *On Liberty* (1859), Everyman's ed. (1910), chap. 3, p. 117.

18. See Skinner's article, "Freedom and Dignity Revisited," *New York Times,* August 11, 1972. And compare K. J. Scott, "Conditioning and Freedom," *Australasian Journal of Philosophy* 37 (1959): 215–20.

19. *Beyond Freedom and Dignity,* p. 157.

20. On this point see Martin Landau, "Redundancy, Rationality, and the Problem of Duplication and Overlap," *Public Administration Review* 29 (1969): 349.

21. *Beyond Freedom and Dignity,* pp. 182–83, 172.

22. *Walden Two* (paperback ed.), pp. 269, 273. Italics in the original.

23. Skinner, "Humanism and Behaviorism," p. 20. This queer definition may help to explain the incredible designation of Skinner as "Humanist of the Year" for 1972!

24. Cf. Neil Postman, "My Ivan Illich Problem," *Social Policy,* January–February 1972, p. 35.

25. "Humanism and Behaviorism," p. 19.

26. Cf. Robert Jay Lifton, *Thought Reform and the Psychology of Totalism* (New York: Norton, 1963); see also Edgar H. Schein, *Coercive* Persuasion (New York: Norton, 1961).

27. From Elie Wiesel, *A Beggar in Jerusalem,* trans. L. Edelman and E. Wiesel (New York: Random House, 1970; Avon Paperback, 1971), p. 52.

Index

American Enterprise Institute, 212
Anarchy, State, and Utopia (Nozick), 139–62
Andrews, Stephen Pearl, 141
Aquinas, Saint Thomas, 148, 201
Areopagitica (Milton), 17, 45
Aristotle, 23, 52, 72, 97, 101, 148, 150, 159, 190; and equality, 113, 115, 116, 118; on man, 93
"Automatic goodness," 175, 178–79

Bacon, Francis, 193
Bakke decision, 132
Banfield, Edward, 208
Bell, Daniel, 123–24, 199
Bellamy, Edward, 109, 187
Bentham, Jeremy: and the happiness principle, 62, 63; and law, 101; and utilitarianism, 52, 55
Berger, Raoul, 126–38
Berlin, Isaiah, 78, 120
Berns, Walter, 210
Beyond Freedom and Dignity (Skinner), 165–97
"Beyond Tolerance" (Wolff), 79–81
Bingham, John A., 128
Blacks, 125–38
Bosanquet, Bernard, 51; and Mill and liberty, 66, 67, 68
Boudin, Louis B., 130, 135
Bread and Wine (Silone), 11
Brown v. Board of Education, 126, 133
Buckley, William, 199

Camus, Albert, 165, 166

Capone, Al, 47
Carlyle, Thomas, 46, 48
Carneades, plank of, 8
Censorship, 16–17
Certainty: and the new conservatives, 210–11; and Skinner, 193
Chamberlain, Wilt, 156–57, 158, 160
Change, and conservatism and liberalism, 27–28
Chapters on Socialism (Mill), 3, 206
Choice, 6–7, 165–66; and Mill, 177, 178; and Skinner, 171–73
Civil Rights Act of 1866, 127, 129
Civil Rights Acts, 133
Class, and Skinner, 183
Cohen, Morris R., 4, 131, 135, 165, 191; and Moore, 83; "The Process of Judicial Legislation," 130
Coleridge, Samuel Taylor, 52
Collective action, and freedom, 29–30
Community, 191; and human nature, 7; and liberalism, 1, 2
Conformity: and Mill, 73–74; and Mill and Tocqueville, 182; and Skinner, 179, 180
Conservatism: and change, 27–28; and liberalism, 25–43; and politics of economic individualism, 204–8; and politics of restraint, 202–4; and politics of virtue, 200–202; and principles, 35–37; and property, 28–30; traditions of, 30–40; and wealth, 32–35
Conservatives, the new, 208–12; and certainty, 210–11; and human rights, 211; observations on, 198–200; and philosophical issues, 208–10

Taft, Representative Robert A., Jr., 26
Taxation, and Nozick, 157, 160
Taylor, Harriet, 46
Theory of Justice, A (Rawls), 140
Thrasymachus, 134, 156
Times Literary Supplement (London), 139
Tocqueville, Alexis de, 71, 155; and conformity, 182; and equality and liberty, 119; and liberty, 72–73, 93; and tyranny of the majority, 48
Tolerance: and liberalism, 1; and Mill, 77–91; and scientific method, 83
"Tolerance and the Scientific Outlook" (Moore), 81–85
Toscanini, Arturo, 8
Toulouse-Lautrec, Henri de, 56
Truth, and Skinner, 188–89
Tucker, Benjamin R., 141, 158
Tyranny of the majority, 48, 50, 73

Uncertainty, and liberalism, 1
U.S. Constitution, 72
Utilitarianism (Mill), 47
Utility, principle of, 139–40
Utopia: fascination with, 193; and Nozick, 161–62

Valjean, Jean, 134
Van Gogh, Vincent, 56
Violence: and freedom, 83; and revolution, 22–23
Voting Rights Act of 1965, 133

Walden Two (Skinner), 181, 183, 188, 189
Walzer, Michael, 92, 94–97, 100
Warren, Chief Justice Earl, 129
Warren, Josiah, 141
Wealth, and conservatism, 32–35
Welfare state, and the new conservatives, 200
"Why I Am Not a Conservative" (Hayek), 207
Wildavsky, Aaron, 208–9
Williams, Bernard, 139
Wilson, James Q., 209
Wilson, President Woodrow, 29
Winthrop, John, 99
Wolff, Robert Paul, 78, 82; "Beyond Tolerance," 79–81
Wolin, Sheldon, 139

Yugoslavia, 115